THE COACH WHO STRANGLED THE BULLDOG

THE COACH WHO STRANGLED THE BULLDOG

How Harvard's Percy Haughton Beat Yale and Reinvented Football

Dick Friedman

LYONS
PRESS

Guilford, Connecticut

An imprint of The Rowman & Littlefield Publishing Group, Inc.
4501 Forbes Boulevard, Suite 200, Lanham, Maryland 20706
www.rowman.com

Distributed by NATIONAL BOOK NETWORK

British Library Cataloguing in Publication Information Available

The Library of Congress has cataloged the hardcover edition of this book as follows:

Names: Friedman, Dick, 1951- author.
Title: The coach who strangled the bulldog : how Harvard's Percy Haughton beat Yale and rein-
vented football / Dick Friedman.
Description: Lanham, Maryland : Rowman & Littlefield, [2018] | Includes bibliographical refer-
ences and index.
Identifiers: LCCN 2017051790 (print) | LCCN 2018005569 (ebook) | ISBN 9781538107553 (elec-
tronic) | ISBN 9781538107546 (hardcover : alk. paper) | ISBN 9781493049097 (pbk. : alk. paper)
Subjects: LCSH: Haughton, Percy D. (Percy Duncan), 1876-1924. | Football coaches—United
States—Biography. | College sports—United States—History. | Sports rivalries—United States. |
Harvard University—Football—History. | Yale University—Football—History.
Classification: LCC GV939.H463 (ebook) | LCC GV939.H463 F75 2018 (print) | DDC
796.332092 [B] —dc23
LC record available at https://lccn.loc.gov/2017051790

♾™ The paper used in this publication meets the minimum requirements of
American National Standard for Information Sciences Permanence of Paper
for Printed Library Materials, ANSI/NISO Z39.48-1992.

CONTENTS

ACKNOWLEDGMENTS

As with a winning football team, a completed book is a tribute to the efforts of a full and varied squad, and *The Coach Who Strangled the Bulldog* is no exception.

Some of the credit (or blame) for this project must go to my friend and former *Sports Illustrated* colleague David Sabino, who now is with ESPN. In 2009, as an editor at *SI*, I was working on the section of the *SI College Football Book* dealing with the 1910s, when David handed in copy that included the entry, "Harvard won three national championships under Percy Haughton, who went 71–7–5 during his time in Cambridge." My God, I thought—I've known this my entire life! And I've walked into the stadium past the frieze honoring Haughton a million times! After determining that there was, amazingly, no work devoted exclusively to the Haughton era, I embarked on my research.

During the ensuing years, Bob Scalise, the John D. Nichols '53 Family Director of Athletics at Harvard, and his staff were generous with their cooperation. I wore out with my requests three Harvard sports information directors: John Veneziano, Kurt Svoboda, and Tim Williamson, plus Tim's superbly efficient staffer, Alli Miller Fossner. It's a measure of their unfailing good cheer that these relationships remain stronger than ever. Jalen Manning, historical research intern for Harvard athletic communications, chipped in with some late photo help.

At *Harvard Magazine*, Craig Lambert had the notion that I might want to replace John T. Bethell as Crimson football correspondent when John decided to step away from the press box in 2014. (Truth to tell, no one really could replace the immortal "Cleat.") Aside from being my editor for my rookie season, Craig became an advisor and unfailing advocate for this book. For that, and for his friendship, I am most grateful.

I cannot thank enough Harry R. Lewis, Gordon McKay Professor of Computer Science, and Marlyn McGrath, director of admissions, for championing this project in its early stages and opening many doors for me, particularly those in Harvard's Widener Library. I benefited greatly from Harry's keen insights about not only Harvard sports, but also college football and its putative amateurism in its formative years.

John P. Reardon, Harvard's former director of athletics and dean of admissions (among other posts in his legendary career), provided vital encouragement. At the Harvard Varsity Club, executive director Bob Glatz and Andrew Chesebro, assistant director of marketing and communications, were ever-gracious in their assistance.

If I had to name a MVP, it would be Barbara Meloni, public services archivist at the Harvard University Archives. For seven years, off and on, Barbara and her efficient colleagues proved unfailingly patient in guiding through the musty past a rusty old grad who hadn't pursued academic-style research in four decades.

When I was still at *SI*, then-managing editor Terry McDonell granted me book leave so I could fully launch the project. Executive editor David Bauer (a Dartmouth guy) read some early pages and had many sharp and vital suggestions.

Two former colleagues, Peter Castro of *People* and Kevin Cook of *SI*, saw early versions of the manuscript and never stopped believing in it. A prolific author (he wrote the classic golf book *Tommy's Honor*), Kevin saw the possibilities from the get-go and took each of my rejections personally—all while urging me not to give up. I owe you, sir.

There were many acquaintances—some who barely knew me—who responded to my requests for advice in navigating the shoals of the publishing industry. Among them were the late Ray Robinson, ever a stalwart cheerleader; Kate Buford, author of splendid Jim Thorpe and Burt Lancaster biographies (it's only practice, Kate); Farley Chase; and Elisa Petrini. Although not my agent, friend-of-a-friend Rafe Sagalyn provided crucial suggestions that helped sharpen the proposal and push it over the goal line.

Several relatives of the men about whom I wrote not only took the time to answer my questions as best they could, but also, in some cases, opened their homes to me. Foremost was Alison Hildreth, granddaughter of Percy Haughton, who put me up (and put up with me) in her lovely Maine home one fall weekend. Over coffee, Ralph and Mary Toran eagerly provided material about Mary's father, Eddie Mahan. Hardwick Simmons took me to lunch and filled me in on his grandfather, Tack Hardwick. Gertrude Burr and Julia Herron-Moore corroborated information about Gertrude's father and Julia's grandfather, Wally Trumbull. A batch of Brickleys—Andrew, Bertha, John, and Matt—helped me out concerning their famous forebear Charlie.

It was a serendipitous day when I called the College Football Hall of Fame to inquire whether Charlie Brickley ever had been nominated for membership—only to find out that a Hall of Famer named Dwayne Nix had beaten me to the punch by a few hours. At this writing, Dwayne (whom I have yet to meet in person) and I have not succeeded in our goal to get Charlie enshrined, but we have built a cherished e-mail bond, all the more delightful for being so unexpected. Thank you, sir.

My good friends at the Ivy League—executive director Robin Harris, associate executive director Scottie Rodgers, and assistant executive director Trevor Rutledge-Leverenz—permitted me to rummage through their office at the beginning of my research. At the National Collegiate Athletic Association, my former *SI* colleague Brian Hendrickson, now director of membership communications, and Ellen Summers, associate director of research, furnished background and statistical materials. Tex Noel, executive director of the Intercollegiate Football Researchers Association, fed me a stream of material about Percy Haughton's place in the coaching pantheon. Richard A. Johnson, curator at The Sports Museum in Boston, was the first to inform me that the 1914 Game was filmed and also provided an illuminating scrapbook from Haughton's final season.

Christen Karniski, acquisitions editor at Rowman & Littlefield, has been the quarterback of this project. She took a gamble on it and has been a brilliant manager throughout, especially when shepherding a befuddled writer through the labyrinthine editorial process.

In assembling photos, the following were most helpful: Gail Friedman (no relation), director of communications at the Groton School; Richard E. Noble, communications manager at St. Mark's School; Pam

McCluskey and Jen McCreery at the Desmond-Fish Library in Garrison, New York; associate athletic director Steve Conn at Yale; at the United States Military Academy, Matthew Faulkner, assistant athletic director for communications, and assistant director Madeline Silvani; and Martha McClintock at Getty Images. The miraculous discovery of the Reggie Brown Notebooks was expedited by assistant librarian Kenneth Kinslow and curator George Rugg at Notre Dame's Hesburgh Libraries.

At the project's outset, I spent a cold and snowy winter in Cambridge being cheered by the warm and convivial hospitality of my landlords, Jonathan Aaron and Rebecca Folkman. Sadly, the ever-encouraging Rebecca passed away in early 2017. I am most sorry she is not here to provide her gentle critiques.

A host of Harvard friends took a great interest in this book. At the outset, Renny Little, the eminence grise of Crimson sports, contributed a number of valuable suggestions. Later, Keith Bender did a bang-up research job. Nearer to my home, the folks at the Harvard Club of Princeton fortified me with refreshment and peppered me with queries, most especially Yuki Moore Laurenti and Jeffrey Laurenti, Mike and Kristin McLaughlin, Jeff and Julia Steinberg. former Crimson offensive tackle Dan Vereb, and fellow Newtonite Jonathan Zoll. Another former Newtonite, onetime Newton North and Harvard quarterback Charles Slack, voluntarily took an active and appreciated role in trying to get the book published.

Several of my classmates provided never-failing encouragement, as well as excellent counsel. My biggest cheerleader was Lawrence Vincent, M.D., a former 'Poonie who shared with me the fruits of his findings about life at Harvard during the Haughton era. Anthony Hill offered candid and insightful comments on an early version that proved most valuable as I proceeded. Rick Wolff rendered his publishing-industry savvy.

Another classmate, Clifford M. Greene, also a dear and lifelong friend, has sat with me at various stadiums in the heat, rain, and snow. Cliff was part of a kitchen cabinet that also included Stephen Bahn; Col. Chris Henes; Nobel Laureate Roger Myerson (yet another Harvard '73 member); and the late Roger S. Sohn, M.D. These gentlemen, friends of more than half a century's standing, unfailingly inquired about my progress and never told me I was nuts to try this, even if they thought I was.

Each person named here was essential to the creation of this book, but, of course, any errors of fact, judgment, or interpretation are my responsibility alone.

I was blessed that the three women in my life indulged me. The most long-suffering is my mother, Edith G. Friedman, who must still wonder where all this sports stuff is leading. The most bemused is my daughter, Leah E. Friedman, who has come to understand that my involvement with Crimson football predates my involvement with her. The one who deserves the most credit is my wife, Meryl Rosen Friedman, who amid many uncertainties agreed to let me pursue this project and follow it where it led. To quote the Beatles, in my life I love them all.

The inspiration for this book is my late father, Robert J. Friedman, who taught me to not only savor football and other sports, but also appreciate their many wrinkles. Although a dyed-in-the-wool Michigan Wolverine, he became the greatest nonalumnus fan the Harvard Crimson ever had. This is for you, big fella.

INTRODUCTION

At the top of the horseshoe end of Harvard Stadium, just below the scoreboard, there is a billboard that reads, "National Champions 1910, 1912, 1913." To anyone who has followed college football only for the past half-century and is aware of Ivy League students' proclivity for practical joking, this sign must seem like the ultimate goof. For a quarter-century, the Crimson has been a very good Ivy League team, but Harvard (or Yale or Princeton) . . . national champs? Yes, really.

There was a time—roughly, from the sport's invention in 1869 to World War I—when the road to the national championship began in Cambridge and ran south through New Haven down to Princeton, ending in Philadelphia: Harvard, Yale, Princeton, Penn. To some degree, this was a creation of the northeastern press (not yet "media"), which at the end of the season somewhat lazily anointed the best eastern team as national champs. (Anyway, without the benefit of films, to say nothing of television, most writers hadn't seen teams or players from the South, Midwest, and especially the West.) On the other hand, most years, the teams from this venerable quartet really were the best—with such occasional interlopers as the Michigan elevens of coach Fielding H. "Hurry-Up" Yost and the teams from Chicago (yes, really) of Amos Alonzo Stagg.

In this book, we delve into the reasons for the early Ivy hegemony. It had ended by the 1920s, when the large state universities of the Midwest, South, and West, as well as private powerhouses the likes of Notre Dame and Stanford, decided to go in for football in a big way. In the

1920s and 1930s, there was the occasional Ivy super team: Princeton's 1922 "Team of Destiny," Cornell's three-season early 1920s juggernaut, Dartmouth's 1925 unbeatens, and Cornell's 1939 powerhouse. Moreover, Penn played a rugged schedule in front of crowds at Franklin Field. But after World War II, the eight schools that eventually would formalize the Ivy League decided to get out of the big-time football game.

I began going to games at Harvard Stadium when I was seven, in 1958, two years after the Ivy League began formal competition. In retrospect, the next 15 years were a transitional time. Many alumni and fans were still around who could recall the early big-time-football days. The crowds remained large, conveying an aura of the old importance. Harvard–Yale—The Game—was a sellout, or damned close if it was at the Yale Bowl. Harvard–Dartmouth and Harvard–Princeton also had packed houses. Even garden-variety early season games drew respectable attendances of 20,000 or more. While the football played was not up to the level of the Big Ten or SEC, it wasn't as far behind as it is now, and it had its own scrappy integrity. Dartmouth's unbeaten 1970 team ended the season ranked 14th in the Associated Press poll—the last Ivy team to be ranked. That 1970 Big Green squad could have played with any team in the nation for a half, before depth would have told.

In 1982, the Ivy League chose to join college football's second-tier division, now called FCS (Football Championship Subdivision). That move reflected and perhaps accelerated the ebbing caliber of play and attendance. Now the average Harvard midseason game is played in front of maybe 10,000 fans—in a stadium that more and more seems like a white elephant.

Which, once again, makes it hard to believe: *Harvard (or Yale or Princeton) really was number one?* Well, yes. Not only that, but the players from these schools were as famous, as nationally known in their day, as Red Grange and Bo Jackson were in theirs. Their coaches, former players, and administrators included such seminal figures as Walter Camp of Yale, Amos Alonzo Stagg of Chicago, John W. Heisman of Brown and Penn, and Glenn S. "Pop" Warner of Cornell—in other words, the men for whom awards and leagues are named. Their stamp on the game remains unmistakable.

Harvard's Percy D. Haughton was considered every bit their peer, but his name is the one even many avid football fans would have trouble placing. This is partly because of his untimely death from a heart attack in 1924, at age 48, and partly because his reign—during the Haughton-ite "Crimson Autumns"—is wedged into a sliver of time between 1908 and 1915.

By now, of course, there is no one alive who can remember this era. As I tried to conjure it for this book, that was my one regret: that I didn't think of this idea 40 or even 30 years earlier, when I could have gotten firsthand recollections from the men who played and coached back then. Nevertheless, as I paged through old clippings and memoirs, I was bowled over by how vivid and sophisticated the sport of football already was. (That also went for its coverage in the press.) I hope I have conveyed the excitement of this discovery in this book—and demystified how Harvard could have been number one. Yes, really.

PROLOGUE

Two Brickleys, a Century Apart

Harvard Stadium, November 22, 1913. Minutes before the scheduled 2 p.m. kickoff, most of the capacity crowd of 46,483 (who have paid $2 a ticket—top dollar) already are in their seats. Another 283 are standing on the stadium parapets, and 127 reporters have crammed the press box. Many of the spectators are gazing at the gridiron, where a power-fully built, bareheaded player clad in a crimson jersey is methodically traversing the field, alternately dropkicking and booting from place-ment, almost unfailingly sending the roundish ball through the uprights.

Charles Edward Brickley is the most devastating weapon in college football. "That Mr. Brickley . . . was quite a showman," remembered syndicated columnist Neal O'Hara, Harvard class of 1915, a quarter-century later. He added,

> During the practice period of each game, he'd start nudging drop-kicks from every angle and every distance up to midfield, moving fanwise around the goal, and making 98 percent of them good—a performance that stunned the opposition. Many a team was licked, psychologically, by Brickley's toe before the opening kickoff. [1]

Standing on the home sideline is a rangy, commanding figure: Har-vard's coach, Percy Duncan Haughton. On this afternoon, Haughton (Harvard class of 1899) sits astride the sport of football. His Crimson team is the defending national champion. His "Haughton System" has revolutionized the way the game is played and taught. Behind the scenes, he has been instrumental in molding the sport's ever-changing rules; however, today the oft-profane Haughton is concerned not with the big picture, but the daily details. Brickley's feat of foot is no happenstance. Haughton has supervised 20 Harvard managers in placing 100 footballs on the field for his star to boot, and he has ordered "Brick" not to miss even one.

The lad from Everett is not fazed. Heck, if he had to, he could nail 'em blindfolded.

As it turns out, he might have to.

◦ ◦ ◦

A paint store in Charlottesville, Virginia, in early 2012. The young man behind the counter admires the windbreaker worn by a tall customer in his mid-60s. "That's a cool jacket," he says, noting the College Football Hall of Fame logo on the left breast. "Where'd you get it?"

"Well," says the older man modestly. "I'm in the Hall of Fame."

"Wow," says Ryan Brickley. He pauses. Then he says, "My family thinks that my great-grandfather should be there, too."[2]

I

P. D. STRANGLES THE BULLDOG

At the dawn of the 1908 football season, Harvard senior Victor Kennard was in the twilight of a mediocre career.

On September 14, the time of year when fashionable men were putting away their straw hats, the scrub Harvard running back and kicker from Brookline, Massachusetts, was one of 45 aspirants assembled in Allston, just across the Charles River from Harvard Square, for the start of practice for the Crimson's 35th season of intercollegiate football. The drills would take place on Soldiers Field, in the shadow of Harvard Stadium, now a maturing five years old. The world's first reinforced concrete structure, the 40,000-seat arena was the grandest sports edifice in the nation—and maybe the world.

Its majesty, however, was in marked contrast to the state of the program, which was in shambles. In 1907, under coach Joshua Crane, Harvard had hit bottom. The Crimson's 7–3 record was deceiving. Its losses had come in its only games that mattered, a season-ending trifecta at the stadium: a 23–15 thriller against a Carlisle team coached by Pop Warner and featuring Jim Thorpe, a 22–0 thumping by Dartmouth, and a thorough 12–0 waxing by archrival Yale. The loss to the Elis was the sixth in a row in the annual match already known as "The Game"; in those defeats, the Crimson had not scored.

For Vic Kennard and his Crimson teammates, the shame was galling, heartrending even. Most came from the tony private and preparatory schools of the East. Their schoolboy chums and foes were playing, and winning, at Yale (where any player worth his sand, as the expression went, dreamed of going), at Dartmouth, at Princeton. For three decades, as more Americans got the time for leisure pursuits, football involving the venerable Eastern schools had evolved from student-only pickup affairs played on a nearby field to an autumn fixture in front of stands packed with sleekly attired patrons and a breathless press corps—testament to the way mass sport already was a driver of newspaper circulation. Football provided crash and excitement, spectacle and noise, and (already) for many, the frisson of the wager. Somehow, defending the honor of one's school on the athletic field (or cheering the team from the stands) had become a rite, a virtue, a near-religious duty that overrode carping about its irrelevance to the educational mission.

By now, these rivalries had assumed paramount importance among many undergraduates and alumni. At clubs and on Wall Street, winners lorded over losers. Why, the mania extended to the White House. President Theodore Roosevelt, Harvard class of 1880, wanted his beloved Crimson to bust Yale the way he wanted to bust the trusts. In 1905, when football's escalating carnage—19 reported deaths—had threatened its existence, T. R. had intervened to help save it, just as he had negotiated an end to the Russo-Japanese War.[1] (That season, his son Ted had his nose broken while playing for Harvard.) Summoning to the White House representatives from the Big Three—Harvard, Yale, and Princeton—T. R. figuratively knocked heads; by the following season, new rules were in place, including the licensing of the forward pass, which bade to diminish the violence. (Widening the field was nixed, partly because Harvard Stadium was set in stone.) Meantime, the youthful football gods on whom so much emotion was expended had become national celebrities, with their faces plastered on the sports pages and even postcards and advertisements.

True, some in the Harvard community were, at best, indifferent (a quality that lingers a century later) and, at worst, hostile to big-time sport. To them it had no place at America's oldest university, whose only proper role was scholarly pursuit. The school's president since 1869, the august and austere Charles W. Eliot, often publicly professed disdain for what he considered a barbaric game. As a collegiate oarsman, Eliot had rowed against Yale in the earliest days of the rivalry, which began in 1852 with a boat race that was the first intercollegiate sporting event in the United States. Eliot even had provided the magenta headscarves that would be the basis of the school color. But of football he would proclaim,

> It's too dangerous for professional players, and college men can't play it for more than a year. They are liable to too many serious injuries—injuries for life. . . . It's different from baseball, and it's worse than prizefighting. The man in the ring doesn't run such a chance of being maimed as the man on the gridiron.[2]

It was not like this at Yale—the school of the fictional Frank Merriwell and the real-life Walter Camp, the hallowed "Father of Football," the smashmouth sport's most fervent proselytizer and also paterfamilias of Bulldog football. In New Haven, school spirit was unabashedly, unanimously, and unequivocally embraced. Then again, being a Yale rooter was hardly a hardship. Between 1876 and 1909, the years of Camp's greatest activity as a player and coach, the Elis won 319 games, lost 14, and tied 16. In doing so, Yale had produced names that already were immortal, among them magisterial lineman Pudge Heffelfinger and mad-dog ends Frank Hinkey and Tom Shevlin.

Kennard was doubly frustrated. He had arrived in Cambridge out of Boston's private Volkmann School (and from a football-crazy family) and, at six feet and 181 pounds, brought impressive size to Soldiers Field. Kennard had snuck into the Yale game as a sophomore at left end, earning the coveted black sweater with the crimson H, which went only to those who saw action against the Elis. But his junior season had been derailed by injuries. Along with several other players from his class—including lineman Rex "Dutchie" ver Wiebe and Kennard's Volkmann chum and fellow back John Cutler—he had become a little-used afterthought.

Kennard could have had scant hope that either his own or his team's fortunes would reverse; the 1908 material looked thin and green. Nevertheless, in the summer before his final season, Vic, a left-footed booter, worked for several hours each day on his dropkicking. Back then, the dropkick—in which the kicker, standing in punt formation, receives the ball and drops it to the ground before booting—was the principal means of scoring a field goal, in that season worth four points. (A touchdown earned five.) If called on, he would be ready.

On this first day of practice on the cusp of autumn, the sun was bright and warm. As the squad broke a sweat, Vic Kennard had reason to wonder if, when the shadows descended at Game's end on Yale Field on November 21, he would once again experience that wintry, hollow feeling—doubly empty, because he would have lost not only a game but also his last chance to experience the warm glow of victory.

Little did Kennard foresee that during the next several weeks, he would become an integral part of the damnedest season since Harvard had begun playing in 1875, one that would see strange bounces, thrilling runs, another White House intervention, the wackiest face-off ever between two future Hall of Fame coaches, and the barehanded strangling of a bulldog. Nor in his most fevered dreams would this humble scrub envision that two months hence he would be a game-changer and that one swing of his good left leg would stamp a new coaching legend.

Perspiring in the heat, Vic looked over the rest of the squad: men from Andover and Groton and Middlesex and Pomfret and St. Mark's and St. Paul's—a few right out of the Social Register—plus a smattering of public schools. Football at Harvard, Princeton, and Yale was close to an exclusive game, one played by a bunch of blue-blooded roughnecks, ready to tear apart the foe for glory. This was probably the only period in the history of American team sports when it was an advantage to be rich; if you wanted to play for one of the Big Three, it was swell to be a swell. The elite private schools were not only the most vaunted molders of young minds, but also the incubators for a sport deemed vital for the inculcation of manliness befitting the ruling class.

To many within and outside these schools, football was a vital aspect of stewardship training—essential, even, to the health of an urban industrial society. As author Michael Oriard noted (with some qualification) in his seminal work, *Reading Football,*

> The game survived, its popularity assured, because of a cult of masculinity best illustrated by Teddy Roosevelt's call to the "strenuous life." . . . Thrust into a new world where traditional masculine traits were no longer meaningful, [the American male] found in vigorous outdoor sports such as football a compensating validation of his manhood.[3]

That manhood was pointedly WASP. "Football is the expression of the strength of the Anglo-Saxon. It is the dominant spirit of a dominant race, and to this it owes its popularity and its hopes of permanence," Oriard wrote, quoting W. Cameron Forbes, Harvard class of 1892, who had been Harvard's coach in 1898 and 1899, and whom Roosevelt had appointed governor general of the conquered Philippines.[4] (If any further validation of Forbes's pedigree was needed, he was a grandson of Ralph Waldo Emerson, Harvard class of 1821.)

Speaking of swells, Vic turned his attention to the tackling dummies, beside which a tall, wiry man in canvas football togs was holding a small megaphone, through which he was barking encouragement and, yes, imprecations. Haughton. Would he find a way to beat the Elis? Or even to score against them?

❀ ❀ ❀

When Percy Duncan Haughton, Harvard class of 1899—"P. D." to his intimates—had been placed in charge of Harvard football the previous February, few were certain he was the right man for the job. Maybe he should have been on the field, not the sideline, for even at age 31, Haughton could lay claim to being one of the best all-around athletes in the United States—if not the best.

Following the debacle of '07, incoming captain Francis "Hooks" Burr huddled with the school's Committee on Athletics, including its newly named chairman, LeBaron R. Briggs, dean of the Faculty of Arts and Sciences. For his coach, Burr wanted Haughton, a familiar figure who had stayed close to the program as a sometime assistant coach. He was one of many; like most schools, including Yale, Harvard football had operated under a coach-by-committee scheme, with the undergraduate captain calling many of the shots. This jibed with the prevailing ethos transported from English sports and honored at least in the breach, if not in the observance. Collegiate teams were to be run by and for the students. Professional coaching was not a fit profession for gentlemen amateurs, and the big-time, highly paid, peripatetic coach was the personification of the evils of college sport.

At the time, Haughton, a bachelor, was making a living as a bond salesman on Boston's State Street. In fact, in 1908, he would take no coaching salary. (He did receive, as his assistant Harry von Kersburg later noted, a "certain sum from interested graduates.")[5] Instead, he demanded something else: total control. Acceding, the committee reluctantly offered him the job.

Percy Duncan Haughton, master of the art of football. Some in Cambridge took issue with his methods (to say nothing of his language), but his vaunted system broke down every element of the game as few had before him. *HUP Haughton, Percy Duncan (4), olvwork376393. Harvard University Archives.*

There was no concern about this bona fides. Haughton bled Crimson. He had been born on Staten Island, New York, in 1876, one of three children of Malcolm, a cotton merchant whose fortunes fluctuated, and Mary Neame Lawrence Haughton. The family eventually moved to Brookline, and young Percy prepped for Harvard at Groton, as would many of his players.[6] In 1951, writing in *The Yale Football Story*, author Tim Cohane invoked three Harvard immortals and one from Yale when he declared, "There is a saying, 'When the Grotons are tough, they are tough.' Like Percy Haughton, Tack Hardwick, Chub Peabody, Gordon Brown."[7]

Haughton may have been the toughest. In the early 1890s, playing football and baseball, he had been perhaps the best athlete the school had seen. Importantly, Groton's coach at the time, beloved master Guy Ayrault, was a forward football thinker who would teach Percy the heretofore unusual scheme of blocking known later as the mousetrap, in which the blocker allows the defender to charge past him, then uses the defender's momentum to bump the would-be tackler off the play. Along with deception, the mousetrap would become a keynote of Haughton's attack.

When it came time to apply for admission to Harvard, Percy labored under two perceived handicaps: He was not wealthy, and according to the authorities at Groton, he was not much of a scholar. Endicott Peabody, Groton's immortal founder and headmaster, declared in a note to Richard Cobb, Harvard's assistant secretary, that Percy was "fairly bright but not interested in his work. . . . He is well-meaning but not a strong character." Another master, Sherrard Billings, said,

> P. D. Haughton is a boy of more ability than his school record or his entrance examinations show. He has never worked very hard at his books, but he looks forward to studying well at college. He has the incentive of being poor, and being sent to college by someone else, all of which is in his favor. A very exceptional athlete, he will be prominent from the start.[8]

Such misgivings for athletes remain to this day.

Despite the skepticism, Haughton was admitted to the class of 1899. As predicted, he was most prominent as an athlete. In football, as a senior in 1898, he would play tackle under another influential coach: Cam Forbes. Forbes countered prevailing practice, emphasizing sen-

Captain Haughton (center, holding football) posed insouciantly with the Groton 1894 squad. One of the greatest all-around athletes the school has produced, he was even more renowned as a center fielder, and baseball would remain his life-long love. *Groton School Archives.*

sible rather than grueling physical training, bringing his team to a late-season peak and stressing speed. As a coach, Haughton would adopt these tenets.

In 1898, his senior season, Haughton's punting ability was one of the keys to victories over Penn and Yale; in a 17–0 thrashing of the Elis at New Haven, he averaged 60 yards booting a rain-sodden ball. An impressed Walter Camp named Haughton second-team All-America. A half-century later, Crimson quarterback Charlie Daly remembered, "What an 'instrument of policy' we had in Percy—[punts] a mile high and sometimes as long as the field!"[9] Not surprisingly, when Haughton became a coach, the kicking game and field position were the cornerstones of his strategy.

Strong as he was on the gridiron, Haughton was even more accomplished in baseball as a batter, outfielder, and relief pitcher. In 1899, he was captain of the Crimson nine. When he became a football coach, Haughton would love baseball players. Melville Webb Jr. of the *Boston*

Globe observed in 1911, "It is a Haughton epigram that any athlete that does not know how to play baseball seldom is a star at any other game."[10]

After graduation, needing to resolve college debts, Haughton became coach at Cornell. His record for the 1899 and 1900 seasons was a decent 17–5, and included a significant victory each season over Princeton. The man he succeeded was Glenn "Pop" Warner. In later years, the two future Hall of Famers would pit their diametrically opposed methods against each other, with memorable results.

In 1906, Haughton won the racquets championship of the United States. He was a tournament-caliber golfer. At 6-foot-1 and 180 pounds, he was exceptionally long and rangy for that era. In 1905, Harvard coach Bill Reid enlisted a film company to make an instructional movie of Haughton illustrating correct punting form. A stills sequence in the Harvard University Archives reveals a splendidly limber athlete with textbook motion and long, high extension—an early-day Ray Guy.[11] At the time, Haughton was in his late 20s, his physical prime.

As a coach, Percy Haughton invariably would demonstrate an uncanny sense of timing. During the next nine seasons in Cambridge, his ability to divine exactly the right moment to insert a substitute or trot out a special play would be instrumental in bringing him a 71–7–5 record and three national championships. By the time he departed following the 1916 season, his vaunted "System"—an integrated method of football organization, from conditioning to practice to final whistle—had redefined the coaching profession. But perhaps never was his timing more propitious than in 1908, when he took the job, as the Crimson's fortunes and expectations were at their lowest ebb.[12] Many of the masterstrokes that would riddle Harvard's foes throughout the next decade would be unsheathed in that first campaign. Likewise, whether by luck or (as Haughton would have it) design, the ball began to bounce Harvard's way and rarely would stop doing so during Haughton's tenure.

On the first day of practice, as he gazed out at his charges, Haughton did not see an athlete of his own caliber. As all were upperclassmen, none were Haughton recruits. Only five prospective members of his squad were returning lettermen, the most prominent being his captain, senior tackle and punter Francis Burr, and junior lineman Hamilton Fish III, a rugged 6-foot-4, 197-pounder who had played decently but not brilliantly in 1907. (In any event, Fish would not report for two weeks, after he had returned from a summer of working out West in a copper mine.) Haughton's best potential power runner and punter, Wayland "Dono" Minot, was academically ineligible. Most important (then as now), he had little clue who would be his quarterback, the man who would drive the attack.

The blank slate was not a disaster but an opportunity. Percy Haughton would whip this bunch of tutti-frutti society boys into champions.

❂ ❂ ❂

Despite his squad's threadbare nature, Haughton had one luxury: time. As it is for the Alabama Crimson Tide in the 21st century, so it already was for the Harvard Crimson 100 years earlier: the ingrained arc of the season for major college football powers. The kickoff came in sunlit late September; the final whistle pierced the gloaming of late November. First came several "preliminary" games against smaller schools (most from New England) eager for the thrill and cash, if not for the drubbing that came with a visit to Harvard Stadium. Played in front of perhaps 10,000 spectators, many were glorified scrimmages that enabled Haughton and other counterparts to tinker with plays and lineups, and, crucially, provide playing time for reserves and the previously untried. Then came the midseason "big games" against sterner foes, some from the far-off Midwest. These attracted crowds of 15,000 to 25,000. Finally, there were the two or three "championship games" that drew capacity crowds and determined not only bragging rights, but also often national honors.

Haughton's task was further focused by the way the game was played: defensively, with points in the major games at a premium. The field was 110 yards long, with no end zones. Game lengths were variable: 40 minutes early in the season, 70 minutes for the major games. A touchdown was worth five points, with a point-after-touchdown obtainable by placekick or dropkick. An extra point actually was a two-part affair, with the ball first "punted out" to the kicker from behind the goal line; this was a remnant of the game's rugby roots. A field goal was worth four points, a safety two. (There were no hash marks, which meant field goals might be attempted from near the sideline.) On attack, teams often resorted to straight-ahead, grind-it-out football, especially because ballcarriers could be helped along by teammates pushing or pulling them. The forward pass, legalized two years earlier, was in an embryonic state and was hampered by restrictions; one, for instance, mandated that the ball had to cross the scrimmage line no less than five yards from where it was snapped. (In 1908, the field was thus marked lengthwise and widthwise—a true gridiron pattern.) An incompletion on first or second down resulted in a 15-yard penalty. Moreover, a pass caught over the goal line was not a touchdown but a touchback; there yet was no end zone.[13]

The gladiators were togged out in wool sweaters with no numbers; numeraled jerseys wouldn't become standard until after World War I. Pants were breeches of brown canvas reaching just below the knee. Shoulder, knee, and hip pads had been refined by Amos Alonzo Stagg, a onetime Yale end named to Camp's inaugural All-America team and now the celebrated coach at Chicago. He had found a hard fiber that afforded protection yet was light enough to permit movement. The rudimentary leather helmets (with ear flaps) were not mandatory; photos of the era generally reveal about half the players wearing them. No one wore a facemask, although some displayed flimsy nose protectors. Their high-topped leather shoes had cleats to provide needed purchase on the oft-bare, muddy fields.

Already the players had benefited from the most up-to-date training apparatus, including the blocking sled and the tackling dummy, both of which the resourceful Stagg claimed to have devised. Moreover, during the season, the varsities were fed lavishly at special training tables and even received massages from a corps of so-called "rubbers."

There were four officials: a referee, a head linesman, an umpire, and a field judge. These often were former prominent players. They were chosen by agreement of the schools, which often would veto an official who previously had displeased them. In 1905, one official who had incurred the wrath of Harvard, Paul Dashiell, had seen his appointment to the faculty at Annapolis held up by President Roosevelt.

An offense only had three downs in which to gain 10 yards. This virtually dictated there would be a lot of punts—which, once they traveled 20 yards, could be recovered by the kicking team. (A short recoverable punt was termed an "onside kick.") Thus, there were premiums on booming punters, speedy ends who could chase punts downfield, and men who could catch punts sure-handedly. Often this last responsibility devolved on the quarterback.

One rule was especially testing: Once a player left the game, he could not return. Men played both ways and through injury. Coaches relieved the first-stringers at their peril. That led to another complication: Coaches only rarely could send in plays. Moreover, in a sport allegedly of gentlemen amateurs, they were prohibited from yelling instructions. The quarterback, then, was entrusted with being the brains on the field.

As a former punter, Haughton banked on field position. This was such an important facet of the game that, when a team was scored on, it usually chose not to take the ball, but to kick off in hopes of pinning the foe deep and forcing a turnover.

Like Haughton himself, his initial corps of top field assistants consisted of recent former Harvard stars. P. D. was unique in delegating responsibility to his corps of lieutenants. Onetime quarterback Charlie Daly (who also had played at West Point) was backfield coach. Harry von Kersburg handled the interior linemen and Dave Campbell the ends. Still young men, they might have been the best players on the practice field. Haughton also employed his onetime teammate Reggie Brown, a keen x's-and-o's man, as his advance scout. Brown spent a lot of time in New Haven watching Yale's games and practices. His notebooks, preserved today, reveal how sophisticated the game and Brown's views were, especially in the days before game films. The brain trust was completed by installing J. W. "Mike" Farley, Haughton's best friend, on a football advisory committee. Canny trainer William "Pooch" Donovan and physician E. H. Nichols had Haughton's ear. Many of these men would be with Haughton during much, if not all, of his tenure, providing invaluable continuity.

During his first preseason, Haughton established his coaching rhythm. While Soldiers Field was not home to a prehistoric Bear Bryant-style Junction Boys camp, it was physically demanding. Haughton began barking at his charges through that megaphone. Already, he was stressing the fundamentals: execution, conditioning, blocking, tackling, following the ball, and pouncing on it if it came loose.

That first autumn established another tenet: After the first few days, practices were held in strict secrecy—literally, behind a fence. This was because Haughton was what we'd today call a paranoid control freak.

There were no exceptions to the secrecy edict: Years later, Haughton would boot Harvard president A. Lawrence Lowell from a scrimmage. "Even the president of the college isn't welcome at secret practice," P. D. told von Kersburg. [14]

It could have been worse: Lowell could have been a newspaperman. In 1955, renowned sportswriter Grantland Rice recounted,

> I recall one day before a Harvard–Michigan game when I was standing with [Wolverines coach Fielding H.] Yost. Haughton spotted some Boston newspapermen at the edge of the field. He had them all chased out of the park. Yost sighed heavily. "Gee," he said, "I wish I could get away with that out West. If I did that they'd run me out of football." As far as Haughton was concerned, one of his most pleasant victories occurred the day he persuaded Pres. Lowell that part of the "overinterest" in the game was due to the presence of football writers at the daily practices. So he persuaded Harvard's president to have them barred. [15]

But P. D. was no mere martinet. Edward Mahan, a Crimson star from 1913 to 1915, later wrote of Haughton (with words that presage Vince Lombardi),

> He was a driver and had a caustic tongue which lashed all alike, yet he had a keen sense of humor. . . . During the first six weeks of the season he was a tyrant and drove, cursed, and manhandled players. After this period of rugged work was over, he would turn around and become affable and seem to be everyone's best friend. He was an excellent teacher and never wasted words. He was able to make men play when they were very tired. He would emphasize this point, and by his driving methods he would prove to you that you still could play 20 percent better than you thought you could when tired. . . . His plan for every game was to wear the other fellow down for three quarters and then win in the last quarter. [16]

Early in the workouts, several positions solidified. Junior center Joe Nourse (St. Paul's), left tackle Fish, left guard Burr, and senior right tackle Sam Hoar (Middlesex) were the building blocks for the line. At one end, a homegrown Irish public-school product, Charlie Crowley from Cambridge Latin, was showing the requisite downfield speed.

Sophomore running back Ham Corbett, a shifty redhead from Portland (Oregon) Academy, was flashing All-America form.

But the scrimmages also revealed deficiencies that could sink a thin squad. A sophomore tackle, Bob McKay, had the size; at 205 pounds, he was one of the Crimson's heaviest men. But he lacked the technique, the fire, the drive. Furthermore, there was no line depth. The best senior sub, ver Wiebe, had been pegging away bootlessly for two years on the varsity B team. Most troubling, no quarterback had emerged. Harvard did not use a huddle. In the Haughton scheme, the quarterback was primarily a signal-caller; he took the snap from center and handed the ball off to a runner. Of the three candidates, junior Gil Browne, a sub end in 1907, was the best all-around athlete and game to try another skill position. He was the early favorite of the coaches. Sophomore Henry Sprague, out of nearby Newton High, brought punting ability.

The third man, John Cutler, was Mister X. Like his fellow Volkmann School product Vic Kennard, he was one of those seniors who had been lost in the shuffle. Cutler was from a Harvard family: His father, Brookline lumber merchant George C., was class of 1879. Two brothers, Eliot and Roger, were varsity crew men. John, too, had been an oarsman—until he was afflicted with a case of boils. His hard conditioning on the Charles had given the 5-foot-11 Cutler strength belied by his 164 pounds. But as a prospective quarterback, he had no resume. John Cutler was a blank slate. Could Haughton entrust his team to such an inexperienced man?

Finally, a reliable dropkicker had yet to emerge; however, the *Boston Globe* did detect a candidate, noting one day, "Kennard is showing vast improvement over anything that has yet been seen on the field."[17]

* * *

Presaging ESPN's midweek games by a century, Harvard opened its 1908 football season on September 30—a Wednesday. In a game with 15-minute halves, the Crimson took on seemingly overmatched Bowdoin. The final score was a mere 5–0. Typically for a first game, Harvard's play was ragged but encouraging, and marred by holding calls. The only score came on a 28-yard scamper on a fake punt by sophomore reserve back Perry Smith, who, "keeping his feet finely,"[18] as the

Boston Globe reported the next day, was hauled over the goal line by his teammates. Gil Browne and John Cutler ran the team at quarterback, rarely taking the wraps off. Browne, who completed two of his three passes, might have had another score but for lack of an end zone. One toss, which end Charlie Crowley snagged nicely, was received over Bowdoin's end line and ruled a touchback.

Three days later, the Crimson was back at it. Some 10,000 spectators showed up at the stadium on a sun-splashed Saturday to see Maine get overpowered, 16–0. They also saw a quarterback take hold. Cutler, who got the start, was beginning to exhibit a cool head and keen initiative. The offense seemed to show snap under his command. Already, he had mastered what was later known as the "audible." As the *Globe* reported, "Twice, when he had signaled for forward pass plays, he was quick to notice that Maine was immediately presenting an adequate defense. Therefore, he kicked the ball once; another time he made an excellent run."[19] Soon, Cutler's main rival for the job, Gil Browne, would be shifted to end, where he would be a standout.

Another Wednesday brought in Bates. Another crowd of 10,000 (with nothing better to do on a workday) witnessed an 18–0 Harvard win—and got its money's worth on one of the most exciting plays in Crimson history. After the first of three Harvard touchdowns, Bates kicked off. Back on his own five, Ham Corbett scooped up the bounding ball and headed directly up the middle, craftily following his interference as his teammates bowled over the pursuing Mules. Near midfield, Corbett veered toward the sideline. He passed every remaining tackler except Bates's safety, "little Cobb,"[20] whereupon Corbett found one more gear and shot by Cobb. Although the Bates man grazed the streaking Crimson back at the 10, Corbett dashed over the goal line. The play covered 105 yards—still the longest return in Harvard history, and likely to remain so.

Against Williams the next week, Cutler went the whole way at quarterback. Burr's stellar punting and a sweet 42-yard placekick were the highlights of a 10–0 win, the Crimson's fourth straight over a plucky little foe.

Vic Kennard did not get off the bench. He had a champion in von Kersburg, who in coaches' meetings continually pleaded his case as a dropkicker. Unaware of this support, Kennard showed his discouragement openly—that is, until he received the proverbial wake-up slap from Percy Duncan Haughton.

Two decades later, Kennard recounted the moment:

> One day, Haughton stopped me as I headed for practice. "See here, Kennard, I'd like a word with you," he said in low, even tones. I can look back to that afternoon and still picture his piercing eyes. I can recall his direct manner and his concise speech. "You've got the physique," said P. D., "and I think you have the spirit, but you'll never get anywhere with that sour look. It's contagious. There's no place on a football field for a grouch. You've got to keep smiling and patting the other fellow on the back. And by the way you've been looking lately, I'll say you'd better be smiling every day at Harvard Square and keep smiling all the way down to the field. Then smile some more. If you do that you'll improve your prospects around here. Another sour look and you're through." That was the extent of our conversation, but it was the best lesson I ever learned. From then on, things came easier. The effect of that two-minute talk has remained with me. . . . Every time I have hit a snag, I'd say to myself, "Smile, damn it, smile!" That short session with Haughton was worth more to me than a dozen degrees at Harvard.[21]

So braced, Kennard readied for the final preliminary game, a certain blowout against Springfield Training School. Haughton was at New Haven, scouting Yale–Army. He left the team in the hands of Dave Campbell and von Kersburg. For the latter, the final score—44–0—was less satisfying than having his faith in a certain dropkicker justified. Years later, von Kersburg recalled his coup with relish. "The psychological moment had arrived," he wrote. "Just as soon as the Harvard team had rolled up a tidy little score, Kennard was sent into the game and instructions were given to the quarterback that he was to signal for a dropkick every time the Harvard team was within 40 yards of the opponent's goal—no matter what the angle might be." Kennard nailed field goals on a dropkick and a placement, and added a point after touchdown. "Nearly all of them were kicked from an average distance of 30 yards and at very difficult angles," continued von Kersburg. "At the next coaches' meeting, serious consideration was given to what Kennard had done, and from that time on he came into his own."[22]

✧ ✧ ✧

It was now late October. The preliminary games were past. Practices began in the bright, glinting New England sunlight. When they finished, chill and darkness cloaked the Charles. In the evenings, Haughton and his staff pored over color-coded dominos, devising formations and defenses, and pondering the roster. They had uncovered a quarterback and a wild-card kicker, and had two steady ends.

Now loomed the meat of the season—a tough game at Navy, home games against Brown, Carlisle, and Dartmouth, then The Game at New Haven. For the Crimson linemen especially, these would be foes worthy of their steel. Haughton thought they needed tutoring, and he had in mind the perfect tutor: Ernest "Pot" Graves. A former star in 1905, and coach in 1906, at West Point, the barrel-chested Graves had spent time in Cambridge in 1907, providing pointers. He was expert in the techniques of the scrum—gaining leverage, even against a heavier man, artfully using hands to avoid holding penalties. There was only one complication: Following his graduation, Graves had been commissioned a lieutenant of engineers. He was stationed at the Washington barracks—and the army was loath to give him leave to coach at a civilian college.

Percy Haughton appealed to the highest authority. Bypassing the secretary of war, William Howard Taft—a Yale man, by Jove!—P. D. sent a note straight to the First Fan in the White House, asking Roosevelt, in his capacity as commander in chief, to transfer Graves to Cambridge. "I was a Harvard man before I was a politician," T. R. told Taft. "Please do what these men want."[23] Pot Graves was posted to Cambridge for the balance of the season.

Graves arrived a few days after the October 24 game against Navy at Annapolis, matching unbeaten, untied, and unscored-upon teams (as did Penn and Carlisle in front of 20,000 at Franklin Field the same day). It was, as the *Globe* later termed it, a "real scrap from beginning to end" and a "splendid test for Harvard."[24] By that standard, the Crimson emerged from the 6–6 tie with a solid B. The Midshipmen boasted two All-Americas on their line's left side: tackle and kicker Percy Northcroft and end Lawrence Reifsnider. (The latter would be a highly decorated commander in both world wars.) Early in the game, the duo figured in Navy's scoring, with Reifsnider snagging a pass from the Harvard 25 and running it over the goal line, and Northcroft booting the conversion. Showing that Graves would have his work cut out for him, Harvard struggled to deal with Navy's low-starting, quick-charging line. The Crimson's only decent drive of the first half petered out at the Navy 14, when Cutler was smothered as he dropped back to pass.

The second half, however, brought a turnover that turned into a turnaround. With Navy on the move, running back Richardson followed Northcroft into the line but was stacked up. Before he was down, Harvard tackle Charles Dunlap knocked the ball into the chest of Crimson center Joe Nourse, who quickly set sail for the Navy goal. He had 30 yards on his nearest pursuer, whom Fish sent somersaulting down the field. Captain Burr thumped through the conversion to give the Crimson a deft escape.

Suddenly and seemingly unaccountably, the tie against a reputable foe edged the Crimson into the conversation for the national title with Yale (unbeaten, untied, and unscored upon) and Penn, whose game with Carlisle also ended 6–6. To impress Walter Camp and other selectors, none of the three could afford a slip. For Harvard, there was the distinct possibility of a letdown against the next opponent, Brown. The Bruins and their fans had come up from Providence 16 times; 16 times they had returned with a loss. But Brown was dangerous because it played a wide-open game spearheaded by quarterback Bill Sprackling, one of football's first great passers. William Earl Sprackling was only a freshman and weighed but 150 pounds. He was nicknamed the "Defiant One," partly for his refusal to wear a helmet and pads. Like Bobby Layne later on, he hollered at both foe and assignment-missing teammate.

In the week before the October 31 game, two events occurred that would profoundly impact Harvard's season. The first came in practice, when captain Francis Burr hurt his shoulder. He was ruled out indefinitely. Haughton named Ham Fish acting captain. Burr's absence meant Graves would have to boost the play of underachieving tackle Bob McKay.

The second, involving struggling second-string lineman Rex ver Wiebe, came courtesy of trainer Pooch Donovan. Recalled Harry von Kersburg,

> One afternoon, one of the line coaches was standing on the sidelines talking with Pooch Donovan about ver Wiebe. Pooch said little but

kept a close watch on ver Wiebe for the next two or three days. At the end of that time, he came out with the statement that if ver Wiebe could be taught how to start, he would rapidly develop into one of the best halfbacks on the squad.[25]

Haughton promptly shifted ver Wiebe to backup fullback.

That Saturday, the move had an immediate payoff. On that Halloween afternoon, the first chill of winter gave the 17,000 stadium fans, said the *Globe*, a "feeling something like satisfaction buttoned-up under their great coats."[26] Harvard supporters were warmed by a 6–2 win that was more convincing than the score would indicate. The Crimson outgained the Bruins 379 yards to 40, with Bob McKay among those leading an aggressive defensive charge. Sprackling made a dandy 25-yard completion but on the next play was smeared and coughed up the ball. Following the Haughton blueprint, Harvard wore Brown down, breaking a scoreless game with a relentless 16-play touchdown drive capped by a three-yard run by back Bob White. And who was the man who hurled White over the goal? Why, Pooch Donovan's find, Rex ver Wiebe—who had subbed for Kennard at the start of the half.

☼ ☼ ☼

November. Along the Charles, the trees were bare, heralding the long, gray New England winter. Now the games would be played in front of banks of dark-coated men in somber-looking derbies. The decisive month for college football and politics was at hand. This was a presidential election year, and on Tuesday, November 3, robust Republican William Howard Taft, from Ohio out of Yale, easily beat silver-tongued Nebraska Democrat William Jennings Bryan. There went Harvard's friend in the White House.

But some undergraduates could be pardoned if they cared less about the Electoral College than the team at their college. Harvard had football fever. Capitalizing on it, Percy Haughton addressed a mass meeting of 450 at the Harvard Union. On the gridiron he took no prisoners, but his rhetoric was straight from the gentleman amateur's handbook. "Cheering does more good than any amount of coaching," P. D. instructed the assemblage, adding,

Don't cheer to rattle the opposing team, and don't do it just when
signals are being given; but by all means cheer for all you were worth
at the proper times. It makes a thrill run up the backbone of every
player and shows them more than anything else can that the undergraduates are with them.[27]

The public utterance was a rare interlude for Haughton, who was
fixed on his next foe: Carlisle. Like Harvard, the Indians of Pop Warner
were 6–0–1. Star runner and kicker Jim Thorpe was in his first stint at
the school. (The second would come in 1911 and 1912.) Carlisle's exciting, lateral-filled style pleased crowds—this day's would number
25,000—and hoodwinked many an opponent. So did the skullduggery
of the slippery Warner. In 1903, Pop had used a then-legal hidden-ball
play (with the football placed under his runners' jerseys) to help his
team upset the Crimson, 12–11.

Haughton was always suspicious of everyone. But to paraphrase an
adage, just because he was paranoid doesn't mean Warner wasn't out to
get him. A stunt earlier in the 1908 season justified Percy's misgivings.
In a game against Syracuse, Warner had duped the Orangemen by
having leather patches shaped like footballs sewn to the uniforms of his
ends and backs. The upshot: The Syracuse players didn't know who had
the ball. Von Kersburg was the first to hear of this, from one of his
contacts in Buffalo.

While von Kersburg was reading the telegram, Haughton and the
other coaches came into the locker room. They saw the grim look on
von Kersburg's face. "Any bad news, Kersey?" they inquired.

"Yes," answered von Kersburg. "It certainly is bad news unless we
are able to develop countermeasures."

Recalled von Kersburg, "After reading the message, Percy pulled off
his cap, slammed it on his chair, and, scratching his head, said, 'Well I'll
be damned! Pop is pulling another trick out of his bag.'" Haughton got
wind that Warner would try the same ruse when the Indians visited
Cambridge.

"Haughton studied the rules and found nothing to prevent Warner's
scheme," later recalled Vic Kennard. When Warner and the Indians
arrived in Boston the day before the game, Haughton and von Kersburg
paid them a visit. Haughton handed Warner the telegram. "Glenn, Kersey received this wire a few days after your game with Syracuse,"
Haughton said. "Is the statement correct?"

Warner grinned. "Of course it is," he replied. "There is nothing in the rules that makes it illegal for our backs to wear those half footballs."

Recalled von Kersburg, "With that, Percy tightened his lips and, saluting, replied as only he could in his brisk, forceful way, 'Very well Pop, we'll be seeing you tomorrow afternoon.'"

Haughton did not vouchsafe his counterpunch.

Taking no chances, however, Haughton worked out a scheme of his own. He discovered that there was no rule which prevented painting the ball red, so he had a ball painted the same color as the crimson jerseys.

The next afternoon during pregame warmups, Haughton and Harvard manager Dick Eggleston walked onto the field with a bag of footballs. Haughton beckoned to Warner, who would be allowed to select the game ball from the batch.

Eggleston opened the bag and began pulling out footballs. Warner's eyes widened. Each ball had been dyed crimson and would blend in with the Harvard jerseys.

"A sickly smile came over Pop's face," wrote von Kersburg. "'Percy, you win!' The half footballs were removed from the Indians' jerseys before the kickoff, at which time a regulation ball was teed up."[28]

The ball could have been purple with polka dots: Carlisle was no match for the most complete Harvard performance in years. The Crimson won, 17–0, holding the Indians to five first downs and smothering a Thorpe placement attempt. Harvard had three long drives for scores, the last one (which, obviously, never will be topped) comprising 108 yards. For observers, three aspects stood out: Harvard's superior conditioning; the smashing, ripping ground game; and Cutler's skill and generalship, testament to Charlie Daly's coaching. Given perfect protection, the quarterback completed two nifty passes to Fish (eligible when he lined up in the backfield). The second, as noted by the *Globe's* W. D. Sullivan, was a prehistoric alley-oop—a "short lob over the rush line and . . . into the arms of the towering Fish."[29]

* * *

The season had dwindled to two games—the so-called "championship games." The next opponent, Dartmouth, had upset Princeton and would arrive at the stadium 6–0–1. The day's real shocker had come in New Haven, where Yale was tied by Brown, 10–10. That made Harvard's victory over the Bruins look even better.

The one unhappy man in the Crimson camp was Vic Kennard, whom umpire William H. Edwards had tossed from the Carlisle game for unnecessary roughness. Vic repaired to his family's home in Brookline, where he felt he could rest more comfortably than in Cambridge. Recalled Kennard,

> I occupied the adjoining room to my mother's and when I was ready for bed always opened the door between the rooms. One night I woke up suddenly and heard my mother talking. Wondering whether something was the matter, I got out of bed and went into her room, appearing just in time to see my mother's arms outstretched. She was calling, "Fair catch." I spoke to her to see just what the trouble was, and she, in a sleepy way, mumbled, "We won." She had been dreaming of the Harvard–Dartmouth game.[30]

Had Yale not existed then, The Game might have been Harvard–Dartmouth. While the team and student body—even then, considered country ruffians by the snooty Crimsonians—descended on the Square from Hanover, New Hampshire, the large number of Dartmouth alums in the Boston area helped make the game, always played in Boston, a perennial sellout. In 1903, the Indians (as they then were known) had christened Harvard Stadium with an 11–0 victory. In '08, Dartmouth came in having not lost in two seasons. Coach John O'Connor boasted two All-Americas, guard Clark Tobin and tackle George Schildmiller, and an African American running back named Leslie Pollard, older brother of future Brown and NFL immortal Fritz.

Haughton expected a tough slog. His strategy was to keep the Indians close and hope to subdue them in the second half. Accordingly, the game featured 25 punts, 13 by Harvard. In the first half, Kennard's boots helped keep Dartmouth penned in. In the second half, he was replaced at fullback by ver Wiebe, by now a key to the Crimson ground game.

The game was scoreless and the hour late when John Cutler seized the moment. The Crimson got the ball on its 23. "It was the machine-like advance which so few Harvard teams have been able to carry so far as their opponents' goal line," reported the *Globe* the next day.[31] Cutler mixed the power running of ver Wiebe, Howard Leslie, and Perry Smith with three sensational forward passes. First, Cutler tossed to Gil Browne for 24 yards. Then came a double pass: Cutler passed the ball to Browne, who started to circle right end, then pivoted and slung the pigskin out to Crowley on the left of the Harvard line for 13 yards. Finally, from the 15, Cutler pitched to Fish, who crashed to the seven. From the three, Leslie followed Fish over the goal. McKay kicked the goal. The drive had consumed 87 yards. Two minutes later, the time-keeper's whistle blew. Writing for the *Globe*, Dartmouth's 1907 captain, John Glaze, was impressed. "Cutler's daring in risking forward passes on the third down was evidence of what the Harvard team can do when it comes to a pinch," Glaze declared. [32]

That afternoon, playing in front of 30,000 in New Jersey, Yale beat Princeton, 11–6. Thus, The Game, a battle of unbeatens, was set for New Haven.

Percy Haughton was 70 minutes from pulling off the biggest miracle in football history.

❁ ❁ ❁

In New Haven, Yale, captained by Bobby Burch, was entering The Game with a swagger both customary and earned. The Elis had not only beaten the Crimson six straight, but also not lost to anyone since 1904, when Army defeated them. Despite Harvard's unbeaten '08 season, there was little reason to think Yale would not prevail, simply because, as their famous song concluded, "Harvard's men will fight till the end but Yale . . . will . . . win!" In the 28 games the schools had played since 1875, Crimson victories were so rare as to be outliers, and the years could be counted on one hand: 1875, 1890, 1898, 1901 . . .

In the week before The Game, a raft of each team's former players would descend upon the practice field to lend advice and counsel. Yale's college of coaches resembled an early-day College Football Hall of Fame: Heffelfinger, Hinkey, Shevlin, punter Billy Bull, and back Gordon Brown. Presiding would be Camp. Yes, Yale was in good hands. Among its students and alumni, the Blue also was renowned for its "Yale spirit"—a unified, schoolwide fervor. Camp didn't have to instruct the Yalies in cheering the way Haughton had the Harvardians. Perhaps it is easier to be spirited when you win all the time.

In Cambridge, by contrast, the Harvards had to find various methods to live with the annual loss. Eminent historian Samuel Eliot Morison (class of 1908), in *Three Centuries of Harvard*, his official history published for the university's tricentennial in 1936, describes what seems like a variation of the famed stages of grief as identified by psychiatrist Elizabeth Kübler-Ross. Morison notes, "A Yale victory on the river or the football field was a subject for mourning, from the early [1870s]." He pinpoints one of the most salient characteristics of the Harvard fan, then and now:

> The famous "Harvard indifference," a quality attributed to the undergraduates from the early [1880s] to the present because they never did "support the team" anything like 100 percent. Their athletes did not water sod with tears of bitterness when defeated, and a mask of indifference had to be cultivated to hide the chagrin of successive drubbings by Walter Camp's teams. Still: Harvard felt a certain loss of manhood in not winning a single football game with Yale in the 80s and only two in the 90s.[33]

There even was a bare hint that if the Crimson's futility persisted, The Game might become Yale versus . . . a school in New Jersey. As the *Harvard H Book of Athletics* related,

> At a banquet of Princeton alumni held in Boston, November 9, 1907, "Pa" Corbin, '89, the famous old Eli player and coach, said, "I hope that Harvard will get a system and method that will make her really formidable in football, but until she does we must count Princeton as our dearest foe."[34]

This was more than rhetoric. As author John Miller related in his book *The Big Scrum*, one Yale coach, John Owsley, wanted Yale to break with Harvard anyway:

> "I am very anxious to see Yale drop Harvard quietly in football," he wrote to Camp. "It is no pleasure for us, at least not for me, to have beaten Harvard and to afterwards hear the lies and whining of their players and some of their graduates." Owsley proposed scrapping the annual Harvard–Yale game and hosting a western team, by which he probably meant Chicago or Michigan.[35]

As with all decided underdogs, Harvard would have to play a perfect game, while hoping Yale brought less than its best. Try to get a lead and hold on for dear life. Percy Haughton knew that on talent and experience and depth, Yale had the edge. Harvard would dress a mere 21 players. The loss of injured Crimson captain Burr, both as a lineman and a punter, threatened to be grievous. The Elis had the best player on the field in junior power back and punter Ted Coy, who used high-knee action to help gather steam; once under way, he was a load to tackle. (He was one of six Elis from Hotchkiss.) Somehow, he must be bottled up. Coy was abetted by his running mate, "Silent" Steve Philbin, and quarterback Allan "Pop" Corey, whose father, William, was president of U.S. Steel. The Crimson had to be mistake-free; Cutler, especially, had to be flawless in handling punts. When Harvard punted, its coverage had to be airtight. It would help to score first so as not to have to take risks later.

But Haughton had three aces up his sleeve. One was misdirection. By shifting left tackle Bob McKay, P. D. would overload the strong (right) side of the line—and run his newfound power back, Rex ver Wiebe, from the head of the tandem to the short side.

The second ace was Vic Kennard.

The third ace was psychological warfare—directed at his own team.

To fire up his undermanned underdogs, Percy D. Haughton choked to death a live bulldog. With his bare hands.

*   *   *

That, anyway, is the urban legend. But dogged research reveals it not to be true, even though everyone who knew the Crimson coach admitted it contains poetic truth. The tale still pops up among casual football fans at the mention of Haughton's name. ("He's the guy who strangled the bulldog—right?") Here's the real story, as related by Harry von Kersburg in 1948.

Two days before the game, the team had arrived at the Elm Tree Inn in Farmington, Connecticut. "Percy went to Hartford on some pretext or other," wrote von Kersburg. He added,

> While he was away, Pooch Donovan took the squad for a long hike
> on the golf course, which was across from the inn. By prearrange-

ment, everything had been timed to the minute, because when the returning squad was on the side of the road opposite the inn, who should appear on the scene but P. D. H., driving a car. Tied to the rear of the car was a long rope fastened to the neck of a papier-mâché bulldog. The dog was decked out with a blue blanket, on either side of which was a large, white block Y. The stunt evoked roars of laughter.

This was the opening salvo in a barrage to keep his charges loose. Von Kersburg continued,

On the day of the bulldog incident, P. D. took the whole team down to the Farmington express office, where there were many packages addressed to the girls attending Miss Porter's School, which was located in the town. The fellows copied as many names as possible, and when they arrived in New Haven the following morning, they sent picture post cards and Yale souvenirs to Miss Porter's girls. Their minds were everywhere but on the game.

The final act of Percy's pregame strategy to keep the men from moping around with their chins cupped in their hands took place in the dining room of the old New Haven House. There were two long tables parallel to each other with a space between just wide enough for the waiters to move about while serving lunch. When the Yale players began to arrive, the waiters had already started to serve the Harvard squad. Percy, sitting at the head of the table, lost no time in starting his horseplay with a rapid-fire line of talk about each Yale man as he sat down.

His comments were made in a voice loud enough for the Elis to hear. Pointing out each man, they ran something like this, "Joe [Nourse], that fellow sitting down is Biddle, whom you will play against this afternoon. I know that you are going to smear him. Ham [Fish], see that 'blue-belly' just sitting down? That's Hobbs. Treat him kindly. I hate to think what you are going to do to him." Percy continued his glib-chatter much along these lines, much to the embarrassment of the Yale men but much to the amusement of the Harvard team. He would now and then interrupt his remarks, when someone at the other end of the table would ask for more chicken, by picking up a piece from the platter and tossing it to him. Such clowning as this kept the merriment of the squad at high pitch.[36]

Harvard men were more easily amused in those days.

* * *

Despite the dismal track record, thousands of Harvard fans (including Vic Kennard's mother and brothers, one of whom was a Yalie) made the trek to New Haven and Yale Field, which would serve the Elis for six more seasons until the opening of Yale Bowl. The bleachers, seating 33,000, were crammed to bulging, with the partisans of each side exchanging school songs and cheers. The late-autumn sun, although low in the sky, was unseasonably strong, and there was no breeze to stir the crimson and blue pennants.

Out trotted the teams. George Trevor of the *New York Sun* took note of the sterling appearance of the Harvards. "All 11 men were stamped from the same die," he wrote, "tall, wasp-waisted, broad-shouldered wolfhounds in human form."[37]

At 2:03 p.m., referee William Langford called captains Burch and Fish to the 55-yard line for the toss, which Harvard won. Taking the north goal for the first 35-minute half, the Crimson kicked off.

The early going belonged to Yale. As the game played out in the Harvard end, the mighty Coy and Philbin pounded out gains, while Coy outpunted Cutler. Three times, the Elis neared the goal line. A penalty set back one drive; a flubbed dropkick halted another; still another stalled as the Harvard defense stiffened. Fish and McKay were stalwart. Still, while Yale had no scoring punch, Harvard seemed to have no punch at all.

Then the field tilted. Ver Wiebe, a nonfactor mere weeks ago, began ripping off big gains through the Yale short side: 12 yards one time, 22 another. But two drives petered out, the way Yale's had.

Late in the half, Harvard took over on its 40. Quarterback Cutler began cleverly alternating rushes by backs Ham Corbett, Bob White, and the relentless ver Wiebe. Throughout the drive, Haughton moved down the sideline, on a line with the ball and with Vic Kennard in tow. Nine plays later, the ball stood on the Yale 14, facing to the left of the goalposts. Third down and four.

Now came the biggest gamble of Percy Haughton's career, and perhaps the cornerstone of his legend. To the dismay of the Harvard stands, he signaled for Rex ver Wiebe, his best ballcarrier, to come to the sideline. His day was done. In trotted Victor Kennard.

During practice, Kennard and center Joe Nourse had hatched a plan. When Kennard halted behind the scrimmage line at dropkicking distance—in this case, the 23-yard line—Nourse simply was to snap him the ball without waiting for a signal. Now Nourse settled over the ball. Belatedly, the Yale defense was hurrying to set up a rush from Harvard's right, as Haughton suspected it might. When Nourse made the snap, the Elis still were not in position. Kennard received the football and dropped it to the ground. Swiftly and unimpeded, he gave the pigskin a thump. As Tim Cohane later wrote, "It soared prettily over the heads of Yale's linemen, who had been caught laggard. On it went, spinning over the crossbar for a perfect field goal and Harvard's first score against Yale since 1901."[38]

It also took a moment for the spectators to comprehend what they had seen, or not seen. When they did, the Harvard fans went wild. The Crimson led—*led!!*—4–0.

Shortly thereafter, the half ended. There were 35 minutes to go, 35 minutes of holding off Coy and Philbin, and history. Moreover, even as they were thrilled with Haughton's brilliant and timely insertion of Kennard, the Harvard supporters wondered if the coach had outwitted not only the Elis, but also himself by pulling ver Wiebe. Why hadn't he kept him in and yanked another, seemingly more expendable player, for instance, end Charlie Crowley? It seemed an abject surrender of the offense; those precious four points would have to hold up.

The second half began. It was played entirely on Harvard's side of the field. With Coy's punts driving Harvard farther back, the Elis kept creeping closer to the goal line. Fish and McKay repelled them. Kennard, now playing as a defensive back, also was a stopper. Eight years later, he recalled the play:

> Five or six minutes before the end of the game, one E. H. Coy decided that the time was getting short and Yale needed a touchdown. So, he grabbed a Harvard punt on the run and started. Yes, he did more than start, he got well underway, circled the Harvard end and, after galloping 15 yards, apparently concluded that I would look well as minced meat and headed straight for me, stationed well back on the secondary defense. He had received no invitation whatsoever, but owing to the fact that I believe every Harvard man should be at least cordial to every Yale man, I decided to go 50–50 and meet him halfway. We met informally. . . . He weighed only 195 pounds, but I

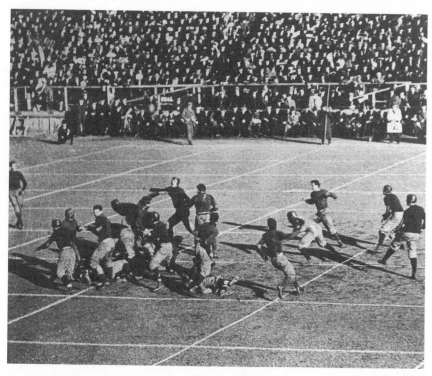

Having virtually snuck onto the field, left-footed Vic Kennard (far right) booted the field goal that shocked Yale, a kick that became the cornerstone of the Haughton coaching legend. *Oscar White/Corbis Historical/Getty Images.*

am sure he had another couple of hundred tucked away somewhere. When I had finished counting a great variety and number of stars, it occurred to me that I had been in a ghastly railroad wreck, and that the engine and cars following had picked out my right knee as a nice soft place to pile up on. There was a feeling of great relief when I looked around and saw that the engineer of that train, Mr. E. H. Coy, had stopped with the train, and I held the greatest hopes that neither the engine nor any one of the 10 cars following would ever reach the terminal.

Kennard's mother was sitting in the Crimson stands with his two brothers. "Mother, who had seen the whole performance, was little concerned with other than the fact that E. H. had been delayed," Kennard recalled. Meantime, her son lay on the field. Kennard continued,

Someone who sat almost directly back of my mother called out loud, "That's young Kennard. It looks as though [he's] broken his leg." My brother, feeling that mother had not heard the remark, and not knowing what he might say, turned and informed him that Mrs. Kennard was sitting almost directly in front of him, requesting that he be careful what he said. Mother, however, heard the whole thing, and turning in her seat said, "That's all right, I don't care if his leg is broken, if we only win this game."[39]

Moments later, after the stop, the Crimson took over—but in the shadow of its own goal line. Here, Haughton made his second seemingly incomprehensible substitution. Out came Ham Corbett, the best backfield defender. Onto the field ran sophomore back Harry Sprague. The frail-looking redhead had been injured for much of the season. Now he dropped back into punt formation. As Nourse snapped the ball back, the Harvard crowd held its breath. All day, no Yale blocker had troubled a Harvard punter, and there was no harassment this time either. *Thump!* The ball went sailing high and deep, all the way to the Harvard 40. For now, the Crimson was out of danger. The fans exhaled.

Time was ticking away. Yale now was betraying confusion, if not panic, as evidenced by delay in play selection. But the Elis had one more thrust and, eschewing a tie, decided to go all in for victory. From the Harvard 25, back Fred Daly assumed field-goal position. But the ball was snapped instead to quarterback Ford Johnson, who heaved it downfield, where Yale tackle Art Brides, an eligible receiver, stood unmolested. Brides snagged the ball and wasn't downed until he reached the eight-yard line. The Yale stands roared, and the Elis raced to the new scrimmage line.

A whistle pierced the din. It was sounded by referee Langford. Standing back at the 25, he disallowed the completion: The ball hadn't crossed the line the requisite five yards from where it was snapped. Again, Harvard was saved.

Haughton had one more master substitution to make: sophomore Howard Leslie for Sprague. As the clock ran, so did Leslie, who proceeded to gain clutch, time-eating yardage.

The timekeeper's whistle sounded.

Validation had arrived for Volkmann products Kennard and Cutler, and their fellow football discard ver Wiebe, for assistant Harry von Kersburg, for Pot Graves and his pupil Bob McKay, and for long-suffering Crimson fans. But make no mistake: The man who had seen the possibilities and limitations, who had driven his men physically, who had instilled the will to win—who had pulled it off—was Percy Duncan Haughton, '99.

"Carried from the field upon the shoulders of their delirious supporters," wrote the *Boston Globe*, "the Harvard football players underwent almost as rough treatment at the hands of their friends as they had previously suffered at those of Yale."[40]

At the White House, T. R. got the news via telegraph on the tennis court. He pushed back his slouch hat and joyfully swung his racket round and round.[41] In Cambridge, the other president, Charles W. Eliot, soon to retire after 40 years as Harvard's chief executive, allowed as how the "result was very satisfactory."[42] ("O! Pshaw!" Taft was quoted as saying.[43])

In New Haven, winter had arrived a month early. Now it was Yale's turn to affect indifference in defeat. As Mel Webb of the *Globe* wrote in his wrap-up, "'Let them have a chance,' I heard one [Yale] fellow say. 'It's only once in seven years.'"[44] Forever after, Ford Johnson would declare he had thrown that pass within five yards out of center. After the game, Walter Camp had accosted referee Langford under the stands. "What was the matter with that pass?" Camp demanded. Langford told him. Camp went back and did some checking. Afterward, he wrote a gracious letter to Langford that said, "I wish to thank you for your work in the game, which was first class."[45] Camp also named Corbett, Fish, and Nourse to his All-America team.

As was customary with Yale captains whose teams had suffered the ignominy of a Game loss, the following fall Bobby Burch was not invited back to help at Elis practices.

A sadder fate befell hard-luck Harvard captain Francis Burr, whose injury had relegated him to cheering on his mates from the sidelines. In 1910, he would die of typhus.

❊ ❊ ❊

Then, as now, the postseason pundits set about asking, "Who's number one?" The only teams in the debate were the usual suspects, the powers from the East and a few from the Midwest. Essentially, if Harvard, Yale, or Princeton was unbeaten, its claim was automatically staked.

(Undefeated Louisiana State University might as well have been playing not in the South, but at the South Pole.) Nevertheless, Harvard was passed over for the mythical national title in favor of 11–0–1 Penn. There are modern football scholars who have pored over records and revived the annual debates. One, James Vautravers, has performed detailed analysis and attempted to rerank teams of that era, posting his thoughts on his website, Tiptop25.com. Writes Vautravers, "I think Harvard's wins over Carlisle and Yale (let alone 6–1–1 Dartmouth) make them a clear choice for number one. . . . I find it strange that NCAA records book selectors retroactively name Penn national champion, while no one selects Harvard to even share the title."[46]

For Harvard, this was but a trifle. In contrast to the previous half-dozen years with their gloomy losses to Yale, the Crimson was back in the football picture, and its prospects were rosy. As Haughton's friend Mike Farley said at the season-ending banquet, "It is not a Crimson sunset, but a Crimson sunrise that we are indeed celebrating."[47]

Most important, Percy Haughton had strangled the bulldog. He would not do so again for four years, but by then P. D. had done something at least as important: help resuscitate and reinvent a dying sport.

Victor Kennard had the shoe with which he kicked his field goal emblazoned as a trophy. The upper part was painted crimson, with the score inscribed. The sole was painted blue.[48]

2

DEATH IN THE AFTERNOON

One of the many considerable pleasures of attending The Game at Harvard Stadium is its timelessness. The edifice, the world's first reinforced concrete structure, has had several facelifts since its opening in 1903. Fashions, of course, have changed; the 21st-century crowd is invariably jeans-, blazer-, and parka-clad, as opposed to the dark-suited, bowler-hatted throngs of the early 1900s. But the late November sun strikes the august colonnade at the same angle; the fickle winds twist and swirl as always. The field is the very one on which strode Charlie Brickley, Barry Wood, and Tommy Lee Jones (for Harvard), and Ted Coy, Albie Booth, and Brian Dowling (Yale). You can imagine yourself transported back, possibly to the 1909 contest, which in its buildup and national significance was the granddaddy of all Games.

The 1909 football season began in businesslike fashion. Even as Cambridge sweltered in late summer, the attitude was purposeful. Harvard had a championship to live up to and the chance to accomplish a first: win a second straight game against Ted Coy and Yale.

But the season, marked by a thrilling, week-to-week pas de deux with the Elis and the most glittering finale the sport had yet seen, would contain a tragic game-changer that threatened its very existence. Harvard, as it had been during the crisis of 1905, again would be at ground zero, this time literally.

In Cambridge, as in Washington, D.C., there would be a new leader. On October 6, Abbott Lawrence Lowell, class of 1877, was inaugurated as the 22nd president of Harvard, a post he would hold until 1933.

Unlike his predecessor, Charles W. Eliot, Lowell, in today's parlance, bought into football. It did not hurt that as an undergraduate he had been a record-setting half-miler. "I believe strongly in the physical and moral value of athletic sports," he declared in his inaugural speech, continuing,

> and of intercollegiate contests conducted in a spirit of generous rivalry; and I do not believe that their exaggerated prominence at the present day is to be attributed to a conviction on the part of the undergraduates, or of the public, that physical is more valuable than mental force. It is due rather to the fact that such contests offer to students the one common interest, the only striking occasion for a display of college solidarity. [1]

Another powerful football backer was LeBaron R. Briggs, dean of the Faculty of Arts and Sciences, who became chairman of the Athletic Committee in 1907. In an influential speech titled "Athletics and College Loyalty," published in the *Harvard Alumni Bulletin* on November 4, 1908—not coincidentally, Percy Haughton's first season as coach— Briggs, class of 1875, declared,

> Football played in America today between schools and colleges is not a mere game; still less it is a mere exhibition of hard-trained strength and skill. It is to the typical undergraduate mind the supreme expression of college loyalty; and everything that touches it becomes a question of allegiance to alma mater. An intercollegiate contest assumes in the minds of players, coaches, students, graduates, and the affiliated public the importance of war. [2]

In 1912, Briggs would be named president of the National Collegiate Athletic Association (NCAA).

Football players, then, were the ultimate warriors. They jibed with Lowell's conception of the all-around, liberally educated man: "The elite should be, if possible, both intellectually and physically superior. That among them some should be in mind and others in physique above the ordinary is not enough."[3] Literally and figuratively, the Crimson footballers were the "Big Men on Campus." Their care and feeding were of great concern. The Harvard Varsity Club had moved into the Harvard Union. In 1914, newspaper columnist Ring Lardner visited before Harvard hosted Michigan at the stadium. "After eating one of those Harvard training table meals," Lardner wrote, "I can plainly see why so many men go out for the football team at Cambridge. And that being just lunch. I wish they'd invite me to dinner."[4]

There were many future notables at Harvard during that era, some of whom already were using campus activities to make their reputations: T. S. Eliot, Walter Lippmann, John Reed, Robert Benchley, John Dos Passos, Frederick Lewis Allen, Joseph P. Kennedy, and John P. Marquand. The professors included some of the most eminent names in academe, for instance, William James, George Santayana (a huge Crimson sports fan), and noted Shakespearean scholar George Lyman Kittredge. But as also was the case at Yale and Princeton, football players were the A-list celebrities. Like many star athletes today, they had reputations even before they entered as freshmen, giving them ready-made constituencies for class offices and influence.

Academically, Charles Eliot had been a liberal, having pioneered the elective system, allowing students a wide range of course choices as they progressed toward a degree. Lowell was more conservative; he insisted on a core curriculum, with a number of mandatory courses. But Lowell also wanted to widen the school's geographical range beyond its traditional New England/Northeast private-school base. Thus, he approved a "New Plan" of admission, one that allowed an applicant to choose either Harvard's standardized admissions exam (heavy on the classics) or a more flexible approach.

Flexibility did not mean leniency, and the average public high school curriculum would not prepare a student adequately. A candidate had to have the proper academic grounding. This could be most readily found at the prep schools that were feeders to Harvard and other Ivy colleges. To be admitted at Cambridge, an athlete, no matter how splendid and bright, *had* to qualify academically; therefore, many public school athletes—even some, for example, the class of 1915's Charles Brickley, who had a solid, if undistinguished, high-school transcript laden with grades in the 80s (essentially, Bs)[5] —were sent to Andover or Exeter for a year or two to get up to speed. (After graduating from Everett High, Brickley spent a year at Exeter.) Some, as their admissions reports in the Harvard University Archives reveal, would be admitted "with conditions." But admitted most were; there still was that craving to beat Yale.

During those years, the United States was experiencing an unprecedented wave of immigration from Southern and Eastern Europe. By some estimates, Jews in the freshman class grew from 7 percent in 1900 to 15.1 percent in 1914—numbers that were swelled by Jewish upper-class transfer students from the Boston area.[6] But you will comb the rosters in vain for a Jewish surname. In 1916, that would change when Harvard would see the arrival of the Horween brothers, Ralph and Arnold, from Chicago; after time out for military service in World War I, this brother act would be a mainstay of the 1919 team that went to the 1920 Rose Bowl and beat Oregon, 7–6. Later in the 1920s, Arnold Horween became the Crimson's head coach. But they were outliers among the Big Three. During the Haughton era, among the few great Jewish players from the Big Three were two Princeton All-America linemen, Harold Ballin and center Arthur "Bluethy" Bluethenthal. (The latter would perish in World War I.)

One handicap to becoming an Ivy jock was financial. The average annual American salary for all industries in 1910 was $574 a year.[7] Tuition at Harvard was $150 a year, a trifle for the son of a captain of industry but an unattainable fortune for the child of a workingman. That meant that many a student from an immigrant family (a number of whom received Price Greenleaf Scholarships of as much as $200 a year) could not afford to live on campus but had to live at home—and, probably, juggle his studies with a job, on campus or off. There just wasn't time for extracurriculars. Another was training: The game was best instilled at the prep schools, which were selective about admitting sons of immigrants.

Still another handicap was, plain and simple, prejudice: Immigrants weren't the "right sort." In the 1920s, Lowell would institute quotas for Jewish students; Princeton and Yale had similar policies. This de facto exclusion played right into the pattern of social organization at Harvard, which Harvard historian John T. Bethell has characterized as "Greasy Grinds and Gold Coasters." The former were the earnest, academically oriented boys—today they would be called "wonks"—who, by choice or exclusion, were out of the social swing. The latter lived comfortably in ritzy private residential halls on Mt. Auburn Street, labeled the "Gold Coast," some with swimming pools and squash courts. Most of the athletes gravitated there. For these grandees, Harvard was a four-year roundelay of games, final clubs, "smokers," and dances, interrupted by enough studying (possibly with the aid of a tutor) to avoid probation or expulsion. As beloved Boylston professor of rhetoric and oratory

Charles T. "Copey" Copeland might have it, it was a life of "sport, shop, and sex."[8] Or, as the mantra of gentlemen who wanted to enjoy their time in the Yard professed, "Three C's and a D, and keep out of the newspapers."

✼ ✼ ✼

Even as the Harvard administration turned over in 1909, in football there was welcome continuity. In March, Haughton had re-upped for another season. As practice began at Soldiers Field on September 13, he had to prove he was no one-year wonder. Although he had done the impossible in 1908, he had done it with men whom he or his presence did not bring to the school. With freshman ineligible, that would be true in 1909, as well. In 1908, he had introduced many of his ideas, but he would not have the proper personnel to refine them for another two, perhaps three, years.

So, he would continue to treat Soldiers Field as a laboratory. His first experiment was to try to make his men quicker. In spring workouts, as the *Boston Globe* reported, he had instituted a new drill:

> There was a dodging practice, a new stunt in Harvard football, in-tended to stimulate quickness. Several men are lined up in a row and the rest of the squad sent on a run the length of the line, dodging in and out between the stationary men. The first man through the line takes up his position as one of the dodging posts, while the last stationary man joins the chase.[9]

Many of P. D.'s 1908 coaches were back, and Leo Leary, who had assisted in '07, returned to coach the ends. (He would become perhaps Haughton's most trusted assistant.) Lieut. Pot Graves, however, would not be able to make a late-season rescue appearance: He now was stationed in the Philippines, safely (for President William Howard Taft and other Yalies) out of Haughton's reach.

Unlike in 1908, P. D. began training with a group of experienced championship players. But like the previous season, he was searching for a quarterback. (This would be a refrain for the next four years.) The heady Cutler was gone. Haughton would settle on a jumpy junior named Dan O'Flaherty, a South Boston lad who had attended Bridge-water (Massachusetts) Normal School. At 176 pounds, O'Flaherty was

12 pounds heavier than Cutler, but he lacked his sangfroid. O'Flaherty did have superb runners in the returning Ham Corbett and Perry Smith, and in Wayland "Dono" Minot, who had spent the '08 season on the second team because he was academically ineligible. The 5-foot-11, 200-pounder from Noble and Greenough School in nearby Dedham, Massachusetts, was larger than most linemen. "For such a heavy man he is very fast on his feet and a regular bull for bucking the line," the *Boston Globe* reported.[10] Minot also was a capable punter. When it came to kicking, however, Haughton was having trouble replacing the departed Victor Kennard. (In a significant rules change for the '09 season, field goals had been devalued to three points.)

At end there was a superb holdover in Gil Browne.[11] But the real strength of Haughton's team was the interior line. Eight candidates were over or near the magic 200-pound mark. Massive 208-pounder Bob McKay was back at tackle, presumably a year wiser after the tutelage of Graves (but maybe not academically; as with several other Crimson players, McKay had to get off academic probation before he would be eligible). Center and left guard would be filled respectively by the brothers Withington, senior Paul and junior Lothrop. The strapping siblings were from Oahu College (now Punahou School) in the territory of Hawaii. "Our island Withingtons," as historian Samuel Eliot Morison later called them, were superb all-around athletes. Paul was New England wrestling champion; one day in practice, in a friendly match, he manhandled P. D. Later, the brothers would team up for a best-selling sports instructional book. (The Withingtons were one of seven sets of brothers dotting the roster that year, joined by the Blodgetts, Brownes, Houstons, Leslies, Pages, and Smiths. Harvard always seemed to be brimming with brothers.) But the heart of the line was the steamrolling right side, manned by sophomore guard (and future two-time All-America) Robert Thomas Fisher and tackle and captain Hamilton Fish.

Two more disparate individuals could not be found. Bob Fisher came out of working-class Dorchester High. He prepped at Andover before taking a year off to earn his tuition; while in college, he continued working as a tutor. He was befriended by another Boston jock of more comfortable means, a first baseman named Joseph P. Kennedy; Joe invited Bob to be his roommate gratis. Ferocious on the field, off of it Fisher was genial and popular, becoming second marshal of the class of 1912. His rise was testimony to what seemed like a budding meritocracy in which financial status was secondary to achievement—the Harvard version of the imagined ideal portrayed in the era's most iconic and influential sports novel, Owen Johnson's *Stover at Yale*. As Fisher declared in the 1912 class album, "Politics played no part in the affairs of the class, and in every competition, whether in athletics or in an election, the best men won out."[12] (Of course, few Irish, Italians, or Jews needed apply; Joe Kennedy would harbor lifelong disappointment about not being tapped for a final club.)

Fisher's running mate seemed a rebuke to that ethos. But although haughty even for a Harvard man, Ham Fish had profitably used every advantage his background had conferred. He was from a prominent Hudson County (New York) family: His father was a Republican congressman, and his grandfather was Ulysses S. Grant's secretary of state. The youngest Fish had attended patrician St. Mark's. As captain, he was lord of the manor, running preseason workouts (under Haughton's supervision) for backs and kickers at his family's estate in Garrison, New York.

Fish was one of the greatest players of his or any era. Entering his senior season, Ham was 6-foot-3 and 200 pounds of sinew. He was looking to cap a career in which he set new standards, not only at tackle, but also when the end next to him shifted to the backfield and made Fish eligible as a receiver, as a sticky-fingered pass-catcher—a prototype tight end. (His size also was an asset because at that time there were no strictures against mugging the receiver while the ball was in the air.)

He glommed on to passes, that is, when O'Flaherty, who snapped off quick flips, could get him the ball. Unfortunately, the black-haired Irish boy was rattled not only by foes, but also Fish. The captain's main fault was his know-it-all overbearingness. Then, as now, football protocol mandated that the quarterback be the commander of the scrimmage line—but Fish often publicly upbraided the Irish lad and changed his plays. (By contrast, Cutler, from an old Harvard family, had held his own against his fellow preppies.)

✿ ✿ ✿

In the preliminary games, such embarrassing disharmony mattered little. In time for the season opener against Bates and six years after it had

CADET EUGENE A. BYRNE
Killed in action at West Point,N.Y.,Oct 30,190

Ill-starred Cadet Eugene "Icy" Byrne, a victim of football's limited-substitution rule in 1909. *United States Military Academy Sports Information. Public Relations Office, West Point, New York.*

opened, the Stadium had been capped with the addition of a colonnade, replete with wooden bleachers and a roof held up by concrete posts that have obstructed the views of befuddled fans for a century and counting. (The colonnade does, however, offer shelter from a storm.) Eleven years before women got the vote, there was also a new ladies' waiting room.

As with 1908, the '09 season opened on a Wednesday, September 29. In a typically ragged opener, Harvard beat Bates, 11–0, with Perry Smith scoring once in each half on short plunges after drives that began in Mules territory. Valiantly, Bates tried to throw the Crimson off with shifts and double passes, to no avail. O'Flaherty failed in his only pass attempt and was criticized for the crudeness of the Harvard attack. That same day in New Haven, Yale, playing without Captain Coy, who would be laid up for several weeks following surgery for what was described as a minor rupture, beat Wesleyan, also by 11–0.

Three days later, Bowdoin invaded. This time, things ran much smoother. The 17–0 victory permitted Haughton to play the subs. But O'Flaherty showed signs of taking hold, completing an 18-yard pass to promising sophomore end Larry "Bud" Smith, which led to one of Harvard's three touchdowns, a plunge by Bud's older brother, Perry. Fish and Fisher smothered any semblance of a Bears' attack.

A sociological observation was more noteworthy in the game report. "So many patrons of football go to Soldiers Field in automobiles," noted the *Globe*, "that additional checking [parking] space has of necessity been provided by the management at the western end of the stadium."[13] In New Haven, Yale beat Syracuse, 15–0.

The following Saturday brought to the stadium unseasonable 70-degree temperatures, the team from Williams—and a shocker. Today, ESPN would have cut in with an "Upset Alert." Fish, suffering from tonsillitis, was not in the starting lineup. Thus, he was not on the field in the first half when an Eph punt went over the hapless O'Flaherty's head and was recovered by Williams on the Harvard three. A touchdown and an extra point ensued—the first Williams touchdown against the Crimson since 1891. The lead held up at the half. Fish, overriding his coaches and the team doctor, E. H. Nichols, put himself in the game and provided a jolt. Dono Minot also came in to see his first significant action of the season. After a long drive against a worn-down defense, he barged in for the tying touchdown. Then, a poor Williams snap on a punt close to its goal line gave Harvard a safety. The Crimson had escaped, 8–6, but the headline was "Williams Crosses Harvard Line." Again, O'Flaherty was faulted for poor judgment. This was the moral equivalent of defeat, particularly since Yale was overwhelming Springfield, 33–0.

The next week, Harvard rolled over punchless Maine, 17–0, but Haughton was not on hand to see it. Instead, he and scout Reggie Brown joined 10,000 spectators at West Point, where Yale was expected to get its first major test against Army, whom the Crimson would face two weeks hence. What they saw was most impressive—and daunting. The Elis dominated, 17–0, as the Cadets could not move on offense. Gingerly working himself back into the lineup, Coy punted and passed but did not carry the ball.

Such a convincing win over a worthy foe proved it: This was shaping up to be Yale's greatest team ever. No one had yet scored on the Elis. The Game was more than a month away, but excitement already was building. Harvard graduate manager of athletics William F. Garcelon reported 718 applications for his personal allotment of seats. He had eight.[14]

* * *

It was October 23. Along the Charles, the leaves on the trees were now russet and yielded easily to the chilly breeze. The big-game portion of the season was at hand, as evidenced by the crowd of 16,000 who turned out for the annual meeting with Brown. The Bruins arrived at the stadium again with star quarterback Bill Sprackling and but one loss, to tough Penn. But they sputtered, as they always did against a deeper and better conditioned Harvard team, which won, 11–0. Both Crimson scores were set up by Sprackling muffs of kicks. There also was a stirring Harvard goal-line stand anchored by Fisher and Fish.

However, the Crimson captain's overbearing ways were on full display, once literally. At one point in the second half, the ball was declared dead. Not hearing the whistle, Harvard back Ted Frothingham scooped it up with Brown's Cy Young in pursuit. Fish caught Young, brought him down, and, with the spectators roaring with laughter, sat on him until Frothingham crossed the goal.

Less risible was Fish's contemptuous treatment of O'Flaherty. As W. D. Sullivan of the *Globe* reported, "Fish repeatedly held up Harvard's play by making O'Flaherty change his signals, which doubtless slowed Harvard's attack." (Imagine Rob Gronkowski doing this to Tom Brady.) Continued Sullivan,

> The South Boston boy [was playing with] decided nervousness. . . . If [O'Flaherty] proved himself incompetent in the selection of plays, Capt. Fish should have sent him to the sidelines and called in another quarterback rather than constantly assert his authority by changing signals. Such tactics persisted in would very quickly destroy the whole team's confidence in their field general, the quarterback.

In the second half, O'Flaherty settled down: "Perhaps Capt. Fish . . . was told by one of his wise and older counselors that he could quickly demoralize [even] the best team that ever walked on a gridiron by the tactics he had adopted in the first half."[15] But in a championship game, such a public rebuke could scuttle a team.

In any case, the victory over Brown paled in comparison to the result from New Haven, where Yale demolished Colgate, 36–0.

✧ ✧ ✧

Harvard versus Army would turn out to be a tragically perfect specimen of football, circa 1909. The October 30 game at West Point was the Crimson's only road appearance of the season. Given the way Yale (which, on this day, would whip Amherst, 34–0) had smothered the Cadets on this same field, the Army game would be closely watched as a measuring stick.

Even before the kickoff there were ominous developments for the Cadets. Three of their best players, including stalwart right tackle and captain Daniel Pullen, were declared out because of injury. Army would now have to put even more pressure on its linemen, particularly left tackle Eugene A. "Icy" Byrne. At 171 pounds, the first classman from Buffalo would be giving away nearly 30 pounds to the man facing him across the line of scrimmage: Fish. Byrne at least would be buoyed by the cheers of a partisan crowd of 7,000, which included the Corps of Cadets and his proud father, John, a Civil War veteran and Buffalo's former chief of police.

The high and mighty Hamilton Fish, a superb two-way tackle, one of football's first pass-catching tight ends, and the last living Walter Camp All-America. Fish was the bane of Harvard foes and, sometimes, Crimson quarterbacks. *Alice Curtis Desmond and Hamilton Fish Library in Garrison, New York, and the Fish Family.*

Since the death-ravaged season of 1905, football had been in a period of calm that was deceptive. There was some feeling that, partly helped by the forward pass, the sport was more open and thus safer. Certainly, the press was less strident on the topic of football violence. Yet, just three weeks before, Navy's quarterback, Edwin Wilson, had been injured in a game against Villanova; he now lay paralyzed in Annapolis, his fifth vertebra fractured. Moreover, many of the elements that had made football so destructive were still extant, including the ability to help a runner by pushing and pulling him, and the rule prohibiting a player who left the field from returning. There was also a feeling that the forward pass, rather than mitigating danger, could add to it: The defenders assigned to guard against a pass would not be available to assist struggling interior linemen, who thus would be "isolated" and worn down.

On this day, amid the cheering, these elements would converge in a deadly manner.

The first half was football as usual—mostly, an exchange of punts. At halftime, Harvard led, 3–0. To this point, the Cadets had played valiant defense, but they also had been unable to develop a sustained attack. The pressure of holding off the Crimson was wearing them down, most noticeably Byrne. "As the game progressed it was apparent that he was not only being outplayed, but that with each play he was growing weaker and less able to withstand the assaults," wrote the *Globe*'s Mel Webb in a literal postmortem. "In the first half, when Harvard was going down the field, Byrne was showing the effects of the hammering he was receiving."[16]

Haughton had taken notice. Early in the second half, Harvard took over at the Army 41 and, in nine straight runs, rammed the ball in for a touchdown. The placekicked extra point made it 9–0. On the drive, the double team of Fish and Fisher opened holes by pulverizing Byrne, who, with the defense "weakened" to guard against the pass, may indeed have been "isolated."

"Several times when play was stopped, Byrne needed assistance," wrote Webb. The Harvard coaches, along with the team physician, Nichols, sent word to Army coach Harry Nelly that Byrne should be removed. Nelly refused, partly because if Byrne came out, he could not go back in.

Later, Fish again proved he could do more than block and tackle. On second down at midfield, O'Flaherty flipped a pass, which the tackle snared—while sitting on his backside. Harvard was threatening to score again. But two plays later, the drive came to a catastrophic conclusion.

On second down from the Cadets 45, Dono Minot, playing fullback, crashed into the line. The teams converged in a roiling mass, with Army backers stepping up to stop the juggernaut. Ballcarriers and tacklers landed in a heap, with Byrne, who had submarined the play, at the bottom. Everyone unpiled—except Byrne. Several teammates tried to lift him. "I can't move," he told them, almost inaudibly. Then he lapsed into unconsciousness.

Nelly and the Army medics ran onto the field and began trying to revive him. The crowd, which had been cheering loudly, was hushed. After 20 minutes, the game was halted, never to finish. The spectators dispersed, and Byrne was taken to the academy hospital.

During an all-night vigil, reports oscillated from hopeful to dire. X-rays showed that Byrne's first and second vertebra had been dislocated and were pressing on his breathing apparatus. He was kept alive through artificial respiration until 6:35 a.m. on Sunday, when he died. Among those at his side was his father.

Two days later, Byrne was buried at the academy cemetery overlooking the Hudson River. He was eulogized as if he had died in battle, which, in a sense, he had. Hamilton Fish was in attendance, representing Harvard. The Crimson team and the school's just-inaugurated president, A. Lawrence Lowell, sent floral wreaths.

✿ ✿ ✿

The real question was whether, at long last, Byrne's death, coupled with the injury to Navy's Wilson, would sound a death knell for football. The second casualty was the remainder of the 1909 Army football schedule, including the ultimate match with Navy, scheduled for Philadelphia and already an annual national event. In an editorial published on the day of the funeral, the New York Times temporized, "Football should not be abolished, but the mass play must go."[17] But in letters to the editor, the antifootball forces were having none of it. Writing from Glen Ridge, New Jersey, popular poet Margaret E. Sangster practically shouted,

"Are we wholly civilized? . . . An overwhelming public sentiment should be awakened at once to arrest this madness."[18]

The next blow came on November 13, when star Virginia freshman running back Archer Christian was critically injured during a game at Georgetown. The next morning, he died of a brain hemorrhage. Now even the *New York Times*, which reported Christian's death on its front page (as it had Byrne's), had had enough. "The public has the right to demand that football be abolished or completely reformed forthwith," the paper editorialized.[19] (Again, a sentiment resonating with today's reader.)

The antifootball chorus was at its loudest and most shrill. There would be 30 reported football deaths in 1909, far bloodier than '05, when Teddy Roosevelt had felt compelled to intercede. The *Times* reported remarks made by Philadelphia's archbishop, Patrick J. Ryan. "Football, as played at present by the college teams of this country, is barbarous and ought to be abolished," declared the prelate. "Instead, they should play association football, as it's called nowadays. It is the kind we played when I was at college, where the players kick the ball and not each other."[20]

Right below that item was another. It began, "Yale and Harvard are staggered at the demand for tickets for their annual game in Cambridge on November 20."[21]

❖ ❖ ❖

Worries that the Crimson would be too stricken to get up for its next foe, Cornell, proved unfounded. The Big Red fell, 18–0, as the Harvard big backs pounded away off tackle, with Minot gaining 135 yards on 26 carries. Ever mercurial, O'Flaherty made a nifty return of a punt but also flubbed two others. His bullet passes were too hot for Fish to handle. Perhaps the most notable feature was a primordial Jumbotron installed at the closed end of the stadium. "In addition to the information which the old board conveyed—the score, the team holding the ball, the number of the down, and the distance to be gained—the new board gives the number of the line in which the ball is in play and the number of the player who goes in as a substitute," the *Globe* reported. "On the score cards, which will be used in conjunction with the board, all the players and possible substitutes will be numbered."[22] In New Haven, Yale beat Brown, 24–0.

Dartmouth descended on Cambridge off of a 6–6 tie with Princeton. That draw was the Big Green's only blemish; indeed, the Tigers' points (on two field goals) were the only ones given up by the Indians to date. The completion of the stadium, plus temporary stands, had made 11,000 more seats available this year than in '08. Almost all of Dartmouth's 1,400 students were among the 37,000 packing the horseshoe. At the open end, a special scoreboard was set up to provide telegraphed reports of the Princeton–Yale game at New Haven.

The press posited a knock-down, drag-out matchup between Harvard's line duo of Fish and Fisher, and Dartmouth's 195-pound left tackle and captain Clark Tobin and its 205-pound left guard, Ralph Sherwin. This would be the Indians' final game, and they were primed. When Captain Tobin went to midfield to meet Fish for the coin toss, he was wearing the sweater Dartmouth's captain had worn at the opening of the stadium six years before—an 11–0 Indians victory.

The battle between the captains, however, would be brief. In the first half, Fish took a shot to the solar plexus that rendered him hors de combat. Once again banking on depth and conditioning, Haughton followed what was by now his winning formula: wage a punting duel, wear the foe down, and play for the breaks. (Perhaps he also did not want to reveal too much to Yale's scouts.) After a scoreless first half, Harvard recovered a punt at the Dartmouth 30 and drove eight plays for a score. Then, when the Indians stalked the Crimson's goal line, Paul Withington picked off a forward pass and returned it 35 yards and out of trouble.

In the second half, O'Flaherty struggled. Haughton had seen enough and yanked him. His sub, sophomore Dick Wigglesworth, tossed a pass to end Francis Houston, who took the ball over the goal on a 15-yard pass-and-run. Dartmouth got a consolation three points on a late Tobin field goal; as the press later noted, that boot won the wagers for those who had bet that the Indians would score.

The 12–3 score was satisfying; in running its record to 8–0, Harvard had used solid play to outscore its foes, 103–9. But within the Crimson there remained unease, plain even to Dartmouth coach John O'Connor. "One fault . . . that Harvard will have to correct before her final contest is the evident friction that seems to exist between the captain and quarterback in the running of the team," O'Connor wrote afterward. "Several times during yesterday's contest O'Flaherty was interrupted in the giving of his signals, and the signal was changed."[23]

In New Haven, Yale beat Princeton easily, 17–0. On the season, the Bulldogs had scored 201 points; they had allowed none. Now they were coming to Cambridge. This year, they would be hard to strangle.

❊ ❊ ❊

The Game of 1909 was one of the earliest of college football's "games of the century." Given how early the century was, it was dubbed the "battle of the giants." Arguably, it was the most important football game played in the sport's first 40 years. The Crimson and the Elis would not enter the finale both unbeaten again until 1968, when Harvard memorably "beat" Yale, 29–29.

Perusing the lineups, the modern observer might at first think these warriors small and slight for football players. Harvard's starting 11 averaged a little more than six feet and 185 pounds; Yale's, a shade less than six feet and 189. Today, these sizes are for scatbacks, but a few years after this game, draftees during World War I would average a little more than 5-foot-7 and 142 pounds. Each '09 team's heaviest player, 208-pound Crimson left tackle Bob McKay and the Blue's 232-pound center, Carroll Cooney, seemed positively mammoth. (Cooney was a veritable Ndamukong Suh or Vince Wilfork.)

Twenty of the 22 starters were prep-school boys. The Yale team, especially, had plenty of pedigree. Back from '08 was quarterback Allan "Pop" Corey, son of U.S. Steel's president. Guard Hamlin Andrus's father was a railroad magnate. Tackle Henry Hobbs, said the *Globe*, was "reputed to be one of the richest men in Yale." Another tackle, Ted Lilley, was the son of a Connecticut governor.

Adding luster, the two well-born, godlike captains, Coy and Fish, personified the football ideal. Yale's All-America runner and kicker, Edward H. "Ted" Coy, out of Hotchkiss, was the son of that school's first headmaster, as well as a member of Skull and Bones and the Whiffenpoofs. He accorded with the image broadcast by popular art. The gridiron warriors were cast in a superhero mold, especially in contrast to the often scruffy, lower-class stars of the national pastime, baseball. The college football player was the masculine counterpart to

Massive Carroll Cooney of Yale, at 232 pounds the heaviest player in The Game of 1909. Cooney broke through to block a Harvard punt, causing a safety that gave the Bulldogs a lead they never would relinquish. *Prints and Photographs Division, Library of Congress, LC-DIG-ggbain-04332.*

the Gibson Girl. Foremost among the image-makers was illustrator J. C. Leyendecker, who created covers for *Collier's* and other mass-circulation magazines (and later would conceive the Arrow Collar Man). As Michael Oriard wrote in his book *Reading Football*,

> The distinctive Leyendecker style from this period—no curves, everything in straight lines, from the creases in the pants to the angles of the limbs, to the contours of the faces—represented football as slashing vectors of force. At the calm center of these whirling forces lies the clear-eyed, square-jawed Leyendecker face, transforming force from potential brutality to heroic mastery. The Leyendeckers' football player has an absolutely undaunted look, no fear or pain in his steely gaze, only determination and coolly calculating intelligence.[24]

Coy was a Leyendecker sprung to life.

Many of the 38,000 spectators who awaited the 2 p.m. kickoff on that sunny and cold day seemingly were dressed more for an evening at the theater than a sports event—a "riot of costly furs, gowns, and hats," said the next day's *Globe*, which also claimed there were "more than $5,000,000 worth of automobiles" outside the stadium.[25] (This at a time when a luxury vehicle could be had for $2,000.) The face value of a ticket was two dollars, but scalpers were getting $35—or more. The East Stands were solidly Blue: Almost 16,000 of the seats had been sold through Yale.

The game was a social event of the first magnitude, with special trains arriving from New York, New Haven, and Philadelphia. President William Howard Taft, Yale 1878, couldn't make it. (Seven years later, his son Charles would be an Eli tackle.) But Taft's vice president, James Sherman, was on hand, as was Taft's niece, Louise, and Mr. and Mrs. Reginald Vanderbilt of the Newport Vanderbilts. For those who couldn't get to Cambridge, a play-by-play account was being fed by "special wires" to the Harvard Club in New York and even to the Heidelberg Restaurant in Berlin for assembled grads of both schools. At nearby Everett High, a senior named Charles Brickley was scoring four touchdowns in a 38–0 romp over Providence Technical. But of equal moment was the wireless installed on the scene by a senior named Harold Powers, which received play-by-play of Harvard–Yale and relayed it to the Everett crowd.[26]

In the stadium's West Stands, the Crimson crowd was being urged on by a head cheerleader from Portland, Oregon, and Morristown (New Jersey) School named Jack Reed, '10. A few years later, as Russia became the Soviet Union, John Reed would be rabble-rousing for another red-tinged cause, one he would stirringly chronicle in his book *Ten Days That Shook the World*.

There was trash talk. Early in the week, Fish, who was still suffering from his solar-plexus injury, declared he would play "unless he was killed." Retorted one Eli wag, "He won't be killed unless he commits suicide when he hears the final score."[27] The bookmakers agreed, although their odds—10-to-9 for the Elis—were narrower than the comparative scores justified.

Just before the team left for Cambridge, Coy stopped by a New Haven tavern to say goodbye to some graduates. Someone proposed to his health and asked him for a toast. Coy, a teetotaler, obliged: "May we cross the line as easily as those [cocktails] slip down."[28]

As in 1908, Haughton prepared for the game at a decided disadvantage. True, in setting up his preferred kicking duel, he had home-field advantage. Thus, his punter, Minot, was familiar with the stadium's wind currents, which usually swirl from the closed to the open end. The problem was, wind or no, Coy was a much better punter. He and "Silent" Steve Philbin also were better than Minot and the other Harvard runners. On the line, Fisher and Fish were impregnable. But Bob McKay, who had played so well the previous year, seemed to have backslid without Graves to goad him. Tellingly, Coy was the best drop-kicker in football. Harvard did not have a 1909 version of Vic Kennard. Finally, given the size equality, it was unlikely that the Crimson could follow Haughton's blueprint of wearing down the foe.

✿ ✿ ✿

Yale won the toss and, for the first 35-minute half, elected to defend the closed end; just as Haughton had thought, the wind was behind the Blue. Per custom, Harvard chose to kick. Paul Withington stood behind the ball at midfield but, in a trick maneuver, yielded to Bob McKay, who dribbled one 25 yards. It was caught by Ted Lilley, who was immediately smeared (in the jargon of the day) by Harvard's left wing. When the players unpiled, Lilley stayed down. He had to be removed from the game, costing Yale its best blocker and one of its best defensive linemen.

The teams commenced playing old-fashioned, smashmouth football, grinding out short gains and battering one another. Tim Cohane, in *The Yale Football Story*, quoted one sideline observer: "It was the most magnificent sight I ever saw. Every lineman's face was dripping with blood."[29] It was magnificent, perhaps, but also disappointing given the buildup.

A football insider would have spotted a couple of wrinkles devised by Haughton. In the "wheel shift," Harvard's interior linemen would move around before the snap, the men from one side stepping in front of the ball, those on the other side stepping behind it. Unbalancing the line or putting the more powerful blockers on one side might indicate where the play was headed, or not. The Crimson also was in the forefront of trap blocking. Forty-four years later, Yale end John Reed Kilpatrick recalled this maneuver patented by Haughton. "It was a delayed play straight through our right tackle," Kilpatrick told writer Allison Danzig. "I stopped it by leaving my position at left end and playing defensive back behind the right tackle."[30] The game devolved into a battle of punts between Coy and Harvard's Minot. On the day, Yale would punt 13 times for a 43-yard average; Harvard punted 14 times for a 34-yard average. The Crimson had trouble handling Coy's boots, especially the feckless O'Flaherty.

Already, the Crimson quarterback was giving off signs of distress. On one series, said the *Globe,*

> Something seemed to be the matter with O'Flaherty's judgment and technique. . . . Capt. Fish asked for extra time for [Dr. E. H.] Nichols to come out onto the field to talk to O'Flaherty. The Yale men clamored that Harvard was delaying the game, but the referee took matters into his own hands and insisted that the Harvard coaches be convinced that O'Flaherty had not been injured. He had not been, and the game went on.[31]

After the game, however, O'Flaherty claimed he had been kicked in the head and thereafter was never the same.

The trash talking picked up. After Fish and Hobbs tussled, the Yale tackle hunched his shoulders and said to himself, "You wait, I'll get you yet." But Ted Coy nipped this in the bud, telling Hobbs, "If you do, I'll get you."[32]

Gradually, Coy's strategically placed boomers and onside kicks put the Elis in position for a 19-yard field-goal try—but Coy flubbed his dropkick. Nevertheless, he was winning the territorial battle. Midway through the first half, Yale got the first break. Minot punted from the Harvard 22. To the ecstasy of the Yale supporters, Carroll Cooney broke through and blocked it; Kilpatrick and Minot scrambled behind the goal line, with the Harvard man falling on it. The result: a safety. Yale 2, Harvard 0.

The remainder of the half was played on the Crimson end of the field. Yale missed two more dropkicks, but finally Philbin speared a Minot punt and returned it 45 yards to the Harvard 15-yard line. Coy stepped back to the 25 for another dropkick, booted not with toe but soccer-style, with the instep. He was only 15 yards from the left sideline, providing an exceedingly tough angle. But this time his aim was true. Yale 5, Harvard 0. The half ended.

There was no halftime show. Each school had songs to sing—*Harvardiana* was new for the Crimson this year—but a marching band wouldn't grace the Stadium until 1914, when Michigan came to town. Fans may well have spent the 15 minutes mulling how difficult it was to cross the goal line, not only because the defenses were so rock-ribbed, but also because even if a defense was backed up to the goalposts, there was no threat of a pass being thrown over its head; it merely had to pack all 11 men near the scrimmage line to stop the offense's thrusts. This made the play cautious and stagnant. For all that . . . well, Harvard was only down by five, the value of a touchdown. If the Crimson could get something going. . . . Meanwhile, Harvard men were complaining that Yale end Kilpatrick continually was lining up offside—to the obliviousness of the refs.

✿ ✿ ✿

As the second half began, the Crimson had a quarterback change: Dick Wigglesworth for O'Flaherty. Briefly, Harvard rallied. Taking the ball on its 25, Harvard gained 20 yards, then succeeded with an onside kick. End Gil Browne plucked it at the Yale 46. Running to the left behind Fish, the Crimson advanced to the Yale 30. The West Stands roared. But there the drive stalled.

Thereafter, even though Harvard had the wind, Yale kept the Crimson bottled up. Another score would clinch it. To get the Elis closer, Coy kept trying onside kicks. Finally, near the close, he stepped back to the Harvard 33 and thumped a dropkick. While the attempt was airborne, Coy "reportedly turned to referee Bill Langford and chortled, 'Mr. Langford, did you ever see a prettier kick than that one? Don't tell me you aren't going to give me a goal.'"[33] It made the score 8–0—insurmountable.

When time was called, the fans in the East Stands doffed all formality. With a great cheer, they charged onto the turf and commenced a snake dance. The lionized Coy got the banner headlines as he "closed his career at Yale in a blaze of glory,"[34] said the *Boston Globe*'s Webb. Some still regard Coy as Yale's greatest player; there is little doubt that its unscored-upon national champions were Camp's greatest team.

Yale's Ted Coy (far left) sweeps right end. The Eli golden boy capped a perfect (and unscored-upon) 1909 season by dropkicking two field goals in The Game. *Yale University.*

Throughout the season, Coy had received marriage proposals from unseen females; one woman in Texas wrote, "Won't you marry me, please, or anyhow send me two football tickets?"[35] He would, in fact, marry thrice, with wife number two being stage star Jeanne Eagels.

Harvard had the consolation of being the only team all season to keep Yale from crossing the goal line. The Crimson had outrushed the Elis by a net 136 to 60 and held the Bulldogs to two first downs, but had been penalized nine times for 105 yards, while the Elis had been whistled once for the loss of a mere yard. (Four decades later, Harvardians were still grousing about the officiating.)[36] Monday morning quarterbacking already was keenly developed. The hapless O'Flaherty was roasted. Said Webb, "He was wretched in handling kicks"; moreover, he "was unequal to infusing the team with real 'go' that would keep continuous its bursts of real speed."[37] His replacement, Wigglesworth, also was skewered for not ordering enough punts while Harvard had the wind.

Six Elis and two Crimson players (Fish and Minot) were named to Walter Camp's first-team All-America; 12 players on the field that day would be All-America sometime during their careers.

A visibly deflated Haughton paid a visit to the Yale locker room. "As the Harvard coach walked into the room, for a second there was a little embarrassment among the victorious Yale men," noted the *Globe*, "but rushing up to the happy Capt. Coy, coach Haughton grabbed him by the hand, and as he shook it with an earnestness that showed he meant what he said, he congratulated the great Yale player on his splendid victory."[38]

Slowly, the great, glittering throng dispersed to their clubs, residences, and restaurants for tea and dinner. (At Boston's Parker House, the menu featured tornedo of venison à la Yale and Harvard—for $1.25.) No one knew it, but this victory, as glorious as it was, would mark the end of Yale's football hegemony.

At Harvard, a season's work was down the drain. Writing in the 1910 class album, Fish called the defeat to Yale "heartrending."[39]

Still, Haughton received an unusually strong vote of confidence. The school previously never had granted a coach more than a two-year term. Haughton was re-signed for three—this time, on salary, for $5,000 a season. (The explanation was that his football duties had put a crimp in his financial business and thus he needed to make up some income.)

So, P. D. would be staying a while. He faced two questions: First, what did he have to do to further raise the Crimson's game? The second: After the death of Icy Byrne, was there any saving the sport—an activity that, like it or not, had become central to college life?

3

HAUGHTON CUTS CAMP OFF
AT THE PASS

The 1910 season often is considered the proper start of the vaunted "Haughton Machine." At this point, the Harvard team was machinelike: grinding, relentless . . . and unexciting. Much like football itself.

Having experienced a spasm of violence and settled down into a rut of dullness, the sport had to be retooled yet again. Football was beginning a brief but crucial period in which it would, in essence, remake the rules as it went. By the time it emerged from this spate of trial and error, it had opened up and become considerably more crowd-pleasing. By decade's end, it would resemble the game we see today and leap in national popularity. And although it would take him a couple of seasons, during which conditions did not permit him to unsheath his genius to the fullest, Percy Haughton was the man who best figured out the "new game"—with the invaluable aid of a remarkable class of players.

☼ ☼ ☼

In the recruiting of college athletes, as in anything else, everyone loves a winner. Before Haughton's breakthrough in 1908, it was axiomatic that the best prep players would be snatched by Yale, then Princeton, then Dartmouth—and finally Harvard. But in October 1909, the *Boston Globe* noted of the freshman classes, "Harvard's [class of] 1913 team has recruited better players than appeared on Yale field for the first time this fall."[1]

57

Then as now, recruiting was a cutthroat business. The four big schools were fishing from the same small pool of prep prospects. Some, of course, were legacies who had been virtually pledged to a school at birth. Yale, especially, benefited from its dynasty and the fictional aura conveyed by Frank Merriwell. And sometimes there were other . . . considerations.

In a remarkable two-part series in *McClure's Magazine* in 1905, muckraker Henry Beach Needham—a former Harvard player and a good friend of Theodore Roosevelt—had uncovered the rock from big-time college sports and revealed its worms. *McClure's* was the nation's leading investigative magazine, renowned for shedding light on corruption and shady practices in business and government. With only slight changes of name and venue, the Needham articles would be exceedingly familiar today. In the service of "winning at any cost," the process had run amuck. Alumni "proselytizing" was rife, abetted by such inducements as Princeton promising its athletes lucrative and cushy jobs as managers of eating clubs. One Andover student, Robert C. Brown, looked askance at Old Nassau's emoluments. "When I graduate," he said, "I want to feel that I earned what I got. A fellow can't feel that way if he goes to Princeton, where they certainly pass it out to you." Brown ended up playing end for . . . Harvard. Yale, in the meantime, provided star tackle James Hogan the cigarette concession on campus; he received a commission on every American Tobacco box sold. Of course, such compensation skirted the rules against athletic departments paying players directly. It could not be sanctioned, but it could be tolerated in the name of victory.[2]

Typically, claimed Needham, Harvard refused to play the game. "At Harvard there is an unmistakable air of self-satisfaction or smug self-righteousness—a 'holier than thou' contentment—which is naturally annoying to men of other institutions," he wrote.[3] Surely, however, Cambridge possessed its ways and means, including having wealthy alumni who could "loan" needy players money for tuition, room, board, and incidentals.

As the tide began to turn under Haughton, Harvard could afford to take the lofty view. All the schools were venerable brand names, but Harvard's was the most venerable. It had the stadium. In contrast to the hermetically sealed small-town environment at New Haven, Princeton, or (especially) Hanover, it had Boston and its many diversions. And suddenly, under Haughton, it had direction. Finally, for the local boys in the large, sports-crazed Boston area, it had proximity to family and friends.

Eight decades later, Michigan's basketball program had a celebrated and successful class of super-recruits immortalized as the "Fab Five." During the 1909 and 1910 football seasons, a similar cohort of remarkable athletes began to point its way to Cambridge and admittance in the class of 1915: the "Group of Seven." Six were within shouting distance of the stadium: at St. Mark's in Southborough, Massachusetts, back Frederick "Peebo" Bradlee and end T. Jefferson Coolidge; at Everett (Massachusetts) High and Exeter, fullback and kicker Charles Brickley; at Groton, back and end Huntington Reed "Tack" Hardwick; at Boston Latin, quarterback Malcolm Logan; and at Middlesex School in Concord, Massachusetts, lineman Walter Trumbull. Not too far south, at the Hackley School in Tarrytown, New York, an immense lineman named Stanley Pennock was making a name for himself. Right behind them was a star back at Andover by way of Natick (Massachusetts) High, Edward "Packy" Mahan. All but Mahan would matriculate at Cambridge in the fall of 1911; Mahan would arrive in '12. As varsity players, the so-named Group of Seven in the class of '15 would not lose a game in 27 outings. Mahan would lose but once.

Back then, to paraphrase the adage about politics of Cambridge's own Tip O'Neill, all sports were local. Hence, the exploits of these schoolboys were given prominence on the sports pages just below the accounts of the Crimson heroes on Soldiers Field. Brickley, especially, was a phenom. He was one of six children of a small businessman. Charlie's nickname upon entering Everett High was "Shorty," but four years later, he emerged as a splendidly muscled, 5-foot-11, 190-pound all-around athlete—the most acclaimed Massachusetts prep player of his or any era. In 1999, the *Boston Globe* named him the state's greatest high school football star of the 20th century;[4] his competition included Heisman Trophy winners Joe Bellino, Angelo Bertelli, and Doug Flutie. In 1908, playing for Everett (whose nickname was, fortuitously, the Crimson), Brickley set school records for touchdowns (eight) and points (47) in one game. His total of 257 points in 15 games would stand as a Bay State single-season record for 87 years. The next season, hampered by injuries, "Brick" scored "only" 107 points for Everett, 11–10 losers to Somerville in a state title game that attracted a crowd of 10,000. Never-

theless, his 488 career points would not be topped in Bay State schoolboy circles for six decades.

Accounts of that title game are a window into not only the frenzied
schoolboy-sports scene, but also the recruiting mania. On hand was
none other than Harvard trainer William "Pooch" Donovan, possibly to
babysit Mr. Brickley. The play-by-play offers several developments that
make a modern reader wonder if the fix was in—and if Brickley was in
on it:

> Everett's inability to kick a goal after its first touchdown also counted
> against it. Norris punted out well, but Capt. Charles Brickley was
> nervous after catching it, and he missed the goal by a few yards. . . .
> Capt. Charles Brickley broke through the right side of the line, and,
> with a clear field ahead, he dropped the ball. . . . Charles Brickley
> tore off a 17-yard run and would have scored had he not stum-
> bled. . . . Capt. Brickley dropped back for a goal from placement
> from the 25-yard line. He missed by many yards.[5]

If one didn't know better . . .

Although he was a solid student at Everett High, Brickley found, as
did most public high school graduates, that its curriculum had not adequately prepared him for admission to Harvard. For polish, he went off
to Exeter, maturing scholastically, athletically, and socially. One of his
recommendations, found in the Harvard University Archives, reads,

> Brickley is a manly fellow. In all my conversations with him, I have
> noted the splendid quality of his ideas and ideals. Of good physique,
> well appearing, and liked by the men he meets, Brickley finds him-
> self invited to all sorts of good places. . . . All of [his] positions he has
> held because of his manly qualities. Lest there should creep in a
> feeling of interest in Brickley because of his athletic ability, I need
> only to say that men from other colleges have offered him many
> things to his advantage, if he would go elsewhere, but at all such
> times, without the slightest persuasion, Brickley has held firmly to
> his wish and determination to go to Harvard College, and it is a great
> disadvantage that he is now studying hard to pass the Harvard en-
> trance examinations, when he might easily go elsewhere. It has been
> the one wish of his father's heart that he should go to Harvard Col-
> lege, and so far as I am able to judge, the question of his athletic

ability has hardly ever been mentioned in relation to Harvard athletics.[6]

Playing for Exeter during the 1910 season, Brickley more than met his match during the traditional season-ending battle at Andover. The star of the day was Eddie Mahan, who scored 14 of Andover's 21 points in the shutout. On Brothers Field, both of Mahan's touchdowns—one on a pass reception, the other on a run—commenced from kick formation, which would become a regular feature of his play on Soldiers Field. For good measure, Mahan dropkicked a field goal and an extra point, and averaged 45 yards on his punts. By contrast, in the final game of his prep career and on the soggy field, Brickley never was able to get going.

For Mahan, this was merely the latest in a series of superlative days that had first occurred at Natick High, where he was a standout in baseball and track, as well as football. Two years after his senior season and after Mahan had completed his time at Andover, the grateful townspeople presented him with an engraved watch at the season-ending game with Milton High.

As a left-handed pitcher, he had shown so much promise that American League umpire Tommy Connolly was touting him as a future big-leaguer, a career path whose payoff arguably was superior to that of college. After all, the same week Mahan was thumping Exeter on the gridiron, New York Giants ace Christy Mathewson had signed for the biggest salary in baseball: $15,000.[7]

Edward H. Mahan—known as Ned or Packy—was the youngest of 11 children born to Patrick and Julia, both immigrants from Ireland. Patrick was a Civil War veteran who had ridden with Gen. Phil Sheridan's cavalry. On his application for a $150 Price Greenleaf Harvard scholarship, Ned noted under family income, "My father is too old to work."[8] In terms of his college choice, Mahan seems to have been more in play than Brickley had been. (It may have helped Harvard's cause that Pooch Donovan was another Irish boy from Natick.) In 1911, the *Globe* noted, "The latest rumor is that Eddie Mahan is going to Princeton. I wouldn't care to wager that he will not enter Yale."[9] Indeed, Mahan had gone so far as to take the entrance exams for New Haven; in his student folder in the Harvard University Archives is a Preliminary Certificate issued by Yale College in September 1911.[10]

Crimsonians can only shudder to think about Mahan in the Eli back-field.

The same week Brickley and Mahan were facing off, four of their future teammates also were in featured roles for their schools. At the Boston American League grounds, Mal Logan, quarterback and captain for Boston Latin, dropkicked a last-minute field goal to beat Mechanic Arts High, 3–0. To the west, the Groton School, led by the virtuoso punting of quarterback Huntington Hardwick, throttled visiting St. Mark's, 11–0, despite the efforts of star left halfback and captain Fred Bradlee and end Thomas Jefferson Coolidge. Following in the footsteps of his future coach Percy Haughton, Hardwick was in the process of capping his final academic year as one of the great athletes in Groton history, having also starred on the ballfield and in shotput. Tall and chiseled, young Hardwick had the aristocratic name and matinee-idol looks that, as a collegian, would be catnip to the newspapers.

But most of all, when Tack Hardwick hit you, you felt as if you had been run over by a freight train.

✲ ✲ ✲

Even as he could read about these high school heroes in the papers, Haughton methodically went about winning a national championship—even if he wasn't all that thrilled about it.

The gridiron calamities of 1909 had brought renewed cries for re-form. Throughout the winter and spring of 1909–1910, committees comprised of members of the "old" rules committee (made up of repre-sentatives from Harvard, Yale, and Princeton) and the nationally orient-ed Inter Collegiate Athletic Association (ICAA) met and tossed ideas back and forth in hopes of making the game less dependent on close combat. One of the most radical would have permitted multiple for-ward passes on a play, but only behind the line of scrimmage, with a ball hitting the ground being declared dead. Moreover, the offense would have been able to send multiple men in motion simultaneously.

The man who forcefully stepped in to intercept these notions was Percy Duncan Haughton. According to John Sayle Watterson in his authoritative *College Football: History, Spectacle, Controversy*, at a meeting of the ICAA rules committee on May 13, 1910, Haughton launched a blistering attack on the rules allowing passes behind the line and men going in motion before the snap of the ball. He argued that these plays would prove both impractical and unsafe. The sheer number of players running around the backfield before and after the play would make the job of the officials nightmarish. Moreover, a return to the momentum style of football [as encouraged by multiple men in motion] might revive the flying formations of the 1890s, resulting in even more injuries. He doubted that it would strengthen the offense because a defender breaking through the line could easily intercept one of these passes and take it for a touchdown. According to the minutes of the meeting, Haughton believed that the "possibilities of the forward pass back of the line was theoretical rather than practical; that the possibility of two forward passes tended to complicate the game."

Eventually (and by a narrow 8-to-6 margin), the combined committee maintained the forward pass, which now could cross the line at any point, although the passer had to be five yards back and the receiver no more than 20 yards downfield from the line of scrimmage. Only ends and backs would be eligible receivers, and (in a significant change) they could not be interfered with past the line of scrimmage. Incomplete passes on first and second down would no longer result in turnovers. (Teams still only had three downs to make 10 yards.)

Just as important, Watterson noted, the overhaul "included the motion passed on the first day, which eliminated mass play by requiring seven men on the line of scrimmage—and by outlawing pushing and pulling [the runner]." Herewith on offense, blocking in *front* of the ballcarrier—or as it was known in the parlance of the day, "interference"—would be paramount (the implications of which Haughton quickly grasped). The length of the game, which previously had varied, was now standardized at four 15-minute quarters. Crucially, the rule on substitutions was modified: Now players who left the game could return at the beginning of a subsequent quarter.

As Watterson reported, "Only one member of the rules committee, Walter Camp, refused to affix his signature to the 1910 rules." His curmudgeonly opposition to the forward pass would herald the start of Camp's withdrawal from the sport he had done so much to foster. In this instance, Camp was not on the side of history. Watterson added,

The new rules would breathe new life into the gridiron game. . . .
Above all, the rules changes marked the watershed between the old
rugby-style version of football and the new, streamlined version that
had less to do with the feet than with the legs and hands, as well as
the space above the field where forward passes would soar.[11]

Haughton immediately saw the upshot: The ideal player now would
not be the big, heavy man, but the mobile, athletic man.

Despite these advancements, scoring in the big games and championship games still proved infernally frustrating. Offenses could gain
yards through midfield but struggled against stacked defenses closer to
the goal line. One problem was they could not throw a pass over the
goal line—so defenders could concentrate entirely on the run.

Ironically, given Haughton's role in preserving the pass, the Crimson
threw relatively little during the next two seasons. P. D. stuck to what
he knew best and what his material dictated: wearing down overmatched foes through the ground and kicking games. Ham Fish was
gone, but a strong cadre returned to the line: Bob Fisher, Bob McKay,
and Lothrop Withington, who was captain. Power-packed Dono Minot
shifted from the backfield to guard. A senior named James "Gag" Perkins was at center; crucially, on defense, Haughton installed him at a
relatively new position, "roving center," playing a few yards back of the
line. In other words, Perkins was one of football's first middle lineback-
ers.

Harvard had its best punter since Haughton himself in sophomore
back-end Sam Felton, a railroad magnate's son from Philadelphia's tony
Main Line who had prepped at Milton Academy. A left-footed booter,
Felton was known especially for his twisting, hard-to-handle "spiral
bombs." He also was an outstanding pitcher. The man who got down
under them the fastest was right end Bud Smith, who also was proving
to be dangerous as a pass receiver. As always, quarterback was unsettled, with two juniors vying for the starting job: Dick Wigglesworth and
Bob Potter. Out of St. Mark's, Potter was the son of one of the owners
of the Philadelphia Phillies and the best friend of a classmate named
Joseph P. Kennedy. Potter had at least one advantage: height. He was a
little more than six feet tall, while Wigglesworth was a bit more than 5-
feet-8. Thus, Potter could see over onrushing opposing linemen on pass
plays, an asset that previously rarely had come into play; however, nei-

ther Wigglesworth nor Potter would need to throw often. Why put the ball in the air when you had a weapon like Percy Wendell?

Referred to as the "Human Bullet," the 5-foot-7, 177-pound Wendell was the first immortal back of the Haughton era. From Boston's Jamaica Plain section and a product of the exclusive Roxbury Latin School, Wendell was well-born and well-connected; he would become first marshal of his class and a member of the Porcellian Club, Harvard's most exclusive final club. He was ideally built for the grind-it-out game. With a literally headfirst, pile-driving style, he was sort of an early day Ironhead Heyward. In his low-slung mode of attack, he was likened to a torpedo. He also had a knack for keeping his feet under him, prompting Dartmouth coach Frank Cavanaugh to term him a "mud

Nicknamed the "Human Bullet" for his headfirst style, diminutive **Percy Wendell** was one of the great line-pluggers of his era and also the bane of the disciplinary dean for his inattention in class. Wendell would meet an early demise, one whose symptoms were suspiciously consistent with those of many modern-day NFL players. *Prints and Photographs Division, Library of Congress, LC-DIG-ggbain-14147.*

horse"[12]—a not-insignificant asset on the chewed-up, oft-swamped gridirons of the era.

The hard-charging Wendell would be named All-America in 1910 and '11. But—again the shock of recognition—from our perspective, he might be most notable as an early sufferer of the brain injuries we are now seeing in profusion in college and NFL players. Wendell's transcript and student folder in the Harvard University Archives reveal a student who apparently had trouble maintaining focus. That sophomore year, for instance, his transcript (with "E" denoting a failure) read as follows:

Ec 1 C
Engineering 11a E
German 25 D
Gov 32 D
Landscape Arch C
Math A D
Physiology 1 C

Wendell's academic difficulties would make him the despair of the school's disciplinary czar, Dean Byron H. Hurlbut. "I am not going to write to you about the meaning of probation, for you have been on probation before," Hurlbut wrote to Wendell on February 28, 1913. (By this time, Percy's playing days were over.) "The situation is extremely grave, both on account of your dilatoriness in electing your courses and on account of your low record. I hate very much to have to report this action to you, for it is extremely unpleasant to have the first marshal incur censure."

One professor, when asked if Wendell were prone to "natural dullness or slowness," answered, "I fancy so."

Writing to a Wendell family friend, Hurlbut moaned, "I have talked until I am tired of talking. He smiles amiably, and that is about all the response I get. . . . I do not know of anything you can do to help him." Then, perhaps, rather tellingly, "He is a man in his 24th year, although he appears to be a child of six. I have heard indirectly that he is much interested in the 'movies.'"[13]

With what we are discovering today about football players and chronic brain encephalopathy (CTE), it is tantalizing to speculate whether Wendell's woes were due not to natural slowness, but to all those knocks on the noggin. Of course, the evidence is circumstantial. Nevertheless, it is not surprising that someone who was getting beaten upside the head every afternoon would have trouble in class the next morning.

✿ ✿ ✿

"The 1910 football squad started work at Fraser's Island [Maine] September 2," Lothrop Withington reported laconically in the 1911 class album.

> About 30 men returned to Cambridge for regular practice, well browned and ready for hard work. The general call for candidates was made September 19. It took a week for things to get in full swing. Two daily practices were held until September 28, when the team met Bates, winning 22–0. The open play promised well for the new rules.
>
> On October 1, after an hour's delay due to Bowdoin missing the train, Harvard played Bowdoin, winning 32–0. The following Saturday, Harvard wiped out the 8–6 score of the previous year by defeating Williams, 21–0. The team began to show power, and it was evident that Harvard would be well represented. Amherst was beaten, 17–0, on a rainy afternoon, October 15. [14]

Amherst coach Heinie Hobbs saw it differently. "We gave them the worst scare they have had this season, anyway," Hobbs told the *New York Times*, which reported that in the third quarter, with Harvard leading, 12–0, "Wendell bored through for two good gains" to set up a 25-yard pass-and-run to Bud Smith for the Crimson's final touchdown. [15]

The preliminary season ended with the Crimson's goal unsullied. Brown made its annual visit, giving All-America quarterback Bill Sprackling another crack at the Crimson. Once again, the stadium was his Waterloo. The Crimson shut Sprackling down and blanked the Brunonians, 12–0. The game was saved in the fourth quarter when, with Harvard clinging to a 6–0 lead, Sprackling mounted a drive from his own 20. Brown reached the Harvard two. On third (last) down, Sprackling dropped back and flicked a pass, which, of course, could not be caught over the goal line. So Sprackling tossed the ball into the flat.

Harvard's Edward Graustein picked it off on the six-yard line and ran it all the way back for a touchdown. On the 110-yard field, it was a return of 104 yards—still the longest in Crimson history.

The next week, the Crimson ventured to West Point. The Icy Byrne fatality of 1909 cast a pall. As the game ground on, Harvard's team doctor, E. H. Nichols, noticed an Army player drooping—just as he had seen Byrne do the year before. In Harvard assistant coach Harry von Kersburg's recollection, Nichols alerted Haughton, who sent word to the West Point coach, Harry Nelly, to remove the man. Nelly conferred with West Point's commandant, Frederick W. Sibley, who ordered that the man remain in the game. This time, even Haughton backed off: He ordered the Crimson not to run plays at the man.[16] The gesture may have saved a player from grievous hurt, but it had little effect on the 6–0 final score. The only points came when Lo Withington blocked a Cadets punt and returned it 40 yards to the house. Harvard outrushed Army 282 yards to 39; the Cadets never crossed midfield. "The game showed little of the new football," the *Times* sourly reported.[17]

To this point, the Crimson was unbeaten, untied, and unscored upon—which meant that after the next week's game, a 27–5 win over Cornell at the stadium, the *Times*'s subheadline read, "Harvard Crushes Cornell 11/Ithacans, However, Score on Crimson."[18] The Big Red touchdown came when the outcome was long decided, after a fumble by Harvard sub Ed Pierce. Starting at right halfback, Wendell made two short touchdown runs, Potter tossed a 37-yard touchdown pass-and-run to Bud Smith, and Felton scored on another touchdown pass. Clearly, with Yale but two weeks away, the Crimson was rounding into form.

That was confirmed the following week, when Wendell scored twice in an 18–0 victory over Dartmouth. "Wendell was simply a steam engine," said the *Globe*, adding, "It was old football with a surfeit of kicking most of the afternoon."[19] Harvard threw the game's only pass (completed).

At Princeton, the newly elected governor of New Jersey, Woodrow Wilson (a former president of the university), attended the Tigers' game against visiting Yale, won by the Bulldogs, 5–3. Thus was set up The Game, in which a Harvard win would cap a perfect season.

Haughton and his staff were uncharacteristically overconfident.[20] Victory on that November 19 seemed likely; the Elis had a startlingly

Wendell plunging for a touchdown. Short yardage near the goal line was especially difficult against bunched-up tacklers until 1912, when the creation of the end zone forced the defense to worry about the pass. *HUPSF Football (237), olvwork376391.* *Harvard University Archives.*

mediocre record of 6–2–1. They had lost at Army, 9–3; been taken apart, 21–0, by Sprackling and Brown; and even (perhaps most shockingly) been held to a scoreless tie by southern upstart Vanderbilt. Yale did boast football's best end in John Kilpatrick, a whiz at "following the ball." The Bulldogs also had a "gadget"—the "Minnesota shift," devised by a former Eli, Dr. Harry S. Williams, now coaching the Golden Gophers. The maneuver—in which backfield men moved, pre-snap, into position behind the place in the line where the play ostensibly was going—was brought East by former star and captain Tom Shevlin, a Minneapolis resident. Its potential for deception had been considered key to the upset of Princeton. One pregame question: Would Haughton, the champion of the forward pass, unbottle this genie?

"The greatest crowd [35,000] that ever jammed into the banks of wooden stands at Yale Field saw the game on an afternoon that was as delightful as Indian Summer," reported the *New York Times* the following day. "Disappointed thousands had to stay away."[21] Among the members of the Harvard class of '11 who would have had an opportunity to witness their final Game as undergrads were Richard Whitney, member of the varsity crew and the Porcellian Club, who as a prominent Wall Streeter and president of the New York Stock Exchange two decades later would be sent to Sing Sing for embezzlement; future *New Yorker* cartoonist Gluyas Williams; Howard Lindsay, later half of the Broadway team of Lindsay and Crouse; Malcolm Endicott Peabody, later the head of Groton, a celebrated civil rights activist, and the father of Harvard All-America tackle and Massachusetts governor Endicott "Chub" Peabody, '41; writer John R. Tunis, who would achieve a considerable reputation penning juvenile sports fiction; future *Boston Globe* managing editor Laurence L. Winship; and Kenneth MacGowan, who, in Hollywood, would produce *Little Women* and win the 1934 Oscar for Best Short Subject for *La Cucaracha*. With his friend Eugene O'Neill, MacGowan would co-found the Provincetown Playhouse.

The Harvard side, in a precursor of the later "card sections," concocted a first: Using white handkerchiefs, the students arrayed themselves to form a large white "H" visible from the opposite stand. When the game began, Harvard proceeded to push Yale up and down the field. In the second quarter, headlined the *Times*, "Wendell, the Battering Ram, Enters." As the paper described it, "Wendell was like a package of firecrackers. He seemed to be on springs. Running low and charging the Yale line like a pile driver, he sent the scrappy Blue forwards tumbling in all directions . . . the Blue forwards bowled over him like 10 pins in his riotous line breaking." Wendell would carry 21 times for 103 yards. "Wendell played as great a game as has ever been seen on Yale Field," said the *Times*. "While he lasted, the Harvard back cut the Blue line to ribbons."[22]

The vaunted "Minnesota Shift" proved not to be a gamebreaker. But Kilpatrick and Yale's defense indeed followed the ball, stifling Harvard whenever it got a whiff of a score. The Crimson repeatedly wasted its chances, fumbling 14 times and losing four, and being penalized nine times.

In the final period, Haughton threw caution and passes (four) to the winds. Per the *Times*, "Wigglesworth hurled a beautiful forward pass to Smith, who raced along the sidelines for 25 yards before he was downed."[23] But the Harvard drive again petered out, and at game's end, the best scoring chance was a desperation field-goal try—by Yale's captain, Fred Daly, which missed badly. If either side had reason to be satisfied by a scoreless tie, it was the Blue.

The lack of points symbolized the sport's biggest problem: It was dull. A letter-writer to the *Harvard Alumni Bulletin* suggested an overtime to break the deadlock, harrumphing, "The death-like stillness of 35,000 people at the Yale game bore eloquent testimony to the boredom of the spectators."[24]

Even with the frustrating finale, Harvard was named the consensus national champion. (Aside from Wendell, Camp selected Fisher and McKay for his All-America first team.) Other undefeated schools could stake a claim, most notably Pittsburgh, which shut out each of its nine foes and piled up 282 points. But to James Vautravers of Tiptop25.com, Harvard was the clear number one. He dismisses the Panthers as follows:

> Sure, Pitt shut out every opponent, but so did 7–0 Illinois. It is a nice feat, but ultimately trivial, especially given that Pitt did not play a top 25-caliber opponent. . . . Harvard suffered a tie at Yale, but Pitt did not even play a team anywhere near as good. Harvard's 4–0–1 record against top 25-caliber teams, though imperfect, is still far better than Pitt's 0–0 record against the same.[25]

In the class album, Captain Withington was restrained. The Yale result, he wrote, "was a disappointment to Harvard, but the season was, on the whole, very successful."[26] Surely this was history's least exultant captain of a national champion.

About the sport itself, the *Times* also was equivocal in its season summary, writing, "The elimination of massing and pushing and pulling has made it easier to see where the ball is going, but . . . the first year of the reformed game has developed little that is new."[27] It would take another season of slogging before there was a real breakthrough.

4

"HERE IS THE THEORETICAL SUPERPLAYER IN FLESH AND BLOOD"

Had a Harvard dropkick not been blocked and run back by a Princeton end named Sam White, the setting of *This Side of Paradise* might have been New Haven or even Cambridge.

For the Crimson, the 1911 season was riddled by bad bounces and worse breaks. In back-to-back weeks, Harvard played two of the signature games in early football history and lost both. All the while, the new arrivals to the Yard—the fabled Group of Seven—waited in the wings.

✿ ✿ ✿

On May 15, 1911, as the Boston newspapers breathlessly reported the next day, Percy Duncan Haughton was wed in Lenox, Massachusetts, to Mrs. Gwendolyn Whistler Howell. The bride, who brought two daughters to the marriage, was the widow of the Rev. Richard Howell, who had died the year before and was renowned as one of the wealthiest clergymen in the United States. She also was a grandniece of artist James McNeill Whistler. "J. W. Farley, a classmate of the bridegroom at Harvard, was best man," the *Herald* noted, without mentioning that "Mike" Farley also was one of the prime behind-the-scenes movers in Crimson football. "The bride wore a traveling dress. Immediately after the ceremony Mr. and Mrs. Haughton started for Grand Canyon."[1]

When he returned and contemplated his 1911 prospects, Haughton was staring at some other large holes. He had to fill them, because the

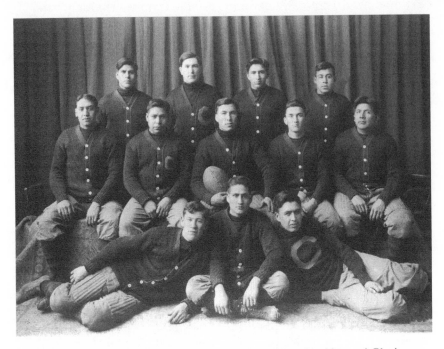

Carlisle's crackerjack 1911 aggregation that stunned haughty Harvard. Playing on an injured leg, Jim Thorpe (bottom row, left) ran the Crimson ragged, booting four field goals and an extra point, while cementing himself in the discussion of the greatest players of all time. Cumberland County Historical Society, Carlisle, Pennsylvania.

schedule included, for the first time since 1896, a Princeton team, one that had worrisome sleeper potential. The week after the Crimson visited the Tigers, Pop Warner's Carlisle Indians, with the virtuosic Jim Thorpe, would visit the Stadium.

As usual for the preseason, Haughton had no commanding quarterback. For better or worse, juniors Bob Potter and Dick Wigglesworth were back and would jockey to start under center. But also as usual, there were the makings of a staunch line to clear the path for the ground-pounding Percy Wendell, one of many short men in the backfield. The linchpins up front were the two returning All-Americas, Bob McKay and the redoubtable Bob Fisher, now the captain. There were large and promising sophomores, Harvey Rexford "Rex" Hitchcock (yet another man from Oahu College in Hawaii), Tudor Gardiner (Groton), and Robert Treat Paine "Bob" Storer (Noble and Greenough). A junior named Derry Parmenter (Stone's School) would be the center/roving center; only 170 pounds, he would have the formidable task of handling two All-Americas, Princeton's Arthur Bluethenthal and Yale's Henry Ketcham.

The ends were crackerjack: Sam Felton had returned to launch his howitzer punts, and Bud Smith was back to cover them.

But there was no surefire field-goal kicker.

Addressing his charges before the start of spring practice, Haughton put everyone, even himself, on notice. Having been named national champion, he acknowledged, had not convinced the football world that the Crimson and its coach were not one-year wonders. Perhaps Haughton himself was not convinced that his methods had taken hold. "Harvard has not made a touchdown against Yale since 1901," he said, continuing,

> Furthermore, the only points we have scored were four in 1908. In all the other years, except last year, we have not only not scored, but we have been defeated . . . this year is a crucial one for the present administration in that the series for the past three years has left Yale and Harvard even. . . . I must say frankly that each year I have been bitterly disappointed in the realization of how crudely we have performed against Yale. I am willing to take my full share of blame for the performance of the team as a whole, but the performance of the individuals lies almost wholly in their own hands, and for the mistakes they have made and for their crudeness of play, they have themselves alone to blame.
>
> If we are to have any hope of being successful over Princeton and Yale, we must start now to improve our methods. I want to assure you that I am doing everything I can to improve the policy of our campaign, but I want assurances from each and every one of you that you will put your energies more forcibly to work toward improving your own skill, so that when you are called on to do your "stunt" you will be able to do it.[2]

Per custom, Haughton used the early games to figure out what he had to work with. Bates was dispatched, 15–0, with Wendell ramming the ball over for two touchdowns. Tudor Gardiner gave a good account of himself alongside Fisher. Haughton played his first team in the first and third periods—which he would not have been able to do under substitution rules even two years earlier.

For Holy Cross the next week, the Stadium unveiled a new feature. "The large Irwin scoreboard, which was used in the football game last Saturday, has been completed so as to show figures which represent each player on both the Harvard and Holy Cross squads," reported the *Harvard Crimson*. "These figures will be published on the score-card [*sic*], which the *Crimson* will have on sale at the game this afternoon. In this way, spectators will be able to determine exactly who makes each touch-down [*sic*] or long run."[3] The Irwin scoreboard was the Jumbo-tron of its day. The brainchild of Arthur Irwin, a former baseball player, it featured a miniature field on which the progress of the ball was continually tracked.[4]

(Perhaps the more notable development that week in the interest of identification came at Princeton. Against Rutgers, the *New York Times* noted, "The men on the Princeton 11 who are eligible to receive the forward pass appeared with squares of white cloth sewed to their backs.")[5]

The spectators at the Harvard–Holy Cross game didn't really need guidance: The only touchdown in the underwhelming 8–0 win was scored by Wendell on a 40-yard run. The quarterback controversy was resolved sadly when Wigglesworth, who had made a scintillating 45-yard punt return, fractured his ankle. Potter, whose field goal rounded out the scoring, now was the signal-caller, with only the inexperienced sophomore Vinton Freedley to back him up.

The next week against Williams, Potter ran the show in an 18–0 victory, going 2-for-4 in passing, including one nice 15-yard completion to Bud Smith. Still, the Crimson was playing mostly straight-ahead football, with Wendell again punching the ball over twice. Ominously, the Crimson missed four field goals. In the following game, a rain-drenched affair contested in front of 2,000 spectators, Haughton mostly played the subs in a scoreless first half, then was forced to put in some regulars, who did enough to beat Amherst, 11–0, with the reliable Wendell blast-ing over for the clinching score.

In the week between these routine, grind-it-out affairs, two astute football analysts saw ominous flaws in the Harvard attack. The *Boston Globe*'s Melville Webb noted,

> So far this season Harvard has used only the simplest variety of forward passing and has done little with onside kicking. . . . The

quarterbacks have had small chance to work out their attack to meet the conditions that they have found when on the field of play, conditions that change so often and so quickly. When two teams come to their final games, evenly matched, there is not a chance in 20 that one can push the other over the last 25 yards of territory by rushing. Something besides power will be needed, except for the final punch plays under the goal posts.[6]

In the meantime, the *New York Evening Post*'s Herbert Reed, writing under the banner "Right Wing" in a piece reprinted in the *Globe*, skewered quarterback Bob Potter:

In the kick formation Saturday, Potter held his hands so that there was a different interval between them from that in evidence when the play was to be a fake. If the change could be seen from the top of the Stadium, how much more easily must it have been seen by the Williams forwards. To catch the starting signal it was only necessary to watch the Crimson quarter's arm, for during the earlier numbers the arm nearest the backs was held out almost straight, swinging in to the position from which the ball was to be taken an instant before Potter gave the starting number. Any set of forwards worth its salt could have caught the instant of the start of the Harvard play to a nicety and timed the charge accordingly. These are small things on the surface, but vital in the long run.[7]

☼ ☼ ☼

It was now mid-October—time for "football in earnest," as the *Crimson* put it. Brown, with passer extraordinaire Bill Sprackling, would furnish, in the *Globe*'s words, the "first real test." It would be Sprack's last crack at the Crimson. Haughton played a wild card, installing Freddie Huntington, a senior and a hockey star, at fullback. Haughton was counting on athleticism and a knack for keeping one's feet to trump football inexperience.

A throng of 25,000 filled the permanent seats in the Stadium, and it was rewarded with a crowd-pleaser, a harbinger of the more varied game of a few seasons hence. Harvard won, 20–6, mixing the runs of Wendell (who scored twice) and the passing combination of Potter to Smith. The Bruins also provided thrills in the first half, with two deft

Sprackling passes setting up a touchdown that temporarily tied the game at 6–6. "The thousands who had accompanied the Brown players to Cambridge were on their feet, yelling like Comanches,"[8] the *Globe* reported. Thereafter, however, Sprackling was repeatedly "smeared" by gang-tackling Crimson defenders, with one hit in the third quarter resulting in a fumble that was scooped up by Harvard's Tommy Campbell and run back for a score. Potter made the final touchdown when the Crimson interference sprung him for a scintillating 68-yard runback of a punt. (Sprackling would recover to eventually become president of the Anaconda Wire and Cable Company, as well as a College Football Hall of Famer.)

The win came with a high price: Sam Felton suffered an injury to his side, which left the Crimson without a varsity-caliber punter, to say nothing of an All-America one. Despite Potter's fine play, there was also some carping; as the *Globe* nitpicked, "One of Bob Potter's weaknesses is that he runs to the right in almost every instance and holds the ball in the arm farthest from the right sideline"[9] (meaning, the left one).

Princeton would be sure to exploit such chinks.

❋ ❋ ❋

The first meeting between the schools in 15 years (the series had been interrupted by an eligibility dispute) would take place in the Tigers' lair—"Jungletown," as the papers referred to it. For those venturing down from Boston, the *Times* provided a revolutionary piece of information: auto routings.[10] When the game had been scheduled in January, Mike Farley, chairman of the Football Committee, had declared to the Harvard Athletic Association,

> The Football Committee believes that under the present rules, or rules substantially similar, that there will be no material additional strain in playing Princeton, as well as Dartmouth, next year. They feel that development of the team for its final game will be in no way injured, and that material advantages will be gained by such a game.[11]

For the next five seasons, Princeton would provide a measuring stick of the Crimson team and Haughton's progress as a coach. In 1911, neither would measure up.

The "Men of Nassau," under William F. "Bill" Roper, came in 5–0–2, and featured All-America linemen Arthur Bluethenthal and Eddie Hart (the captain), plus a golden boy in all-purpose sophomore back Hobart Amory Hare Baker, soon to be known to the ages as Hobey. Despite Harvard's being installed as a 10-to-8 favorite, former captain Ham Fish, writing in the *Globe*, was skeptical of the Crimson's chances. "The game is expected to develop into a punting duel," predicted Fish, "with Harvard perhaps an aggressor in the smashing attack, and Princeton playing safe and on the lookout for an opportunity to get one of her fast backs off for a long run . . . Wendell will be a marked man," Fish wrote. "The outcome is likely to depend on the ability to kick field goals . . . as neither team has the punch to carry the ball for a steady advance and then to push it over."[12]

Fish had it mostly right. In the first game ever photographed from an airplane,[13] Princeton, the season's most opportunistic team, won, 8–6, victimizing Harvard on one of the most famous plays in early football history. In the second period, the Crimson had driven to the Tigers' five, and when the drive stalled, Paul Hollister attempted a dropkick. Princeton's Joseph Duff blocked it. End Sanford "Sam" White, out of Fall River, Massachusetts, and Exeter, who was partially screened from tacklers by referee Bill Langford, scooped the ball up and ran 105 yards for a touchdown.

"Line after line White romped across, until he finally threw himself over Harvard's goal line for a touchdown," Webb wrote in the *Globe*.[14]

In attendance that day was a student at Newman School in Hackensack, New Jersey. The young man was in the process of finalizing his college choice. Afterward, Francis Scott Key Fitzgerald wrote, "Sam White decides me for Princeton."[15]

The play was not happenstance, but the result of keen scouting. As Webb noted the Monday after the game,

> Harvard's defense for the kicker had been watched carefully, and the Tigers put on a block kick formation, which has just been handed down by Pennsylvania State College and which has blocked more kicks this fall than any team on record. Harvard had two men in tandem between the kicker and the rush line, and on the right in front of the kicker's feet. There was one man for protection at the left. Princeton, Saturday, sent three men, both ends and a halfback, to their right, and when the ball was passed all three of them darted

in toward the kicker. One Harvard blocker had to attend to the three
Tigers. At the same time, these Tiger guards pulled the center aside,
and Bluethenthal dashed through. Also, the men tackling on the left
wing came through to engage the protectors on the left. The result
was that three men at least had a chance to block the kick unless the
pass was absolutely true and the kicker quick as a flash. Hollister
wasn't quick, and the result was that the kick was blocked and that
there were three Tigers on the spot, one to get the ball and two
others to go on the field to interfere. [16]

In future seasons, Haughton would make sure to drill kickers to get
their ball off in a flash.

The Crimson kicking game was a disaster all day. As Captain Fisher
reported in the 1912 class album. "Harvard began the contest without a
kicker, and allowed Campbell, the little halfback, to do the kicking.
Considering his lack of kicking experience, the work was well done. But
Campbell was soon put out of the game by a bad muscle bruise." [17]
Receiving proved equally hazardous. "White's run" was followed in the
third period by "White's safety," a play on which the Princeton end ran
down under a punt and tackled Harvard's Harry Gardner on the Harvard two, then knocked him back over the goal line. The play would
prompt a rule change declaring the ball down where the punt receiver
caught the ball. [18]

Huntington scored the Harvard touchdown, barreling over from the
three early in the fourth quarter, but the Crimson could not get over
the hump. Princeton was impotent on offense; the Crimson outgained
the Tigers 213 yards to 40, and completed four of the seven passes it
tried. (The threat of the pass also set up some nifty runs off of fakes.)
But Harvard squandered four field-goal chances, in some cases because
their best kickers either were injured or had been removed earlier in
the period and thus could not be reinserted for the boot. The consensus
was that Harvard was "outgeneraled"—a smirch on the reputation of
Haughton.

The trip back to Cambridge was particularly subdued. Bob Potter
and Tudor Gardiner had sustained season-ending injuries; Gardiner's
broken arm threatened to be career-ending. "Championship games"
with Dartmouth and Yale loomed. Given the battered and bruised state
of his squad, Haughton would be forced to treat the following Saturday's game as a respite, a breather, a day of healing. The opponent was

Carlisle, featuring the coach's old nemesis, Pop Warner, and a halfback named Jim Thorpe. Thus, the seeds were sown for one of the most storied performances in college football history.

* * *

The symbolism of the matchup was undeniable: the poor and dispossessed Native Americans versus the powerful and (let's face it) snobbish swells. But Carlisle was not tiny—at times it had 1,000 students—and it loomed particularly large in college football. The Indians, who had visited the Stadium 12 times previously, were the game's most entertaining traveling show, barnstorming the nation and receiving large financial guarantees. (Harvard assistant coach Harry von Kersburg claimed that Warner lopped a cut of Carlisle's share for himself.)[19] For this match, according to Harvard Athletic Association records in the University Archives, Carlisle, having bargained for a 50-percent share of the gate, took home a check for $10,399.67, a munificent sum in those days.[20]

In 1911, its team was superb. The Indians arrived at the Stadium with a 9–0 record. Hence, it wasn't as if the tiny Native American school was an underdog. For a football analog today, think perhaps Boise State against Oklahoma. This was, if not the game of the year, at least one of them.

Haughton, however, did not necessarily see it that way. Given the battered state of his squad, he chose to treat the Carlisle game as a de facto practice game, leaving it to his second-teamers to go up against the Indians. Haughton saw no need even to be on hand; instead, he would travel to New Haven, scouting Yale as it played Brown. He instructed assistant Leo Leary, who would run the team, not to insert the starters unless absolutely necessary. Haughton harbored hope that his scrubs would win and Leary could tweak Warner by inserting the starters for a cameo.

Admittedly, this was a gamble. Warner's team, composed mainly of light, quick players, ran his ingenious brainchild: the single wing. The formation bamboozled brawnier foes with laterals (often more than one on a play), reverses (single and double), and occasional passes, or at least the threat of them. The attack featured All-America quarterback Gus Welch and two other stars, fullback Possum Powell and end Samson Burd. Tackle William "Lone Star" Dietz, later a coach at Washington State and of the NFL's Boston Redskins, was the best Indian interior lineman.

Above all, Warner could deploy the all-around talents of Thorpe. Previously, Thorpe had played football and run track at Carlisle in 1907 and '08, but he left school discouraged. He was lured back by Warner's promise to help him train for the 1912 Olympics in Stockholm. Large for the time, at six feet tall and 185 to 190 pounds, and classically proportioned, he also was one of the world's fastest humans, running 100 yards in 10 seconds. To his speed, he added uncanny instincts. Said the *Boston Globe* in a pregame "Football Notes" column, "Charley Wharton, the old Pennsylvania line veteran . . . says that of all the football whirlwinds he has ever seen in an open field, Thorpe of the Carlisle Indians is the whirliest."[21] Thorpe could run, pass, punt, defend, and, above all, placekick.

As with Harvard, Warner had a major bruise to deal with: Thorpe's. Two weeks before, in a 19–0 victory over Lafayette, he had suffered an ankle injury. On this day, he would play with a bandage on his right (kicking) leg.

Spicing the buildup even further was the history of distrust between Warner and Haughton. Thus, there was more than usual anticipation as 25,000—some sitting in temporary stands—crowded into the Stadium on a sunny afternoon. Carlisle had sold 443 tickets,[22] and the *Globe* noted that the team was "urged on by the Indian girls in the stand." The fans settled in to watch what the *Globe*'s Mel Webb would the next day describe as a "wonderful vaudeville football show on Soldiers Field."[23]

Harvard took the field quarterbacked by sophomore Vinton Freedley, who, shortly after the Crimson kicked off, produced the first break—for Carlisle. Freedley mishandled a kick. The Indians recovered at Harvard's 22 and drove to the Harvard five, where they eschewed a field goal. The Crimson held, but after a punt, Carlisle, behind 10-yard gains from power backs Thorpe and Powell, was back inside the five. Again, the Crimson stiffened. This time, Thorpe backed up to the 13. He employed the placekick. It sailed straight through. Carlisle 3, Harvard 0.

Later in the period, Harvard answered. From midfield, backs George Morrison, Ken Reynolds, and Robert Blackall (who reeled off an 18-yarder) bowled through the light Carlisle defense and advanced the ball to the 21. On third down, Paul Hollister dropped back to the 28 and sent a dropkick through the uprights. Carlisle 3, Harvard 3.

As the second period began, Thorpe riposted. Again, the hapless Freedley was the goat, mishandling a kick that rolled out of bounds at the Harvard four. The Crimson immediately punted it away, and after a holding penalty, Carlisle started at the Harvard 44. Two plays brought the ball to the 35. Rather than take a chance on losing the ball on downs, Carlisle again unsheathed its ultimate weapon. Thorpe stepped back to the 43 and sent his placement cleanly through the uprights. Carlisle 6, Harvard 3.

Next came the game's only untoward incident. A Harvard tackle, Ashfield Stow, slapped an Indian with the back of his hand. "After the match Stow manfully apologized to the referee for his roughness and was sportsmanlike enough to implicate no Indian as a mutual offender," reported the *Globe*.[24] Shortly after the slapping, Thorpe fumbled, and Hollister pounced on the ball just past midfield. On second down from the Carlisle 46, Harvard's Ken Reynolds headed around left end and was slammed to the turf by Welch. But under the rules of the day, Reynolds could continue until he was fully halted. He got up and kept on going, all the way to end zone. It was good for five points, and Hollister's dropkick conversion added another. At the half, it was Harvard 9, Carlisle 6, and it seemed as if Haughton's audacity in resting the starters might be rewarded.

But in the second half, the Indians took the wraps off—"played their whirlwind football," as the *Globe* put it. Early on, Harvard punted from the Carlisle 40 to the 15, where Thorpe gathered it in. He weaved his way back to the original line of scrimmage. "Then," said the *Globe*, "began the slaughter of the substitutes. The Crimson line was like paper before the hard-punching plays of the Indians and their splendid end runs, which were made possible by the finest of interference."[25] Alex Arcasa and Powell worked a nifty crisscross play that gained 25 yards around Harvard's right wing. Thorpe gained five yards, Powell 10, and then he and Arcasa worked another lateral and crisscross for 10 more. Three more plays brought the ball to the goal line, from which Powell barreled across. Thorpe slammed home the point. Carlisle 12, Harvard 9.

After Harvard's kickoff, which Thorpe returned to the 35, Carlisle kept at it. Thorpe sailed through the Crimson for 24 yards to the Harvard 51. (Remember, this was a 110-yard field.) The drive stalled at the Crimson 30, whereupon Thorpe stepped back to the 38 and banged another three-pointer. Carlisle 15, Harvard 9.

The period ended, and Leary had seen enough. He sent in the cavalry—eight of the starters. Out trotted the redoubtable fireplug Wendell, Fisher, center Bob Storer, and tackle Rex Hitchcock, among others. Furiously, the fresh troops began to gain a territorial advantage, reversed only by an interception tossed by the hapless Freedley. Carlisle clearly was being worn down. There was only one thing to do: Hang on for dear life and hope Jimmy Thorpe's weary leg could supply some insurance points.

His opportunity came in the middle of the period. After an exchange of punts, Carlisle had the ball at Harvard's 40, second down and six. Thorpe backed up to the 48. As related in Kate Buford's *Native American Son: The Life and Sporting Legend of Jim Thorpe*, Thorpe said to Arcasa, "Set the ball up. I'll kick it."

Buford recounted Thorpe's later recollection:

> The pain sort of helped me because it made me more deliberate. . . .
> As long as I live . . . I will never forget that moment. There I stood in
> the center of the field, the biggest crowd I had ever seen watching
> us . . . I was tired enough so that all my muscles were relaxed. I had
> confidence, and I wasn't worried. The ball came back square and
> true, and I swung my leg with all the power and force that I had, and
> knew, as it left my toe, that it was headed straight for the crossbar
> and was sure to go over.[26]

According to newspaper accounts, the ball was not dead center—it snuck inside one upright—but it would have been good from 10 or 15 yards farther back.

The points were needed, because a few minutes later, Storer blocked a punt and ran in for the touchdown. But after Carlisle withstood a final Harvard passing flurry (the Crimson tried five passes in the game, the Indians none), the 18–15 score held up. In the final moments, Warner pulled an exhausted Thorpe, to a universal ovation. "Fancy What Would Have Happened If Jimmy Thorpe Hadn't Been Lame," mused a *Globe* headline the next day.[27]

But perhaps the most impressive tribute came from the absent and hard-bitten Haughton. "I realized," declared P. D., "that here was the theoretical superplayer in flesh and blood."[28]

The performance cemented Thorpe's place in the discussion concerning the greatest football player ever.

Neither Haughton nor anyone else knew this: Harvard would not lose again for the next 33 games, spanning four years.

* * *

Taking Carlisle lightly had snuffed any faint hope the Crimson had of defending its mythical national title. The next week, 37,000 at the Stadium saw Harvard regain some confidence by beating Dartmouth in the mud, 5–3. The only touchdown was scored early in the first period when, after Bud Smith blocked a punt by Dartmouth's Fred Llewellyn, Freddie Huntington, inserted that week as center rush, fell on the rolling ball 30 yards behind the goal line. (Beginning the following season, a touchdown so far back of the goal would not be allowed.) On the play, Haughton cagily had split his line, leaving the middle uncovered. The rest of the game, mudder Wendell hurled himself into the line, helping the Crimson control the ball. However squeaky, the victory at least provided some momentum going into The Game.

On November 25, more than 40,000 showed up at the Stadium on a sunny day. The cloudy result highlighted not only the Crimson's Achilles' heel, but also what was wrong in the sport that season: yet another scoreless tie. It was a chippy game. Each side made only five first downs. Paramount were the booming punts of Harvard's Felton (16 kicks, 37-yard average) and the line-drive responses of Yale's Walter Camp Jr. (18, 30). The Crimson's best chance came in the first period, when, with the ball on the Yale eight, quarterback Bob Potter tried a pass that was picked off by Yale's Jesse Spalding.

The toss was risky for many reasons, not least being that it could not be received over the goal line, but instead would have to be caught in front of it and run in for a touchdown. Thus, it had to be thrown in front of the defenders. Former Harvard player Dudley Dean wrote in the *Globe*,

There will be a lot of carpers even about Saturday's game. "Harvard should have won," they will say. "Potter should never have tried that forward pass on first down on Yale's 10-yard line in the first quarter. He should have used up two downs, anyway, getting the ball squarely in front of the posts and then have dropkicked a goal." Beautiful! Now just suppose, for a brief argument, that Potter had done all the carpers had wanted him to do—but alas, Yale had blocked the dropkick or Potter had missed it? It's the old story of success succeeding and that alone—and of what might have been. Bob Potter has played baseball. Further, he knows the "chance" in "new football." He took that chance. What better time to catch Yale unawares within the very shadow of Yale's goal line, and with [Yale's Arthur] Howe's reputation as a dropkicker what better chance to tick off six points for the Crimson, against which the Blue would have struggled in vain?[29]

Harvard, which was six times inside the Yale 35, undid itself with penalties and three missed makeable field goals. Yale botched two. "Never did a game show more plainly and prove more conclusively the value of good dropkickers," wrote the *Globe*'s W. D. Sullivan.[30] As Mel Webb summed up, "The game ended—an anticlimax—everything a hush—no enthusiasm—nothing but disappointment and dissatisfaction over a game that neither team could win."[31]

In a postmortem, Webb (echoing critics throughout the country) put his finger on the sport's main flaw. He wrote,

In the last six important matches of the year, Harvard–Princeton, Dartmouth–Princeton, Yale–Princeton, Harvard–Dartmouth, Harvard–Yale, and Army–Navy, there have been only four touchdowns

The Game, 1911. The standard packed house at Harvard Stadium went home frustrated by a second consecutive scoreless tie—symbolic of the sport's major problem as a spectator attraction. *Prints and Photographs Division, Library of Congress, LC-USZ62-130692.*

scored, four goals from the field, and one safety. Not much of a tribute to a game the basis of which is supposed to be the ability to carry the ball by rushing—that is, if it is agreed that football is still football and not some other game under the same name. Two of the four touchdowns were made by Sammy White of Princeton, both on long runs after an opponent's mistake; Harvard scored on Dartmouth by blocking a kick, and against the Tigers by splendid work on a forward pass by Gardner and Reynolds, together with a hard punch for a few-yard gain to cross the goal line. . . .

With the forward passes eradicated when close to the goal line, except as a tremendously long shot, and with the impossibility for the attacking team to use an onside kick, the team that is holding its goal need figure only on how to stop a rushing attack. This is mighty easy with the secondary defense drawn in and the inability of the attacking team to help its runner along over any part of the 10 yards that is as necessary to gain down the field as it is out in the open to secure first down. . . . The game is all right between the 25-yard lines, but to make it right from these lines to the goals more rule tinkering is needed.[32]

Deliverance was at hand. Two crucial innovations would bring forth a torrent of points. And Harvard's kicking salvation was already in Cambridge. On the same day that the Crimson varsity was failing when within sight of the Princeton goalposts, Charlie Brickley was accounting for all the game's points in the Harvard freshman team's 12–0 win over the Princeton frosh. Brickley dropkicked three field goals (one from 53 yards away) and placekicked one, from the 36, at a "very difficult angle," reported the *Crimson*. "The ball went straight and true, being the best kick seen at Princeton this year."[33]

The Men of Nassau soon would be all too familiar with this sight.

5

THE DA VINCI OF THE DROPKICK

On April 16, 1912, the *Titanic* went down. Among the more than 1,500 who perished was Harry Elkins Widener, Harvard '07, whose passion was book collecting. In his memory, his mother, Eleanor, commissioned the construction of a grand new repository: the Harry Elkins Widener Memorial Library would open in 1916.

Seven days before the tragedy, across the river from Cambridge, the Red Sox had broken in their spanking new baseball palace, Fenway Park, with an exhibition game—against Harvard. In cold and snowy conditions, only 3,000 showed up. On the mound for the Crimson was ace Sam Felton. Known on the gridiron for his hard-to-handle punts, Felton was suitably wild, issuing 10 walks, but he permitted the Sox only four hits. With Boston leading 2–0 going into the bottom of the seventh, the game was called. That season, the BoSox would win the World Series.

The year 1912 was also a presidential election year, one with a decided Big Three tinge. The incumbent, Republican William H. Taft, was a Yale man. He was opposed by former president Theodore Roosevelt, of Harvard, running on the Bull Moose ticket, and Democrat Woodrow Wilson, governor of New Jersey and former president of Princeton. All three were enthusiastic backers of their respective schools' teams. Somewhat surprisingly, given the conservative bent of the student body, a straw poll of Harvard undergrads and law students (which had them order their choices) gave the nod to Wilson—perhaps presaging the split in the conservative ranks that handed the election to

the Princetonian.[1] (But not all was progressive that year: For its cotillion, the Junior League in Boston banned the turkey trot.[2] The next
year, the city prohibited the tango.)

In 1912, the National Collegiate Athletic Association named its first
president: Harvard dean LeBaron R. Briggs. Hoping to produce more
scoring, the football rules committee—with Harvard coach Percy
Haughton in the vanguard—made several changes. A touchdown was
now worth six points instead of five, the ball was made slimmer in hopes
of furthering the passing game, and passes now could be thrown longer
than 20 yards. The onside kick—the punt that could be recovered by
the kicking team after going 20 yards—was eliminated. The offense was
now given an extra down, for a total of four, to make 10 yards. The
dimensions of the field were altered: Instead of 110 yards, the gridiron
was shrunk to 100.

In the long run, however, the most crucial move may have been the
introduction of two 10-yard end zones. Previously, a pass could not be
caught past the goal line. Now, it could—which meant the defense had
to loosen up to cover potential receivers. The change would not take
hold immediately, but within three seasons most teams would take full
advantage, boosting the game into the modern era.

* * *

For Harvard varsity football, 1912 saw the first appearance of its trans-
formational class of sophomores, the Group of Seven, who were of
diverse and splendidly complementary talents. Five—save quarterback
Mal Logan and end Jeff Coolidge—would appear at least once on a
Walter Camp All-America team.

Back Charlie Brickley already had celebrity, and even notoriety. He
was a marvelous all-around player, capable of scoring on offense and
defense. But what made him special was his right foot.

Whether by placekicking or dropkicking, extra points and short field
goals were not the pro forma affairs they became in the latter part of the
20th century. Although the ball was rounder and softer, and presented a
larger surface to contact, unlike today's pigskins it often was in play the
entire game. Especially on rainy days, it would become waterlogged.
Moreover, it was harder for the snapper to send it back with accuracy
and velocity. Because of limited substitution, the kicker was not a spe-

Charlie Brickley demonstrating the fine points of the dropkick, which he mastered more proficiently than most, if any, others. Thanks to unceasing practice, "Brick" could bang his boots through the goalposts from any angle, and even half-blind, as he would prove against Yale in 1913. *Harvard University Sports Information.*

cialist, but a hard-used back or lineman often booting with a weary leg. The men who mastered this difficult art, then, were coveted.

Brickley began refining his unique talent as a lad in Everett, eventually making it such an art form that he became the da Vinci of the dropkick. He began seriously booting at age 13; "many a neighbor's windowpane suffered as a consequence," he wrote later.[3] "I practiced dropkicking every day for 10 years, summer and winter," Brickley told Arthur Daley of the *New York Times* in 1948. "Nowadays the kids throw the ball. In my day we kicked it."[4] He had many role models, even if, unlike the booters of today, he merely could read about them.

✧ ✧ ✧

The dropkick had been part of the game since the rules convocation of 1876 modified the old Rugby Union code accordingly:

1. A drop kick, or drop, is made by letting the ball fall from the hands and kicking it the very instant it rises.

2. A place kick, or place, is made by kicking the ball after it has been placed in a nick made in the ground for purposes of keeping it at rest.

6. A goal may be obtained by any kind of a kick except a punt.

In the early days of football the point values of touchdowns and field goals kept fluctuating, but the difference often was small, thus the worth of the dropkicker. Perhaps the first great practitioner was Princeton back Alex Moffat. Weighing less than 140 pounds, "Teeny-bits," as he was affectionately called, could smack 'em through with either foot. In the October 20, 1928, issue of *Collier's* magazine, famed coach John Heisman wrote,

> Here was a youth with wings on his heels. He could stop dead from a hard run and in that same moment boot the ball, frequently 65 yards. Either of Alex's feet could send the ball 50, 60, 70 yards. Against Harvard in 1883, he dropkicked four field goals—two with the right foot and two with the left.[5]

That season, in addition to scoring seven touchdowns for the Tigers, Moffat kicked 16 field goals and seven extra points.

While thumping the ball around the vacant lots of Everett, young Brickley surely heard the legend of (and maybe emulated) Pat O'Dea, a near-mythical figure whose story has echoes of Roy Hobbs's in *The Natural*. Heisman called O'Dea the "most prodigious of all the dropkickers." O'Dea arrived at Wisconsin in 1896 with his brother Andy, the school's crew coach, having traveled from his native Melbourne, Australia, where he had been recognized in Australian Rules Football as the greatest kicker in the Antipodes. Quickly dubbed the "Kangaroo Kicker," the 6-foot, 170-pound O'Dea, in the 1897, '98, and '99 seasons, startled the Badgers and their opponents with his feats of feet. In '97, according to Allison Danzig, he dropkicked a field goal of 60 yards against Chicago and one of 42 yards on the dead run against Minnesota. In 1898, in a driving blizzard, he was credited with a 62-yarder against Northwestern; one teammate, Eddie Cochems, later said it actually came from 65 yards and the "ball went between the goal posts two stories high and over a fence 10 yards behind the goal posts." O'Dea was also an expert placekicker and punter. "Seventy- and 80-yard boots were the rule for O'Dea," said an Associated Press story in 1934. In '99, "while returning a punt against Minnesota, O'Dea saw the Gophers closing in on him and so—on a dead run toward the sideline—he wheeled and scored a goal on a 60-yard dropkick."[6]

Post-football life only enhanced the legend. O'Dea coached Notre Dame, then practiced law in San Francisco until 1917, when he apparently vanished. Rumor had it he had joined up with the Australian army as it passed through town. The truth wasn't discovered until 1934, when he was located in Westwood, California, living under the name Charles J. Mitchell and working as a statistician. He had made the switch because he thought his fame was a handicap in his business affairs. "As Pat O'Dea, I seemed very much just an ex-Wisconsin football player," he said. "Probably I was wrong. Mrs. Mitchell, that is, Mrs. O'Dea, always said I was."[7] He died on April 3, 1962—the day after he was inducted into the College Football Hall of Fame.

Also making his mark as a dropkicker was future baseball Hall of Famer Christy Mathewson. Playing for Bucknell in the 1890s, Mathewson was a "better football player than a baseball player," as he told author William H. Edwards. When Matty was playing summer baseball, he would tote along a football and, he said, "occasionally had an opportunity to practice kicking when I was through with my baseball work." The practice paid off when "Big Six" showed his pinpoint control by dropkicking 35- and 40-yard field goals against heavily favored Penn and scoring another at West Point "from a difficult angle."[8]

When young Brickley was getting his first kicks in at Mt. Washington Elementary School in East Everett, the most celebrated dropkicker in the land was Chicago's Walter Eckersall. Had there been a Heisman Trophy in 1905, the 5-foot-7, 142-pound quarterback for Amos Alonzo Stagg's national champion Maroons almost certainly would have won it; as it was, Walter Camp would place him on his all-time All-America team. Eckersall dropkicked five field goals in a single game twice—in 1905 against Illinois and in '06 against Nebraska. The latter performance, good for 20 of Chicago's points in its 38–5 win, came in the final game of his career, after which "Eckie" was carried off the field by cheering Maroon rooters.[9] Later, Eckersall became a sportswriter and prominent football official, particularly in games involving the Notre Dame teams of Knute Rockne; Eckersall had been the first hero for the

Rock, a Windy City product. Alas, Eckersall lived hard, and he died of cirrhosis of the liver in 1930, at age 43.

Having heard of the exploits of such inspirational dropkickers, young Charlie began systematically breaking down the mechanics. In many ways, he was like a golfer trying to perfect his stance, swing, and impact, all the while figuring out, through trial and error, how to "work" the ball. Later, he would receive hands-on instruction from former punter extraordinaire Percy Haughton, who would carefully (that is, without messing it up) help refine his technique. In 1915, the year after his Harvard career had ended, Brickley distilled his wisdom into an article for his syndicated newspaper column. The main elements were as follows:

Grip and drop. "The best method of holding the ball is to keep one hand on each side of it. The ball should be held as closely as possible to the ground in front of the kicking foot and should be dropped perfectly straight."

Stride and toe position at impact. "If a right-foot kicker, the left should be back at the start. Then, as the ball is snapped back from the center, the left foot comes forward in a position so that the right foot can meet squarely with the weight of the body behind it. Meeting the ball squarely! In this many dropkickers fail. There are so many chances against hitting the ball squarely. The step may be wrong; the ball may not be dropped perfectly straight; the eye may be taken off the ball; the ground may be uneven; the kicker's attention may be diverted—the chances are against the kicker unless he is absolute master of the situation."

Focus. "The eye should be kept on the ball and not on the goal posts. The time to look at the posts is just before the ball is passed from the center. If the kick is made from an angle, great care must be exercised. Once the post is sighted then all attention must be put on the ball."

Receiving the snap. "In the big college games, the ball must be kicked within two or two and a half seconds from the time it leaves the center's hands or it will be blocked. The best way to practice is to have someone hold a stopwatch. I found that during my junior year at Harvard I averaged slightly less than two seconds for the kick. But form should not be sacrificed for speed.

Get the form and accuracy first, and the speed will come later on."

The man holding the stopwatch for Brickley, of course, was Haughton. According to a 1930 article in *Boys' Life* magazine by former Penn coach Sol Metzger, P. D. helped resolve the ongoing debate as to whether the dropkick was superior to the placekick in favor of the former thanks to one vital tweak: having Brickley receive the snap leaning forward and catching it knee-high. This not only saved precious milliseconds, but also often resulted in better contact. "The error in dropkicking," wrote Metzger, "is usually due to the kicker catching the ball so high that in its longer fall its long axis is tilted to one side or another and the ball is not struck true."[10]

The literal upshot, according to Brickley: "I found that during my junior year at Harvard I averaged slightly less than two seconds in the kick."

> *Distance control.* "I have always made it a point to practice short-distance kicking more than long. I have always claimed that a man could guide the course of a football from 30 yards or nearer just as a [baseball] catcher controls his throw to second. But out beyond the 35-yard line the distance makes this accuracy almost impossible."
>
> *The "Brickley toe."* "I discovered I could better control the ball the blunter the toe of the shoe. I was of the opinion that a perfectly square toe would be better than a blunt one. So I had an old shoemaker rig me out with a square toe to slip over my regular shoe. . . . I was surprised that nobody had realized the possibilities of this before. Within a year at Harvard everyone who did any kicking had what they called a Brickley toe. Hobey Baker of Princeton heard of my shoe and in the first game he used it got a dropkick against Yale from the 48-yard line in that memorable 6–6 game of 1912."[11]

Those were his precepts. By the time he arrived in Cambridge, Brickley had a veritable Ph.D. in bootery.

☼ ☼ ☼

Entering Harvard in the autumn of 1911, Brickley played freshman football and also competed in track and field. In the summer of 1912, before suiting up for the Harvard varsity, he traveled to Stockholm for the Olympic Games. A member of the U.S. track and field team (along with decathlon gold medalist Jim Thorpe, who would become a lifelong friend), Brickley finished a creditable ninth in the hop, step, and jump. But it was on Soldiers Field that he would make the leap to fame.

Brickley began to wow the Stadium crowds with his artistry. He had become so proficient that he could stand on the sideline and nonchalantly curve the ball through the uprights. "Bend 'Em Like Brickley" preceded "Bend 'Em Like Beckham" by eight decades. Apparently, as time went on, some teammates came to resent Brickley's showstopping displays; there was grumbling that he was showboating, that "Brickley didn't play for Harvard; he played only for himself."[12] It's possible there was a class-based aspect to the complaints against an uppity Irish American. But no one could argue with the results, or the aesthetics. Many accounts speak of Brickley's "pretty" field goals, the way today we speak of certain passers, for instance, Joe Namath, throwing a "beautiful" or "sweet" ball.

Like an artillery siege gun that could shell the enemy from well behind the lines, he was a threat to produce three points any time the Crimson got beyond midfield. In his first season, the "King of Kickers" thumped 13 field goals—still tied for most in a season at Harvard. (Amazingly enough, however, he kicked only two extra points in his entire Harvard career because Haughton, in a rare bit of coaching myopia, thought the PAT unworthy and would ruin him for field-goal work.)

In 1912, the Crimson would need every one of them. In a normal season, Haughton would try to bring his team to a peak for Yale. This year, however, almost every game was a "big game." As college football historian James Vautravers notes, "[Harvard's] schedule was incredibly difficult, featuring seven top 25-caliber teams in nine games, four of them top 10-caliber."[13] (A mitigating factor: Every game, save one—the finale at New Haven—was at Harvard Stadium.)

But this season, at last, Percy Haughton had the horses to put his "system" into full play. Added to the holdovers, the Group of Seven— men who had come in as Haughton recruits—provided unparalleled athleticism. The linemen were fast enough to block downfield. Every back was a threat to break a long run, making it impossible to key on only one. Most important, even after a play began, the opponent never knew who the ballcarrier was. Was it Wendell through the middle? Tack Hardwick off tackle? Brickley around end? Haughton also now had several men who could kick, a true asset in an age of limited substitution.

Percy Wendell was the captain; unfortunately, he also was hobbled by injuries, perhaps a consequence of all his hard-won yardage. It's possible, however, that in just a few short months, his type of back, the valiant mud horse, had become a dinosaur, supplanted by the next evolution of back suited to a suddenly modern game, the taller, faster, multipronged Brickleys and Hardwicks.

Wendell could afford to sit and rest: Sophs Brickley, Hardwick, and Fred Bradlee were primed. The line had lost Bob Fisher and Bob McKay. But their replacements were future All-Americas Stan Pennock (although there was initial worry that, at a chunky 5-foot-9, he was too short) and Wally Trumbull. Rex Hitchcock, Derry Parmenter, and Bob Storer furnished experience. At end, Sam Felton would catch passes and plaster his punts.

Of course, this being Harvard, there was no strong quarterback. Sophomore Mal Logan was judged not ready. Seniors Bob Potter and Harry Gardner at least could be counted on to manage the game.

There was one crucial difference between this year's squad and its recent predecessors. The 1912 Crimson had a field-goal kicker.

Boy, did it ever.

* * *

An all-Group of 12 running-back corps—Bradlee, Brickley, and Hardwick—started the 1912 opener on September 28, against Maine, as Wendell sat. Brickley got the first points of his career on a first-quarter plunge set up by his own 20-yard run. In an unusually tough 7–0 win, the score held up, but only because a Maine pass toward an open receiver in Harvard's end zone struck the goalpost (which was on the goal line). "This play was interesting," noted the *Harvard Alumni Bulletin*, "because it was the first exemplification in Cambridge of the new rule which allows a forward pass to be completed in a zone extending 10 yards back of each goal line."[14]

Against Holy Cross the next week, Brickley misfired on his first career field-goal attempt, from the Crusaders' 35. But he, Hardwick, and Wendell each scored a touchdown in the 19–0 win. Already, Hardwick's brilliance was evident. "His quickness in turning and dodging, and his ability to throw off tacklers are remarkable," noted the *Bulletin*.[15]

Brickley's first field goal came a week later, one of two in a 26–3 win against Williams, during which he also scored a touchdown. The next week, in a 46–0 walkover against Amherst, the Lord Jeffs did not cross their own 35. Brickley ran for three scores, and Hardwick dashed 60 yards for another. Although the foe was not worthy, the downfield blocking was something for future foes to fear. The Crimson Machine truly was in gear.

October 26, with the trees along the Charles shedding the last of their leaves, brought the true start of the season—and scoreboard watching. As always, the opponents to keep in sight were Carlisle, Yale, and Princeton. On this day, all would remain unbeaten, with the Indians and Jim Thorpe beating Georgetown and the Elis taking down Washington & Jefferson. In Jungletown, the Tigers, Harvard's next opponent, whipped Dartmouth, 22–7, to run their record to 6–0. A Harvard victory over Brown would set up a battle of unbeatens in Cambridge the following Saturday.

Bill Sprackling was gone at last, but the typically entertaining Bruins trotted out another scrappy and even more diminutive quarterback, 134-pound George "Kid" Crowther, who at season's end would be named to Walter Camp's All-America first team. But Brown had brought a lightweight to battle heavyweights. In an action-filled 30–10 Harvard win, more than 15,000 onlookers witnessed Brickley scoring on both sides of the ball. He intercepted one of Crowther's tosses and took it 53 yards to the house. He dropkicked three field goals, one set up by his own 40-yard dash. In this game, Haughton began to open things up, to unfurl possibilities for prospective opponents. He had punter Felton fake a kick and toss a 33-yard pass to soph Jeff Coolidge. Later on, reserve quarterback Ev Bradley threw a 50-yard scoring pass to Eddie Graustein.

By the second half, the game was a rout. Kid Crowther, however, showed no quit. He would use the opportunity against the Crimson reserves to become a member of an exclusive fraternity: Players Who Told Percy D. Haughton to Go Screw Himself.

As the score mounted, Haughton sent word to Brown coach Edward Robinson that he might want to take his undersized quarterback out lest he risk getting hurt. As William H. Edwards related in his book *Football Days*,

> Crowther, however, was like an India-rubber ball, and not once during the season had he received any sort of injury. Robby told Crowther what Haughton had suggested, and smiling, the latter said, "Tell him not to worry about me; better look out for himself." On the next play, Crowther took the ball and went around Harvard's end for 40 yards, scoring a touchdown. After he had kicked the goal, the little fellow came over to the sideline and said to Robby, "Send word over to Haughton and ask him how he likes that. Ask him if he thinks I'm all in? Perhaps he would like to have me quit now."[16]

Between the scoring and the shenanigans, the game lasted until after 5 p.m.—well after the sun had set over the West Stands. "Long before that time, thousands of spectators were lighting matches in mimic attempts to see what was going on on the playing field," noted the *Alumni Bulletin*. "It looked as though the seats in the Stadium were occupied by countless fireflies."[17]

✲ ✲ ✲

In early November 2012, a back named Johnny Manziel truly announced himself to the college football world by leading his team, the Texas A&M Aggies, to a victory over the defending national champion, Alabama.

In early November 1912, a back named Charlie Brickley truly announced himself to the college football world by leading his team, Harvard, to a victory over the defending national champion, Princeton.

A sunny, bracing afternoon—perfect football weather—saw arguably college football's first great game of its new era. It featured 32,000 enthralled fans (including 500 who made the trip from Princeton), lead changes, long gainers, artful kicking, and, if not a plethora of passing (14 attempts total), then the ever-present possibility of the pass—or an interception, of which there were five.

Above all, it had Brickley. He was, wrote the *New York Tribune*, the "rock on which the Tigers split." [18]

Princeton had the better of the early going. Only Sam Felton's brilliant punting, including a 65-yard boomer, kept the Tigers at bay. Felton's 19 punts that day remain the all-time Crimson record. His opposite number, John DeWitt, struggled all day, unable to get a handle on the stadium's fickle winds. Felton averaged almost 40 yards; DeWitt, punting 18 times, averaged a shade less than 30. A poor DeWitt punt set up the first score, a 15-yard Brickley dropkick from a difficult angle. But a few minutes later, Princeton riposted spectacularly. Its quarterback, Walter Andrews, completed two passes. The second was a 25-yarder to E. C. Waller. Shaking off Harvard's Harry Gardner, Waller rolled over the goal. The touchdown gave Princeton a 6–3 lead, which it nursed until halftime.

In the third quarter, the Crimson again worked the ball down close, and again Brickley dropkicked a field goal, from the 18-yard line. Then came the game's pivot point. DeWitt punted for Princeton, and Gardner made a fair catch at the Tigers 47. This entitled the Crimson to a free kick. Brickley was primed. Reported the next day's *New York Tribune*, "Carefully he measured the distance; carefully he directed the placing of the ball." Hardwick, the holder, stretched out on the turf with his finger on top of the ball. "Taking only two short steps, [Brickley] drove it over the goal with the accuracy of a sharpshooter for as pretty a goal as has been seen in many a long day." [19] Some said it would have been good from 20 yards farther. Harvard led, 9–6.

The Tigers spent the rest of the game bottled up in their own end, smothered by Derry Parmenter and the Crimson defense. Desperately, they flung passes; four were picked off, one by Brickley, another by Tack Hardwick. Brickley proved to be mortal; he missed three field-goal attempts. Gradually, inexorably, the Crimson moved closer to the clinching score. It was first and goal from the four. Three times, quarterback Gardner handed the ball to Brickley, who tried to barge through. He gained a mere yard. Fourth down. A field goal was out: even if successful, it would leave the Tigers within a touchdown.

Then came what soon would come to be recognized as signature Haughton trickeration.

The ball was snapped. Gardner again handed the ball to Brickley, who headed toward the left, followed by every Princeton tackler. But wait . . . Gardner had held the ball, then slipped it to Hardwick, who charged unmolested into the end zone, then booted the extra point. When the final whistle blew, it was Harvard 16, Princeton 6.

Utterly depleted, Brickley staggered off the field. According to the *Tribune*, "Brickley was cheered by 30,000 people today in a way that comes to few athletes. Even the men of Princeton were generous enough to applaud this dashing, brilliant player."[20]

Charles Edward Brickley had arrived in the spotlight. For better and worse, he never would leave it.

✻ ✻ ✻

During this era, teams from the Midwest and South provided some variety for Harvard, Princeton, and Yale. They invaded the Big Three with two goals in mind. One was a nice payday, guaranteed even if the visitors were massacred; the other was exposure and even glory. An upset could give an upstart school national credibility. This happened with Carlisle in 1911; in 1921, little Centre College of Kentucky would be the giant-killer.

In 1912, however, Vanderbilt was not the usual sacrificial lamb. Although perhaps not in the Crimson's class, the Commodores were the South's best team, having not lost in six games, and were coached by the respected Dan McGugin, who had played at Michigan under the already legendary Fielding H. "Hurry-Up" Yost. Harvard's regulars were exhausted from the effort against Princeton. Hence, as he had done against Carlisle in 1911, Haughton treated the Commodores contest as a practice game, playing the subs heavily. This time he got away with it, winning 9–3, weathering a puzzling Vandy attack in which McGugin sent men in motion toward the flank, then had a back blast up the middle. At one point, the Commodores' Fred "Rabbi" Robbins bolted for 25 yards and was hauled down only by Harvard's last man, Vinton Freedley. Vanderbilt headed back to Nashville with its only defeat of the season, but with heads high.

That day in New Haven, Yale shut out Crowther and Brown. At West Point, Carlisle kept pace by beating Army, 27–6. In that game, the football career of a promising Cadets back named Dwight D. Eisenhower ended when he was injured while tackling Thorpe.

The final Crimson home game, against another good Dartmouth team, posed a dilemma. Yale, of course, loomed. How much to expend against the Indians? "Although Harvard wants very much to win from Dartmouth," wrote the *Alumni Bulletin*, "Saturday's game will be unhesitatingly sacrificed if the coach and captain believe that by so doing they can improve the chances of defeating Yale."[21]

An overflow throng of 43,000 saw Harvard cut it close. The game was a bare-knuckle brawl. Hardwick ferociously covered Felton's punts. Wally Trumbull stymied the Indians' ballcarriers.

Arthur Daley wrote in 1948,

> Frank Cavanaugh was coaching the Green that season, and the Iron Major had a tremendous team. The Dartmouth tackles crashed through on every play, and these ferocious giants smothered two Brickley field goal attempts in the first half. "How are we going to win," barked Haughton, "if Brick doesn't get protection on his kicks?" [Haughton] scowled. "I'll kick one, coach," interposed Charlie mildly, "if I only get another chance. . . ." "Which you won't get," snapped Haughton.
>
> But Brickley already had decided not to take his extra step before booting, and he'd also decided to give the ball all the loft he could. That's what a consummate artist he was. So, he kicked one as planned. Final score: Harvard 3, Dartmouth 0. Brickley insists that the Dartmouth fray was the hardest and toughest he ever was in.[22]

That same day in Philadelphia, Carlisle sustained its first loss, to Penn. In Jungletown, Princeton and Yale played to a 6–6 tie. Of all the major title contenders, Harvard was the only one left unbeaten and untied.

To win it all, the Crimson now only had to defeat two traditional rivals: the Elis—and the ghosts.

✿ ✿ ✿

"Never has there been a more critical moment in Harvard's athletic career than will be marked by the game tomorrow afternoon," editorialized the *Crimson* on November 22, 1912. "Since Coach Haughton took charge of the team, the series with Yale has resulted in a victory, a defeat, and two tie games. A victory tomorrow will prove to all that the

Ever clutch, Charlie Brickley provides just the right amount of loft to his field-goal attempt against Dartmouth in 1912. The kick supplied the only points in an often-brutal battle, which Brickley ranked as the roughest game in which he ever played. *HUPSF Football (243), olvwork376383. Harvard University Archives.*

rejuvenation of football at Harvard is a permanent matter and not a mere flash in the pan."[23]

A loss, however, would have been the iceberg to Haughton's *Titanic*. It would have provided a field day for practitioners of counterfactual history. Yale would have recaptured its now-presumed role as the nation's dominant football school. Harvard's unbeaten streak would have ended at a modest 10. Haughton, who was not signed past the 1912 season, might have chosen not to return—or been dismissed. The names Brickley, Hardwick, and Pennock would be footnotes, if that. There would be no Haughton System.

"Does it have to be recalled to your mind how afraid we all were that Harvard would not win?" captain Percy Wendell would write in the 1913 class album, invoking the familiar refrain, "A better team, perhaps, but they never seem to be able to beat Yale!"[24]

The Elis, coached by the 1911 captain, Art Howe, did not constitute the juggernauts previous Yale teams had been; however, they had given up but 12 points all season—10 fewer than Harvard had surrendered—all on field goals. Their line had two All-Americas. Douglas Bomeisler was a superb end, although he had an injured shoulder and would play wearing a harness. At center, junior Henry Ketcham was what later would be termed a stud. His opposite number, Derry Parmenter, would have his hands full.

The Bulldogs had home-field advantage, although half the crowd would be Crimson. The real 12th Man was the bogeyman, history. Harvard had not scored a touchdown in The Game since 1901.

There was also psychological warfare, some of it nasty. A former coach at Exeter apparently was spreading the word that Charlie Brickley had a yellow streak. Although this seemed improbable given Brick's manful performances against Princeton and Dartmouth, Yale was of another order. The person most upset was a lady in Everett, Massachusetts: Mrs. William Brickley, Charlie's mother. The accusation might have been bogus, but it also was a distraction.

Percy Haughton cast about for any sign to break the spell. According to the *Globe*, the master psychologist found one. Haughton "had a 'hunch' when he saw that the number of the car in which the Harvard players went down to New Haven was 1898. It was in 1898 that Harvard beat Yale in New Haven, 17 to 0, and Haughton played a most prominent part."[25]

Now on a sunny, warm day, 35,000 were at Yale Field waiting for the kickoff. At 2 p.m., Bill Langford, back to referee the game despite a litany of prior complaints, called captains Wendell and Jesse Spalding to midfield—this year, for the first time, the 50-yard line, rather than the 55. Langford tossed the coin. Yale won. The Elis kicked off. The ball went over the end line for a touchback and came out to the Harvard 25.

That, for all intents and purposes, was the closest Yale got.

Haughton's strategy was simple. He would use Sam Felton's punts (sometimes on first down) as the artillery, pinning Yale deep. The reconnaissance, Harvard's cover men—Hardwick, Hitchcock, Storer—would follow the ball and pounce on fumbles. The infantry—Brickley—would administer the final punch, with toe or legs.

On Harvard's first play, Felton skied one that ended up on the Yale 25. A poor return punt put Harvard in business at the Yale 35. Six plays later, Brickley, hurried, missed an 18-yard field goal. The relieved Blue fans roared. The Crimson was unworried. There would be more where that came from.

Then it was Tack Hardwick's turn to be a game-changer. Gardner fumbled a Yale punt. With Bomeisler bearing down, Hardwick, standing alongside, went not for the ball, but for the Eli end, blocking him off. This smart bit of interference enabled Harvard to recover—and, by the bye, demonstrated Tack's keen football instincts.

A few minutes later, punting from his 30, Felton lofted one to the Yale 40. The Elis quarterback, Nat Wheeler, settled under it. The ball reached his arms at the same instant as did Hardwick, running full force. Smash! The ball came loose and took a bounce—right into the arms of oncoming Bob Storer.

The Harvard tackle now could live a dream known to few other Crimson players: to be against Yale with the ball in his hands and nothing but green grass before him. Storer's crimson stockings twinkled as he streaked unimpeded over the goal line. Hardwick kicked the extra point. Harvard 7, Yale 0. It was the first time in 11 years the Crimson had crossed Yale's goal.

A few moments later, Felton sent another punt downfield. Wheeler muffed it again, and Harvard's Rex Hitchcock fell on it at the Yale 45. Wheeler was yanked from the game in favor of Tommy Cornell, a former Exeter teammate of Brickley's. Gardner again called for Felton to kick on first down. As the ball was heading downfield, so was Crimson end Frank O'Brien—until he was tripped by a Yalie. The ensuing penalty gave Harvard the ball at the Yale 25. On two punts, the Crimson had traveled 55 yards. Three plays later, standing on the 33, Brickley essayed another dropkick. This time he made it. Harvard 10, Yale 0. The first quarter still had several minutes to play. It was all over but the shoutin'.

"The suddenness with which the superiority of Harvard's team, which was moving like well-oiled machinery, had overwhelmed the disjointed efforts of the powerful Eli giants, had hushed the Yale stands into absolute silence, while the Crimson host settled back in perfect contentment to enjoy the rest of the exhibition, in a full realization that Harvard had won the game," wrote W. D. Sullivan in the next day's *Globe*.[26]

The rest of the half was scoreless. Bomeisler, spent and hurting, retired early in the second quarter.

Hoping for a rally, Yale put in fresh men to begin the second half. Haughton stood pat. Early on, Felton boomed another punt. This time it was Tommy Cornell who muffed it. Rex Hitchcock fell on the ball at the Elis 18. On the next play, Gardner pitched to Brickley, who swept around left end. Ahead of him was a convoy of Hardwick, Hitchcock, and Frank O'Brien. Shrugging off tacklers, Brickley crossed the goal at the corner of the end zone. Hardwick kicked the goal. Harvard 17, Yale 0.

Now the Elis had to pull out all the stops. A Harvard fumble gave them the ball just past midfield. Spalding faded to pass. Shadowing a Yale receiver, Brickley "jumped the route," as we now put it. Leaping, he plucked the ball from the air and headed downfield. He did not stop until he had reached the Yale 24.

Here, quarterback Gardner pulled some legerdemain. He ordered Brickley back in dropkick formation. But instead, Parmenter snapped the ball to Gardner, who took three steps back and tossed it downfield to a wide-open Felton, who lugged it to the nine. The Brickley dropkick that followed was virtually automatic. Harvard 20, Yale 0.

Brickley might have scored more points. A potential long gain was curtailed when he ran into the umpire, who later said he felt as if he had been hit by an automobile.

For the rest of the game, Harvard's well-drilled line dominated. Stan Pennock played his first great game, penetrating the Yale backfield and dropping runners in their tracks. Parmenter, using Haughton's specially designed silent signal code, held his own with Ketcham. In the backfield, Wendell burrowed in behind Hardwick for yardage off tackle.

There was one more bit of heroism left for Sam Felton. With its fans pleading to break the shutout, Yale drove from its own 25 to the Harvard eight before the Blue was repulsed. On the second down after Harvard took over, the big end stepped into the newfangled end zone and punted the Crimson out of trouble.

Wendell later exulted about "how in the last few minutes, as Yale was going to try a goal from the field, they became confused and were unable to get it off before time was called."[27]

Replaced in the fourth quarter, the Human Bullet could run off the field in the dying sunlight for a final time with sweet satisfaction; he and classmates Felton, Gardner, and Parmenter had turned it around. Soon thereafter, time was called. The Crimson fans began their happy snake dance around the goalposts.

⁕ ⁕ ⁕

By acclamation, Harvard was national champion. As historian James Vautravers puts it, "Harvard is indeed your 1912 mythical national champion, and they're not sharing it with anyone."[28] On December 6, the squad was feted by 600 at the Harvard Club of Boston. As the *Alumni Bulletin* reported,

> When Mr. Haughton rose to speak, Dean Briggs, on behalf of the Boston graduates, gave him a great silver loving cup appropriately inscribed. After the speaking Major [H. L.] Higginson, for the Boston Harvard Club, presented to every one of the men who took part in the Yale game a miniature gold football.[29]

On Hall Street in Everett, Mrs. William Brickley was happy that her boy had vigorously proven he was not yellow. A few days after the Harvard Club banquet, the Boston papers reported,

> Charlie Brickley, the famous Harvard halfback, was the honored guest at a banquet given by the citizens of Everett last night. [He] was toasted by state, church, and city representatives as a model son, a model man, and an athlete of which his city could be proud. . . . Brickley himself was apparently under a great nervous strain, as he sat and listened to the fine things said of him by the speakers of the evening. As he himself said, in his neat little speech, "I am heartily sick and tired of all this notoriety. You people must pity me. I would much rather have each of you meet me on the street and then I would do myself justice."[30]

Had there been a Heisman Trophy that year, the choice would have come down to Brickley and his Olympic teammate Thorpe, who had again performed brilliantly for Carlisle. As it was, Brickley, Felton, and Pennock were named to Walter Camp's All-America first team.

Yale had not seen the last of Hardwick during that academic year. In June, he delivered a game-winning hit to help the Crimson knot its annual best-of-three baseball series with the Elis, then closed out the deciding contest at Ebbets Field with a nice running catch.

His gridiron teammate Felton also put a double whammy on a football foe, striking out 15 in a 7–0, three-hit win over Princeton. Performances such as this prompted Philadelphia Athletics manager Connie Mack to offer Felton a three-year contract. Mack is said to have been of the opinion that Felton would be "one of the greatest pitchers in the history of the game," and the $15,000 bid was the biggest ever offered a collegiate player. Railroad scion Felton turned Mack down. Had he accepted the deal and joined the eventual World Series champion A's, he could have played for the baseball and football champions in the same year. Instead, he went home to Haverford—within hailing distance of Shibe Park—to pursue a business career. (Felton also blew off his finals and did not receive a degree.)

For Harvard football, the most welcome announcement came in April, when Percy Haughton was re-signed as coach for three years, with a significant pay bump. Harvard maintained its $5,000 salary, and a

Sam Felton's powerful punting leg helped win the Yale game of 1912, but his right arm might have been more impressive: Connie Mack offered Felton $15,000 to pitch for his hometown Philadelphia Athletics. *Prints and Photographs Division, Library of Congress, LC-DIG-ggbain-10761.*

group of influential alums—what today would be called "boosters"—kicked in a like amount. For the times, a five-figure coach was rare, if not unique.

In the view of the *Alumni Bulletin*, P. D. had more than earned it—and not merely by victories, welcome as they were. "We believe he has put it on a more sane footing than has hitherto existed anywhere," the publication declared, adding,

> The wearing drudgery of practice has been to some extent transformed into real fun, and the athletes who used to look forward with dread to the work of the afternoon have come to anticipate it with pleasure. Common sense has cast aside the old methods, which led to mental and physical exhaustion long before the end of the schedule. [31]

The *Alumni Bulletin* was on to something. As if by wireless, word was spreading throughout the world of football about something called the "Haughton System." During the next three seasons, it would be honed to a fine sheen and become the sport's scourge, and its pride.

* * *

On October 21, 1913, as the newspapers reported, Samuel Morse Felton III, Harvard '13, of last fall's Harvard football team, of Haverford, Pennsylvania, was married to Anne Nelson, of Marlboro Street and Cohasset, at "Trinity Church . . . in the presence of a large gathering of representative Bostonians." [32] Among the ushers were teammates Dick Wigglesworth, Percy Wendell, and Harry Gardner. Significantly, the nuptials were on a Tuesday, so no one would have to miss the following Saturday's game against Penn State.

6

THE SYSTEM

When analyzed, football is nothing more than a complicated game of human chess.—Percy Duncan Haughton, *Football and How to Watch It* (1922)

It is often a great deal easier—and the results are much better—to take a bright student with a reasonably good physique and teach him the physical part of the game than it is to take a man who has all the physical equipment but is not mentally up to the task.—Haughton, address to the Harvard Division of Education, May 27, 1916

Being in politics is like being a football coach. You have to be smart enough to understand the game and dumb enough to think it's important.—Sen. Eugene McCarthy, as quoted in the *Washington Post*, November 12, 1967

Percy Duncan Haughton figured out football the way Henry Ford figured out the assembly line.

In the sport's early days, coaching was largely a one-man job, and to some degree it was simple, monotonous, even primitive. In the fall, you sized up likely prospects—the huskier the better—put them through brutal, Hunger Games-like scrimmages that weeded out the weak, then sent the survivors smashing, often artlessly, into their opponents. In this respect, the game's methods resembled the military meat grinder perpetrated by the nations that soon would hurl their youths against one another in the Great War.

This is not to dismiss those, for example, Glenn "Pop" Warner, who truly were imaginative, even radical, particularly in formation and play design. But they were so rare as to stand out, then as now. And Haughton had his flashes of invention and gadgetry. But what stamped him was his creation of a *system*, one befitting the dawn of the age of industrial management. Haughton was the first to step back and break down the game into its components, not only those on the field, but also those involving preseason and pregame preparation. As his assistant Harry von Kersburg described the method, "Football had been put through the laboratory and reduced to a science."[1]

Much of the Haughton philosophy is spelled out in his 1922 best seller *Football and How to Watch It*. It might be considered *The Little Red Book* of football. Published six years after his final season at Harvard and a year before he became coach at Columbia, the book distills Haughton's thinking. Not coincidentally, because Haughton had served in the U.S. Army as a major during World War I, it is studded with military analogies.

What Haughton lays out is now commonplace, even mandatory, as modern-day football at every level features large coaching staffs and administrative apparatuses. Back then, however, his schemes of organization were revolutionary. Haughton had three advantages other coaches, especially those who were employed year to year, did not. First, with or without football fame, his school was the most prominent in the United States. Second, his raw material was promising: a large student body whose best football candidates had learned the game in prep schools. The wealth of talent enabled Haughton to withstand injuries and maintain keen intrasquad competition. Third, as time went on, he exploited continuity, in his staff and his rosters. He began instilling his doctrines to freshmen who would hone them through their senior years. Thus was the machine fed. In essence, Haughton's was, if not the first, one of the first *programs*.

As the 1913 season kicked off, Haughton's method was fully invested. He had the players to fit it; he had the victories to validate it. It's tempting to say it wasn't foolproof. But from mid-1911 to mid-1915—a span of 33 games without a loss—it was.

In the Haughton System, every aspect was accounted for. Nothing was left to chance. The following are its hallmarks.

By the 1910s, the blocking sled was a fixture of football training for Harvard and its rivals. *Prints and Photographs Division, Library of Congress, LC-DIG-ggbain-09729.*

Time Management

"The football season is a race against time," Haughton declares in his book. Even more precisely: "One football season begins the day after the last season ends."[2]

Practices were scripted to the minute (literally, minutely). Even the prepractice routine was planned. As von Kersburg described, Haughton "developed [everything] . . . such as having the headgears lined up so that players could quickly pick out their own."[3] Again, this is standard today. Back then, it was groundbreaking.

As Haughton wrote, "Should the spectator peep into the notebook of a football coach, he might find a schedule of a day's practice, as follows":

Tuesday, October 12. Squad assembled at 3.30 dressed in uniform.

3.30 to 3.50 Blackboard demonstration.
   a. Additional plays No. 14 and 15 diagrammed and explained.

b. Change in assignments of plays No. 5 and 6 diagrammed and explained.

c. Outline and theory of defense vs. "shift plays."

3.50 to 4.00 Squad at tackling dummy.

Three tackles per man, right, left, and head on. Accent on the man "beyond."

4.00 to 4.15 Practice at a walk additional plays and change of assignments.

4.15 to 4.30 Offensive and defensive assignments of punt and dropkick.

4.30 to 5.00 Scrimmage teams A vs. B. Accent on new plays and assignments.

5.00 to 5:30 Scrimmage team C. vs. second team. Accent on defenses 4 and 5.

Likewise, each day of the week had a purpose. As von Kersburg outlined,

> Monday was the easiest day of the week. The players usually relaxed. There were blackboard talks before practice and occasionally after the evening meals. The game of the preceding Saturday was reviewed, and the mistakes made were pointed out. If the game had been a close one, this day was designated as Blue Monday. Tuesday was devoted mostly to hard individual work and signal practice. Wednesday was scrimmage day. Thursday was polishing up day for the individual work of the players and the correction of their faults which showed up in scrimmage. Dummy scrimmage was held on Friday—plays were walked through with no bodily contact.

Haughton even scripted the weeks building to the Yale game. Recalled von Kersburg,

> The critical season was divided into four parts. Accuracy Week— which included a complete rehearsal of all fundamentals. Fight Week [when starting jobs were up for grabs]—any Harvard football player who has ever been through it will never forget it. Speed Week—when everything really moved. And finally *Joy Week*—the week before the Yale game, when the pressure was taken off, the guards played quarterback, and the quarterbacks played guard—anything for a laugh. His teams always went on the field loose and relaxed.[4]

Details, Details

Many of Haughton's methods, and much of his thinking, had been influenced by the progressive approach of his 1897 and '98 Harvard coach, Cam Forbes, particularly concerning a punter named Haughton. Wrote Forbes,

> Percy was supposed to get the ball off, kicking from a stand without advancing. He was protected in 1898, by two defensive backs, to cover the kick. I checked him with a stopwatch, and he usually got the kick off in 1 5/8 seconds from the snap. I don't think it was blocked once during the year.[5]

Thus indoctrinated, Haughton was way ahead of his time in his obsession with what now are termed *measurables*. As he wrote, "If the player is fast, he can move on the field at least seven yards a second" (which, alas, would work out to a 5.7 40, which would be awfully pokey today).

In 1955, Grantland Rice related an anecdote that conveyed Haughton's finicky nature. "One Saturday, Sam Felton, the famous end and star left-footed kicker, booted the ball 60 yards. Haughton jerked him out of the game. 'I told you to kick 40 yards,' Haughton said. 'The ends can cover at that distance. Forty yards doesn't mean 39 yards or 41 yards. It means 40 yards.'"[6]

Athleticism

During an era in which brawn was prized above all else, Haughton went against the grain. "The 200-pound fat boy is fast disappearing," he declared in his 1922 book. "The present game calls for a far more athletic player than in the old days, because the backfield and the ends must be adept at handling forward passes, and the other linemen are called on to cover more territory than heretofore." What's crucial is that he had discerned this 10 years earlier and filled his teams accordingly with such all-around athletes as Charlie Brickley, Sam Felton, Tack Hardwick, hockey star Freddie Huntington, and, beginning in 1913, Eddie Mahan.

To condition them, he believed in a gentle break-in period and would have deplored today's year-round programs: "It is better to return [to school] overweight," and then work into fighting trim. Haughton also shunned weight training: "Gymnasium work is not well suited to the football player, as it tends to make a man musclebound."

In this, he was abetted by his longtime trainer and confidant, William "Pooch" Donovan. "[Haughton] never went against Pooch's advice," wrote von Kersburg, continuing,

> When Donovan said a man had had enough, his decision was never questioned. . . . Pooch insisted that his players should have at least nine hours sleep every night. He would never allow the men to eat too much at the training table but insisted upon a well-balanced diet that built up strength and did not tax the digestion. Furthermore, they were made to relax by resting 15 or 20 minutes before dinner.

Underscoring his strategy of wearing foes down in the first three quarters and beating them in the fourth, Haughton sometimes stinted on football drills in favor of physical training. "He felt that condition won more football games than any other single factor," said von Kersburg.[7]

The pace of practice was brisk. "No Harvard player could walk on the field," wrote Rice in 1955. "He had to be running." Counter to prevailing custom, contact was held to a minimum. Recalled Hardwick to Rice, "We were all so fresh and keen by Saturday that we wanted to murder somebody. Harvard teams were never battered up in practice. They were always fresh."[8]

The Ladder

Using his vast manpower, Haughton instilled never-ending and fierce intrasquad competition. He broke his squads down into varsity A, B, and C, plus a second team, which learned the opponents' plays and formations, and practiced against the varsity. Although the second teamers knew they would not play on Saturday, they nevertheless understood their role and took pride in it.

The big stars, of course, had safe berths, but others did not. Complacency was forestalled. Especially with injuries, players constantly moved up and down the ladder. The most famous model of perseverance was halfback Bob King, who began as a scrappy second-team scrub and ended as a 1915 All-America.

The tackling dummy was important in teaching technique, but it also helped Haughton's players stay fresh by minimizing contact in practice. *Prints and Photographs Division, Library of Congress, LC-DIG-ggbain-10956.*

Position Coaches

Again, Haughton did not invent this concept, but he used it as well or better than any head coach of his generation. He trusted valued lieutenants such as Leo Leary (who coached the ends) and von Kersburg (the linemen), and gave them considerable discretion, clout, and input. Leary received Haughton's highest accolade when P. D. said after the 1912 Yale game that he "put the fun in fundamentals."[9] From West Point, he imported Ernest "Pot" Graves, who was the guru of how to use the hands on the line. Haughton paid his staffers $2,000 to $3,000 a season—more than many head coaches (and professors!) made.

Simplicity

"Some teams have as many as 40 plays, but far better is it to have a few plays well learned, for it is the execution, rather than the nature of the play, which makes it successful," Haughton preached. His playbook contained *exactly* 25 plays: 16 rushes (10 plunges/slants/sweeps, 3 reverse plays, and 3 tricks); 7 forward passes; and 2 kicks. Each, however, could be run out of any of four formations (close, open, loose, wide)— or from kick formation. Thus, opponents' defenses could be presented with 125 "looks." In some ways, the play's design mattered less than how it was run. Haughton, said von Kersburg, "was the first coach to insist that a play perfectly executed would result in a touchdown from any point on the field."[10]

Much like Vince Lombardi with his Green Bay Packers of the 1960s, Haughton relied on straight-ahead, fundamental vanilla football, and he molded his talent accordingly. Although Haughton had some gadget plays in his bag, he thought they too often "acted as a boomerang," writing, "The elements that insure the victory are the inherent strength of a team and the soundness of its fundamental policy." But—also like Lombardi—Haughton was not averse to tossing in some experimental wrinkles, on either side of the ball, wrinkles that would keep the foe sweating and guessing.

At a time when the seven-man line was standard on defense, Haughton went to a five-man front, dropping two men as proto-linebackers. Athletic, versatile players like center Derry Parmenter and end/back Tack Hardwick were ideal in such a scheme, which proved especially useful with loosened rules on the forward pass.

Using blackboard diagrams and colored dominoes, Haughton and his coaches refined the playbook and the numbered signals (which Haughton had first learned playing under Cam Forbes in the 1890s), and then indoctrinated the Crimson players. Related von Kersburg,

> In the days long before the huddle, specifically 1908, 1909, and 1910, Percy would assemble the squad on the second floor of the Locker Building and, using a metronome, have the quarterbacks take turns in practicing cadence in their signal calling. When the starting signal was given all of the squad as one would clap its hands. If this was not done simultaneously, woe betide the man or men who had clapped just a fraction of a second too soon or too late.[11]

Drill. Drill. Drill.

In his speech at the 1915 postseason banquet, Haughton said, "We trained our players to such an extent that their subconscious minds enabled them automatically to perform their various assignments, while their active or conscious minds were dealing with the unforeseen exigencies which happen during the game."[12]

Wally Trumbull, one of Haughton's star linemen in the 1912–1914 era, recalled,

> One example which [Haughton] used to give in defending the constant, unrelenting drilling of a football team concerned an actress. "If you go to Keith's and watch a ballet dancer and applaud her at the end of her performance, remember that she probably has spent months in perfecting her steps," he would declare, and he would continue, "Remember that we must drill, drill, drill to achieve the same results of the ballet dancer." He felt that constant drill was justified, and the results proved him right.[13]

Haughton once took it a step further by inviting musical-comedy star Julia Sanderson to observe the Crimson. "He asked her to watch particularly the synchronous movement, stressing that, as a norm, she should always have in mind the perfect timing and unified movement of the chorus,"[14] said von Kersburg.

Haughton himself invoked another benefit. "We did employ various forms of psychology," he said at the 1915 postseason banquet. "To illustrate, we studied the chorus girl, and we found that while she was doing most wonderful gyrations upon the stage, she was all the time smiling at the bald-headed man in the front row."[15]

Of course, in allowing Sanderson to set foot on Soldiers Field, Haughton was violating his own policy that practices were to be secret. At the time, P. D. was a bachelor, so who knows his real motives. Still, the number of times Haughton invoked chorus girls and burlesque leads one to believe he spent much time studying them—purely for research purposes, no doubt.

Haughton relished the slave-driver role. As he wrote, "The author was once reminded that he has compelled an 11 to repeat one play 17 times before he felt satisfied that it was properly executed." If a play was not run to his liking, recalled von Kersburg, Haughton "would often stop a practice scrimmage and introduce formally the defensive backs to the center, thus calling attention to the fact that each should know what the other was doing."[16] In this, he would have his celebrated successors in the likes of Lombardi, whose teams endlessly rehearsed the power sweep, and Bud Wilkinson, whose Oklahoma teams of the 1940s and 1950s were renowned for their metronome-like execution.

Play for the Breaks

"Other things being equal," Haughton wrote, "the team that makes the fewest mistakes usually wins." Thus, field position was paramount. Even during an era when ground was not gained in large chunks, if a team had the ball between its 20 and 40, it should "always punt on fourth down with more than two yards to go, because although you are theoretically surrendering the ball to your opponents, you gain 30 to 40 yards in doing so."

Even more to the point, Haughton did not believe in wasting offensive energy when his team was in its own territory. Better to kick it away, wait for the opponent to make a mistake 40 or 50 yards downfield—then pounce.

Identify and Overwhelm Weak Spots

This job fell to the quarterback, who in an era of limited substitution and prohibitions on sideline coaching truly had to be Haughton's extension on the field.

During the Haughton era, the quarterback was a field general first, a passer occasionally, and a ballcarrier almost never. "The ABC of quarterback training . . . varies in elasticity even as the conventions of auction bridge," Haughton wrote. He elaborated,

> In auction, conditions are constantly changing, because not only are there different cards in every deal, but one's decision is always dependent upon such things as whether the player is dealing, or sits number two, three, or four position, also upon the score and whether it is "free double," and so on. . . . Apply these principles to football and we get the elasticity of judgment required to the quarterback. It always devolves upon the quarterback, with a warp of long training and a woof of common sense, to weave the various component factors into a fabric which shall fit the exigencies of every situation.

On the attack, the "quarterback endeavors to attack a defensive position by numerically and consequentially physically superior offensive force," Haughton wrote. (The quarterback began the play crouched with his head next to the center's butt.) To overwhelm the foe, Haughton's favorite weapons were the following:

Attacking in force. In one play illustrated in the book, Haughton practically licks his chops in his caption: "The offense has thrown six interferers against three of the defense who are [the ones] most likely to stop the runner without gain."

Isolation. Haughton loved nothing better than to put the opposing defensive back on what today we would call an island—unsure of whether the ballcarrier was going to run or throw, and in which direction. The hapless defender is "between the devil and the deep blue sea," Haughton exulted.

Unbalanced or indecipherable formations. While most teams of the era ran plays from a tight T formation, Haughton developed unbalanced formations, designated as "formation right" or "formation left." Two backs were placed in a tandem; the up man usually (but not always) was the lead blocker for his trailer, just like a fullback in today's NFL.

The ruse. Haughton summed up this approach at the 1915 postseason banquet. "We studied our opponents' defensive methods and proceeded against their weakest point, varying this principle by pretending to attack the weak spot and developing toward what, without the fake, was theoretically a strong territory," he declared. [17] Especially when he had backs who also were kickers, for example, Mahan and Brickley, Haughton would have his team line up in punt formation on nonpunting downs. They might kick . . . or they might not.

The forward pass had its place in the attack, and Haughton was one of the first coaches to have his passers throw to zones (as opposed to pitching directly at a receiver). But the toss was primarily a tool of deception. "Forward passes," he contended, "are an invaluable weapon of attack, not only as a means of gaining distance, but also as a constant threat, thus weakening the defense against rushes and kicks." It was the threat, the threat—something other coaches had to account for—that would keep coaches up at night.

Deception

Other than perfect execution, Percy Haughton relished nothing better than the artful feint. "Artful is the word!" was one of his mantras. In today's parlance, Haughton wanted to mess with your mind. His aim was that the other team would never know where the play was going and which Harvard player had the ball. He also wanted to be one step ahead. His innovations were not always flashy, but they often were crafty. For instance, he helped develop "mousetrap" blocking. Grantland Rice recalled that before one Yale game, he mentioned to Haughton that the Elis had a big, hard-charging line. "I only wish they were twice as fast," Haughton responded. "We'll let them through and then cut them down."[18]

The mousetrap helped beget Haughton's patented hidden-ball play. He often tried out his plays on his wife and daughters, and even on the family dogs. (As corroboration, Haughton's granddaughter, Alison Derby Hildreth, told me that her mother, Alison Haughton Derby, often recounted the times she tossed the football on the lawn with her dad.)[19] Von Kersburg elaborated,

> The story is told by Bill Cunningham, columnist of the *Boston Post*, that when Percy had perfected the hidden-ball offense he had been working on and when his teams had mastered all its deception and guile, he summoned his wife and several other ladies to the practice field, and spaced them in front of the Harvard team, more or less in the normal defensive positions. Then he had his team run its plays, and after each he'd check with the women to see if they could tell him who had the ball.
>
> Convinced that the ladies were thoroughly mystified, he then brought out a couple of big, but very smart dogs, who had been carefully trained in the fine art of chasing a football. After letting them cavort with the squad until well acquainted, he again lined up the varsity with the dogs held in front of it, and again the plays were run off. The dogs were turned loose each time and told to get the football. When it developed that they were running in circles unable to decide where it was, Haughton considered his offense a success. This it proved in games to be, for no team could stop it.
>
> The reasoning behind all this strange experimentation was that Haughton had somehow arrived at the conviction that a woman's eyes and instincts were quicker than a man's, and that a keenly

trained dog's were quicker than a woman's. When those plays completely fooled the ladies and then went on to fool the dogs, he figured no ordinary football player would ever be able to follow them.

A dog was also responsible, the story goes, for the development of Haughton's spin play. The "97" and "98" play inside a moving tackle won many a crucial game. P. D. got the idea of the spin play from his pet fox terrier. Percy would spin with the ball to see if the terrier would move, and he did—to the outside. He reasoned that if he could fool a dog, he could fool a tackle—and why not?[20]

As with his straight plays, of course, Haughton's trickier plays relied less on deceit than execution and timing. Haughton devoted an enormous amount of time and energy to signals. Plays were called not in a huddle, but barked by the quarterback at the line of scrimmage. Haughton gathered his team and, using a metronome, rehearsed snap counts. The players were to clap on the starting signal. No one wanted to risk P. D.'s wrath by going too late—or too early. At the 1912 post-season banquet, as the *Alumni Bulletin* reported, P. D. regaled the assemblage with a signals tutorial. He called on his victorious quarterback, Harry Gardner, to go through a count. Began Haughton,

> Note that he will not use a word, but that each of the signals consists of figures. In each of the figures he will give there is contained the following bits of information: first of all, the specific formation which he desired; second, whether that formation is to be to the right or to the left; third, the spot or place where the play is to go; fourth, the player who is to carry the ball; and fifth, when the ball is going to be snapped. The team cannot well prove to you that they know the first four of these signals, but they will conclusively show you that they know the starting signal, and they will show you by clapping their hands together when the ball is supposed to be snapped.

Gardner, the quarterback of the 11, and Bradley, the substitute quarterback, then called off several signals, and the players clapped their hands in perfect unison when the time came for putting the ball in play.

Haughton continued,

> The Harvard defense was more intricate than usual, because we found ourselves against so many different kinds of offense. Here again it would be impossible for me to explain in this short time the

entire defensive system. Suffice it to say that this Harvard team was required to know intimately five different defenses, each of which had variations; that these defenses were used in different parts of the field always with respect to the number of the down, the distance to be gained, and the formation which the opponents assumed. The signals for those defenses were given by the Harvard center [usually soundlessly, with a series of semaphore-like arm movements], and he was so thoroughly versed in the strategy of the game that he could very often anticipate the nature of the opponent's next move. Thus, with the opponents in possession of the ball in a certain place in the field and with a certain distance to go, I have seen seven or eight Harvard men on the defensive line of scrimmage, and at other times I have seen, and I am sure you have seen, only four men on the line of defense.[21]

Of course, a century later even the most casual football fan is familiar with a snap count and its permutations. Back then, even many devoted fans had no clue.

The Follow-Through

When football was mostly played close to the line of scrimmage, what happened downfield often was irrelevant. That changed when the game opened up, and Haughton recognized it. Hence, one of the hallmarks of the System was that every man was to carry out his assignment on every play

> irrespective of the fate of the runner on the assumption that he will need their assistance if his path has been cleared to that point. Only on rare occasions does this occur, but when it does this interference [against] the third and even fourth line of defense converts a gain of, say, 10 yards into a really long run, which often as not results in a touchdown.

This so-called "forward interference," focusing on the "man beyond," became a trademark pioneered by the Crimson, particularly by rugged end-back Tack Hardwick. (Eddie Mahan once recalled one of Haughton's adages about the benefits of effective blocking: "Anyone can carry a ball through a bunch of dead men.")[22]

Intelligence

This was the term for scouting back then, and Haughton had one of its most adept practitioners in advance man Reginald W. P. Brown, Harvard class of 1898. In the late 1890s, Reggie Brown had been Haughton's backup at fullback for the Crimson. Now it was his job to keep tabs on future opponents, either by seeing them in person or through a network of correspondents. (His nickname, for some reason, was "Subway," and his day job seems to have been working in the family export–import business in Boston.) It was Brown who, in 1914, would suggest the strategy that would humble the supposedly unstoppable lateral attack of Yale coach Frank Hinkey.

Evidence of Brown's meticulous craft is revealed to us through a serendipitous discovery: his 1911 and '14 scouting notebooks, which have been hiding in plain sight in the Joyce Sports Research Collection at Notre Dame. (Not a big football school.) They are something of a Rosetta Stone of early football, and they attest, above all, to how sophisticated the game already had become, even in an age before complicated pass plays.

Brown recorded formation after formation, sometimes with comments. "All short side plays failed," he said of the Yale practice of November 22, 1911. In the days before newsreel highlights, jersey numbers, and the use of film, he often felt a responsibility to provide recognizable physical characteristics. Of Yale's tackle, H. E. Perry, he wrote, "Light hair. Legs and body trifle slight for a tackle, but he has enough dash to offset. Refined face."[23]

Brown's work was not quite cloak-and-dagger; everyone knew who he was, and other schools had scouts, too. Leafing through the books, a football fanatic can imagine Brown sitting by himself on chilly bleachers and sketching formations, or in lonely fleabag hotel rooms filing his reports to P. D. It's likely that Harvard's overwhelming talent and Haughton's mastery of the fundamentals often made Brown's work superfluous. But the notebooks are testament to this: In the System, little was left to chance.

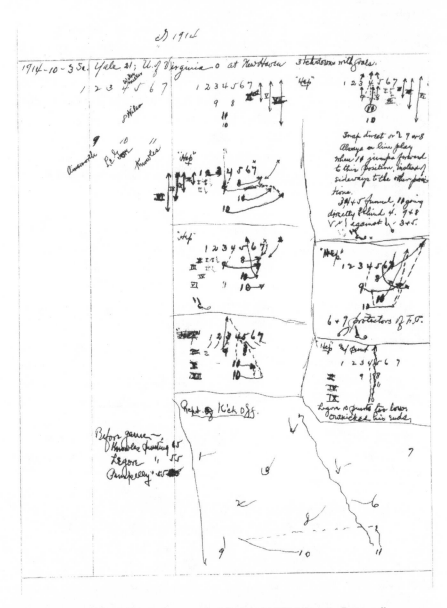

Having scouted Yale's 21–0 victory over Virginia in 1914, Reggie Brown diagrammed the Elis' formations for the benefit of Haughton and the Crimson team. *Notebook, Reggie Brown Collection, Rare Books and Special Collections, Hesburgh Libraries of Notre Dame.*

Photos

On Mondays, the squad examined pictures of the previous Saturday's game, taken by Warren Colby of the *Boston Transcript*, the newspaper of the Brahmins, and spiced by commentary of the journal's learned sports editor, George Carens (who also moonlighted refereeing Crimson junior varsity games). "Haughton coaches a great deal by the use of photographs, which are taken in practice, as well as regular games," Mahan wrote in 1916. "He would get us all together and coach from the pictures—point out the poor work. Seldom were the good points shown."[24] The paranoid P. D. did not, however, allow practices to be filmed, lest the footage fall into the wrong hands.

Psychology

Aloof, hard-driving, and coldly brilliant as he was, Haughton also had the capacity to back off, as demonstrated by his ability to clown around with his team during Yale week. He also showed his human side at the finishes of Yale games by making sure to conspicuously insert hard-working senior scrubs, even if only for a few plays, so they could win their "H." The times he let down his guard came to be part and parcel of his mystique. Tack Hardwick recounted one such moment:

> We were preparing a series of new plays to be used on the following Saturday. Progress had been slow, and P. D. had been hurrying things along in his race against time. In the scrimmage, a certain player was not giving his best efforts on every play. P. D. noticed it and rushed onto the field, grabbed him by the neck, and shook him until his teeth rattled. "Get over to the sideline. The trouble with you is that you perspire. We want men who sweat!"
>
> Later in the afternoon, the same player was put into the scrimmage again. He played like mad. After a dozen plays or so, time-out was called, and the same player was seen lying injured on the field. The trainer commenced to work over him where he lay. Out rushed P. D. "Take him over to the sideline, this is no field hospital." A substitute sprinted out on the gridiron, and immediately play was resumed.
>
> The race against time must not be lost. It sounds cold-blooded, almost brutal. But who was it that hurried into the Locker Building the moment practice was over, ran upstairs to the doctor's room

where the boy was lying down being bandaged, put one hand on his shoulder, gently ran his other hand across the boy's brow, and remarked, "That's not perspiration, son, that's sweat!" Who was it that left a suffering boy with tears of happiness welling in his eyes because he had exonerated himself in the eyes of the man whose good opinion meant so much to him? That was the real P. D.[25]

Real or not, P. D. could get away with being selectively kind because he was winning football games. His players almost had to buy in (as we now would put it). Mahan, who lost but one game in his career, put it best: "A few players hated him, but a big majority liked and respected him. Personally, I hated him at first but got to like him and found him a good friend."[26]

These were the elements Haughton polished until they shone. As he said, football was nothing more than a complicated game of human chess—but one in which the stakes had assumed an irrational importance.

7

BRICKLEY 15, YALE 5

On Monday, September 15, 64 men reported to Soldiers Field for the first practice of the 1913 Harvard football season. In most cities and towns, the early drills of a defending national champion would dominate the sports news—and perhaps all the news. But the Crimson's workouts were eclipsed by at least two events: Boston mayor John "Honey Fitz" Fitzgerald outlawing that morally compromising dance known as the tango[1] and the astonishing developments at another sporting event, one taking place seven miles from the Stadium, on Clyde Street in Brookline. There, at the Country Club, a 20-year-old amateur named Francis Ouimet was turning the golf world upside down. Ouimet, who had grown up across the road from the course, thrillingly topped British professionals Harry Vardon and Ted Ray in a playoff to win the U.S. Open. For a few days, the gridiron would have to take a back seat.

Even as Ouimet was triumphing, at Soldiers Field there was another intriguing battle of shotmaking titans that was less publicized. Harvard coach Percy D. Haughton invited two of the stars of his 1908 team, kicker Vic Kennard and center Joe Nourse, to Cambridge to tutor the booters and snappers, respectively. P. D. made one exception: Kennard need not coach dropkicker par excellence Charlie Brickley. Haughton may have had an ulterior motive. Whether he did or not, an ensuing duel would bring Mr. Charles E. Brickley down a peg.

Kennard had a hunch beforehand that Brickley would suggest an informal dropkicking contest. Accordingly, Vic began practicing in earnest—and in secret. It's not as if Kennard, then in his mid-20s, were a gimpy geezer; he was able to get up to speed quickly. Near the end of Kennard's tutoring stint, Brickley did challenge him to a friendly boot-off. (History does not record if there was a financial wager.) At first, Vic demurred, claiming he was rusty. But finally he agreed, with the proviso that there be rules, judges, and witnesses.

There were to be 25 dropkicks each, booted nearly simultaneously, from 25 yards out. Nourse and one of the Harvard centers each would snap to both men, so there would be no advantage. Fittingly for the week, the scoring would be like match play in golf. A kicker would win a point if he split the uprights and the other man did not, or if, with both men being successful, one ball went through the uprights first.

Standing behind the men, Harvard trainer Pooch Donovan fired his starter's gun. The men commenced kicking. When the smoke cleared, the winner was . . . Victor Kennard, by an astonishing 18 up.

Brickley, as usual, was still cocky. "Vic," he hollered over, "that was your distance. How about a competition at my distance—35 yards?" Kennard assented but requested that this time there be only 15 kicks. The two dropped back and fired away. This time the old grad won— four up.[2]

It was the last time at Harvard anyone got the best of Charlie Brickley at dropkicking.

❀ ❀ ❀

After the 1912 season, there was recognition among players, coaches, writers, and fans that the game of football was beginning to stabilize, to gel. For 1913, the major rules alteration involved substitution: Henceforth, a player who had been removed prior to the fourth quarter could return any time during that last quarter, not just at the beginning. Aside from promoting safety, the freer substitutions were a boon to the larger schools with more depth.

That season, there were two storied games that still reverberate a century later. The first occurred on November 1, at West Point: Notre Dame's 35–13 shocker over Army, during which quarterback Gus Dorais and end Knute Rockne convincingly demonstrated the potential of the forward pass. Dorais completed 14 of 17 tosses for 243 yards and three touchdowns, including a 40-yarder to Rockne, to that point thought to have been the longest pass ever completed. The performance's game-changing nature was summed up in a headline in the next day's *New York Times*: "Notre Dame's Open Play Amazes Army."[3]

The second headline-maker was authored at Harvard Stadium three weeks later, in the biggest game of the year, by the right toe of Charlie Brickley. The Crimson junior's five field goals, all of Harvard's points, in its 15–5 win over Yale on that afternoon in 1913, conferred immortality; Hall of Fame college and pro coach Clark Shaughnessy, writing in 1943, considered this game the third greatest in football history to that point, behind only the six-touchdown day of Illinois' Red Grange against Michigan in 1924, and Michigan's 6–0 victory over Minnesota in 1910.[4]

The major addition to the Harvard team in 1913 was significant: Charlie Brickley's heralded prep school rival, Eddie Mahan, was ready for the varsity. He would round out a backfield that on paper included holdovers Brickley, Fred "Peebo" Bradlee, and Tack Hardwick. Haughton made the accommodation for Mahan by moving the versatile Hardwick into the graduated Sam Felton's end position; essentially, it was replacing one All-America with another. In the meantime, Mahan seamlessly slipped into Felton's other role, as punter. (Mahan also fit the Haughton mold in that he also was a star baseball player, in his case a right-handed pitcher who would give the Elis fits on the diamond as well as the gridiron.)

Some thought Packy Mahan already a better player than Brickley. Even Brickley thought Mahan was at least his equal; in 1915, he called Mahan the "greatest player I ever saw."[5] Where Brickley was a power runner, Mahan, who was a change-of-pace ballcarrier, was described as "elfin footed." (They were an early day Thunder and Lightning.) Mahan himself once gave Tack Hardwick his method of befuddling a tackler. "It's a cinch," said Eddie. "All I do is poke my foot out at him, give it to him; he goes to grab it, and I take it away."[6] As the forward pass became more of a factor, Mahan also revealed himself to be one of the sport's first true triple threats, throwing halfback passes, punting brilliantly, and even sharing field-goal kicking duties with Brickley. Moreover, he was a comedian, keeping the other fellows loose. (A modern analog might be wisecracking Paul Hornung.) Photos show Mahan as outsize, with a huge lantern jaw, enormous coat-hanger shoulders, and an unfailingly erect bearing.

Of course, as excellent as Mahan was reputed to be at punting, he had a stern figure to convince: P. D. Haughton. Trainer Pooch Donovan recalled Mahan's early efforts. On the first day of practice, Haughton asked Donovan, "Where is that Natick friend of yours? Bring him over to the Stadium and let's see him kick." Donovan corralled Mahan. The trainer recounted the rest:

> Mahan [booted] the ball 70 yards, and Haughton said, "What kind of a kick is that?" Mahan thought it was a great kick. "How do you think any ends can cover that?" said Haughton. Mahan thereupon kicked a couple more, low ones, but they went about as far. "Who told you you could kick?" quoth Haughton. "You must kick high enough for your ends to cover the distance." "Take it easy and don't get excited," Donovan was whispering to Mahan on the side. "Take your time, Ned." But Mahan continued kicking from bad to worse. Haughton was getting disgusted and finally remarked, "Your ends never can cover those punts." Mahan then kicked one straight up over his head, and the first word ever uttered by him on the Harvard field was his reply to Haughton: "I guess almost any end can cover that punt," he said.[7]

Haughton's toughest opponent was overconfidence. Indeed, the surest sign Harvard was now regarded as the bullyboy of the sport was a story in the *Boston Herald* (reprinted in the *Harvard Alumni Bulletin*) headlined "Harvard's Football Team Is Overrated." The article gives every indication of being ginned up by an editor looking to sell papers by stirring the pot. "There is much talk of this or that star, but the stars of one season are never equally effective the next," claimed the author, continuing,

> The most crucial position is that of quarterback. . . . Bradlee, Logan, and Freedley all have serious weaknesses. . . . The backfield is generally supposed to be Harvard's strongest point. Yet, it can be said with absolute certainty that no combination of players now eligible can be made as effective as last year's trio. Mahan's playing has been striking, but it is the kind of playing that shines against weaker teams. . . . Meanwhile, Yale, Princeton, and now Penn State are studying those weaknesses and bending every effort to take advantage of them.[8]

And so on.

While picking nits, the writer did have a point: The conspicuous hole—not an insignificant one—was at quarterback. Harry Gardner having graduated, Haughton once again would have to find a man who could learn on the job. The three main candidates were senior Vinton Freedley, who was a career backup, and juniors Fred Bradlee and Mal Logan. Bradlee was the best athlete and, weighing 176 pounds, heavier than his rivals by a good 20 pounds. But he was denigrated as being too focused on the "technical points of play and the signals." In any case, he would be useful elsewhere. The pepper pot Logan was the choice. He was the sixth member of the Group of Seven to crack the starting lineup. Jeff Coolidge, playing at end behind senior Frank O'Brien, was the only one waiting his turn. (There was some worry neither man had enough stamina; other coaches would have been thrilled if they had such a problem.)

Juniors Stan Pennock and Wally Trumbull (now at center) joined seniors Rex Hitchcock and captain Bob Storer as holdovers on the line, which was completed by a 186-pound sophomore from Exeter, Joe Gilman, and the return of Tudor Gardiner, trying his comeback after his 1911 arm injury against Princeton. The line followed the Haughton formula: no 200-pound fat boys. The heaviest man, Pennock, was listed at 195, and various accounts claimed the chunky "Bags" (his middle name was Baggs), who seemed to have lost some quickness, could stand to lose some weight.

Among the members of a B-team "pony backfield" was a handsome, well-knit sophomore named George Alexander McKinlock Jr. The son of a financier and the president of the Chicago Electric Company, and the former Marion Rappleye, now a society doyenne, Alexander McKinlock had spent happy times on horseback at his family's summer manse, Brown Gables, in tony Lake Forest. He had prepped for Harvard at St. Mark's, where he had played fullback under coach Daniel Woodhead.

In some ways, the 5-foot-8, 169-pound McKinlock had picked a bad time to try out for the Crimson squad: The backfield was groaning with All-Americas. Yet, given the Crimson's power, there might be blowouts that would afford playing time, even against Yale—the game a player had to enter if he wanted to receive the coveted "H." Yes, Alexander McKinlock might very well see some action.

Prime members of the class of 1915's never-beaten Group of Seven, Charlie Brickley (right) poses with quarterback Mal Logan. The peppery Logan became coach Percy Haughton's trusted brains on the field, responsible for adjusting his play-calling to ever-changing game situations. *Bettman/Getty Images.*

Despite the daunting depth chart, for McKinlock the familiar sights of the Yard and Soldiers Field were welcome. He and his mother had spent the summer on a six-week trip to Germany, during which Alexander saw the sights and studied the language. The American lad looked down his nose at the Germans. "The people, especially the women, are coarse, poorly dressed, and pasty-faced, with the exception [of] those whose faces are bright scarlet," he wrote his father. "They appear to have no interest in athletics. The men drink lots of wine and every afternoon have coffee and kucken [*sic*] and an assortment of cakes."[9]

Like the rest of the world, Alexander McKinlock soon would encounter the Germans in a very different guise.

¤ ¤ ¤

The schedule was easier than it had been in 1912. Hard feelings still existed toward Dartmouth after the rough treatment of Brickley; the Indians wouldn't return to the slate until 1922. In the first six games, there was plenty of excitement, but only a little drama. The ho-hum nature of most of the games obscured a realization that perhaps dawned only slowly and might be appreciated best in retrospect: In terms of the talent assembled, the Stadium throngs were seeing the 1910s equivalent of the 1927 Yankees, the 1960s Packers, or the 2010s Golden State Warriors.

Saturday, September 27, brought Maine to the Stadium for the opener. In 1912, the Black Bears had held the Crimson to a 7–0 score. Now on a typical Boston mild, dry early fall day, 10,000 fans rose for Maine's kickoff. They were still standing afterward. Mal Logan gathered the ball in at the 15. Some 85 yards later, he was over the goal, untouched by any foe. Then, the first time Mahan touched the ball, he ran 67 yards for a score, the first of his two TDs. It was 21–0 after eight minutes. Brickley scored a touchdown, and with Haughton substituting liberally, even Alexander McKinlock got into the end zone for the final points in a 34–0 win.

The next week saw Bates and a steady rain that held the score to 14–0. Seeing his first action of the season, Tack Hardwick scored the only touchdown, on a 12-yard dash through the slop. Brickley and Mahan each kicked a field goal. After the game, a still-ailing Tudor Gardiner declared himself done with football. He would move on . . . to become governor of Maine and, as we shall see later, a hero in two world wars.

Williams, the Crimson's bugbear during the Teddy Roosevelt administration, showed up next, and for three quarters the pesky Ephs went toe-to-toe with the champs. Heading into the fourth quarter it was 3–3, with Harvard's only points coming on a Brickley 22-yard field goal. Passing craftily, Williams also gave Haughton some of his own deceptive medicine: an option-play attack that sounds familiar to today's fan but was a revelation back then. As the *Globe* explained it,

> The backs started off with the ball as if for an end run. But when the man with the ball was just about to be tackled by the Harvard end, he would toss the sphere over to the accompanying halfback, who would then perhaps have a clear field or who could at least win his way as far as the Harvard secondary defense. Sometimes the pass was forward and sometimes it went a little back, but it served its purpose in deceiving the defensive end. [10]

In the end, depth told. Haughton was able to sub for his starters and reinsert them in the fourth quarter, when a rested Brickley and Mahan each scored a touchdown in the 23–3 result.

Haughton's former assistant, Harry von Kersburg, had taken the head job at Holy Cross, and on October 18, he came into the Stadium with his Crusaders. It seemed as if Kersey had picked a good day to visit. Brickley, Bradlee, and Hitchcock were out with injuries. Things started well for the Cross: With only two minutes gone, Vinton Freedley, starting at quarterback that day, mishandled a punt on the Harvard six. Holy Cross's fullback, Eugene Donovan, scooped the ball up and ran it across the goal. Just like that—Harvard was behind. It would not happen again, in this game or any other. A deluge of 47 unanswered Crimson points followed.

(Vinton Freedley would shrug off his miscue to become one of Broadway's leading theatrical producers. His credits included Gershwin's *Lady Be Good*, with the Astaire siblings; *Tip-Toes*; *Oh, Kay!*; *Funny Face*, for which his old Hasty Pudding pal Robert Benchley, '12, wrote the book; *Girl Crazy*, with Ginger Rogers and introducing Ethel Merman; *Hold Everything*, introducing the now-standard "You're the Cream in My Coffee"; and, collaborating with a Yalie named Cole Porter, *Anything Goes*. "Unlike some of my confreres in this hazardous business, I quit when ahead of the game," Freedley wrote in his class's 50th anniversary report. "It has been exciting and can be rewarding if you know when to cash in the chips.")[11]

Even though the foe was not grade A, this was Eddie Mahan's first great game as a triple threat. Aside from being Harvard's primary ballcarrier, he punted and dropkicked two field goals, one from 18, the other from 40. For good measure, he tossed a touchdown pass to Hardwick.

Thus ended the "preliminary season." It had gone about as expected, and a star had been born in Mahan, but it is a measure of how far football under Haughton had come that there was an undercurrent of griping. How could anyone complain about a team that had not lost in almost two years, that now had run its unbeaten streak to 15 games and had outscored its first four (admittedly overmatched) opponents 118–10? In Cambridge, discontent is practically a requirement for graduation. "The progress of the team as a whole has not been satisfactory during the past two or three weeks," wrote the *Harvard Alumni Bulle-*

tin. "There are so many veterans on the squad and so few places are in doubt that the competition has not been as keen as it should have been. The old men in many positions have not been pushed hard by the other candidates and therefore have been inclined to take things too easily."[12]

The next two games were meant to be sterner tests. But again in the rain, Penn State—not the gridiron force it would become after World War II—was vanquished, 29–0. Mahan scored on a 50-yard run around right end. Brickley added two touchdowns, one on a 35-yard "dash through a big hole in the center from fake kick formation,"[13] as the *New York Times* put it. The bamboozled Nittany Lions defense had no idea what was coming, as evidenced by another play from kick formation; this time Brickley dropkicked a 35-yarder through the uprights.

The next week, in front of 15,000 at the Stadium and with Mahan sitting out because of a spider bite, Cornell made headlines. Proclaimed the *Times*, "Cornell Crosses Harvard Goal Line."[14] The first (and, as it turned out, only) touchdown scored from scrimmage against the Crimson the entire year came in the fourth quarter, on a plunge by Big Red quarterback Charley Barrett, who was vying with Mahan for recognition as college football's best sophomore. Two years later, Barrett would bedevil Mahan and the Crimson. But today, his tally came against the scrubs, with the game tucked away, and made the final score 23–6. Before that, Harvard had shown a balanced attack, with quarterback Logan cleverly mixing or threatening passes and plunges. All three touchdowns were scored by Brickley on runs; Brick also had started the scoring with a 17-yard field goal "from a slight angle." Moreover, the Big Red had tried to counter Crimson power by opening up the game with passes; Brickley, showing an uncanny nose for the ball, picked off three.

✳ ✳ ✳

Now it was November, the month when championships are won. Harvard was one of a handful of unbeaten teams in the country: Chicago, under Amos Alonzo Stagg; Auburn, the best of a weak Southern field; and, for the first time on a national stage and fresh off its dismantling of Army, Notre Dame. To accomplish a repeat title, the Crimson would have to knock off its Big Three rivals Princeton and Yale, with Brown sandwiched between.

Princeton was the season's only road game. The Tigers were 5–1–0 and captained by Hobey Baker, polishing his immortal career in football and hockey, and bulwarked by junior All-America lineman Harold Ballin. Leaving no stone unturned, Haughton had embarked on one of his favorite ploys: working, flattering, and cajoling the officials. In correspondence with referee Bill Langford, maintained at the College Football Hall of Fame, Haughton first is unctuous and even conspiratorial. "I am delighted to hear that you are to act as referee in the Harvard–Princeton and Harvard–Yale games," Haughton writes. "As you know, I have tried to effect this for the past three years and now feel that I have really done you a service by this accomplishment." Then he gets to the point: preemptively protecting any attempt to mess with his sacred "wheel" formation. "It has been reported to me that you took exception to the manner in which Holy Cross executed this same evolution, and I am desirous of knowing where the trouble lay."[15] In his return note Langford is reassuring: "Your shift is permissible, but care should be taken to see that players do not advance beyond their line of scrimmage."[16]

Once again, the Princeton game would illuminate Haughton's coaching acumen. This time it would ratify his genius—in substitution, in strategy, in deception, and in his thorough inculcation of football fundamentals. These and Charlie Brickley's right foot would win the day.

The game at Osborne Field took place in front of 25,000 rain-soaked (again) spectators and, thus, was a mudbath. It also was a bloodbath. According to Arthur Daley in the *Times* in 1948, "Haughton kept a private box score on the number of times the Tigers slapped down Brickley when he didn't even have the ball. The count reached the quite incredible total of 168 times."[17] Eight years after the game, Brickley gave a lower number. "Official statistics verified by a correct counting of my bruises show that I was knocked down 78 times," he said. "Thirty-eight times it was Ballin who was the catapult force that took me off my pins. Ballin weighed 220 pounds. I tipped the scales at 180. When the game was over I had gone down to 168."[18]

The Tigers had the better of the early play. On the day, Baker, booting for the Tigers, was unable to lift the soggy ball. He would miss on five field-goal attempts. Brickley failed twice and made one—the only one he needed. It came in the second quarter, after one of Haughton's patented breaks. Princeton's Buzz Law went back to punt. The ball was snapped. Law's foot hit the pigskin at the same time as did Harvard's onrushing Bob Storer and Frank O'Brien. Smack! The ball flew backward and bobbed toward the Tigers' goal, with the three men in pursuit.

If Percy Haughton had taught his men anything, it was how to follow the ball. O'Brien performed the same maneuver employed by Tack Hardwick the year before against Yale: O'Brien sacrificed his body and hurled himself in front of the foe, in this case Law, permitting the Crimson's Rex Hitchcock to recover on the 20. On fourth down from the 11, Brickley stepped back to the 20 and—"coolly and carefully," said the next day's *Times*—kicked the sodden ball over the crossbar. "Capt. Storer of the Harvard team—dripping with mud—wiped his grimy hands on young Brickley's perspiring, dirt-stained face," continued the account, "and said something which no one but Brickley will ever know."[19]

Thereafter, the teams maneuvered for field position. Haughton had left his ace in the hole, starting Bradlee instead of Mahan. "Just the time when Princeton was doing its best parading through the Harvard team [Haughton] rushed Mahan into the game," said the *Times*.[20] "The effect was instantaneous. Just the presence of Mahan seemed to put more vim into the Harvard team. Knowing Mahan's great ability as a dodging back, the Princeton defense was forced to spread out." Sure enough, Mahan flipped the field, returning a punt 50 yards before (in a meeting of immortals) Hobey Baker ran him down. Wrote Brickley two years later, "Mahan gave the finest exhibition of running on a wet field that I have ever seen. . . . Mahan ran along as if he were wearing spike shoes on a cinder track, while the rest of us were floundering around hardly able to stand up, let alone run."[21]

On this day, Haughton had thought of everything. At the beginning of the second half, the Crimson trotted onto the field in clean, dry togs, while the Tigers reappeared in the same sodden, mud-caked uniforms they had worn in the first half.

In the fourth quarter, after Baker's final field-goal miss, Brickley and Mahan combined to bail out the Crimson. Their derring-do hinged on Haughton's ability to keep the foe guessing as to who would get the ball. Mahan stepped back as if to punt, but the ball was snapped to Brickley, who barreled 61 yards down the right sideline to the Princeton 23. This "romp from scrimmage, in which he scattered Princeton tacklers right and left, was about the most brilliant piece of open-broken field running he has ever done in college," said the next day's *Globe*.[22] This was the backbreaker; unlike two seasons before, Harvard had made a great escape in Jungletown.

There was one more way in which this Princeton game confirmed Haughton's coaching genius. When Mahan was out of the game, Hardwick, a line-drive kicker, had done the punting, but unsatisfactorily. Clearly, Mahan, who could boot the ball high and deep, was the man for the job. And here Haughton, who had been trying to mold Mahan as a punter in his own image, conceded his error.

As the *Globe* later would report,

> After the game at Princeton, Haughton went to Mahan and said to him, "Young man, from now on you kick that ball in your own way. Boot it the best you know how, and I'm sure you'll do the trick by the time we play Yale." Haughton explained his change of base in this way: "In baseball, it is conceded that it is folly to try to change the style of a good hitter. He should be allowed to develop along his own lines. Now I had been told that I was once a great punter, and naturally I have tried to teach men my style. But this man Mahan is not only a natural athlete, but a natural punter. Why should I run the risk of spoiling his usefulness by trying to teach him my way of kicking, when he had an effective style of his own?"[23]

Two weeks later, that flexibility would pay dividends.

Brown provided a needed laugher. There were 25,000 on hand on a chilly day at the Stadium, but Haughton was not one of them. He, Mal Logan, and Wally Trumbull went to New Haven to scout Yale against Princeton. Harvard did not need them for the 37–0 blowout, during which the B-teamers got copious playing time. The Crimson showed many looks to the hapless Bruins. With the ball at the Brown 16 in the first quarter, Brickley went back for a dropkick—but instead the ball was snapped to Mahan, who darted for 14 yards to the two, from where Brickley went over. In the second quarter, with the play starting from kick formation, Mahan and Hardwick combined on a 28-yard halfback pass-and-run for a touchdown. After quarterback Freedley made a fair catch at the Brown 38, Brickley put the ball down and drilled a placekick through the uprights. It was an augury. To the delight of the crowd,

Lewis Mills, a popular senior scrub tackle, grabbed a Brown kickoff and lugged the ball 83 yards to the end zone.

Now, as had been the case since time immemorial, it came down to Yale.

✧ ✧ ✧

The Elis, coached by Howard Jones (later to make Southern Cal a power), were finishing a down year. Jones, Yale class of 1908, was his school's first paid head coach, at $2,500 a season. He was brought in as part of a shakeup instigated by captain and All-America center Henry Ketcham that relegated Walter Camp to figurehead status. In addition to a draw with Princeton, the Elis had played scoreless ties with Maine and Washington & Jefferson. Most ignobly, they had been beaten by Colgate, 16–6. This mind-boggling defeat would be akin today to Michigan's 2007 loss to Appalachian State. The Yale malaise was treated by the press the way today's media discuss losing streaks of the Cowboys, the Yankees, or the Lakers. The conclusion: Yale was still Yale. The Blue had a very worthy booter in Otis Guernsey, who might be able to match Mahan punt for punt and Brickley dropkick for dropkick. Aside from Ketcham, they had another All-America in tackle Nelson "Bud"

Having snared a pass from halfback Eddie Mahan, Tack Hardwick barrels goalward in the blowout over Brown. A superb all-around end, blueblood Hardwick, above all, was a ferocious hitter. *Courtesy of Hardwick Simmons.*

Talbott, and a rugged line that Haughton wasn't sure his offense could penetrate. P. D. also had his assistant coaches and advance scout Reggie Brown feverishly trying to figure out a way for the defense to counter Yale's scheme of cross-blocking. Yale also had a clever quarterback in Alex Wilson.

Each side had men pawing the ground by the bench for a chance to win a letter and, if fate cooperated, become an unforeseen hero. In addition to McKinlock, Harvard had a senior end from Groton named Duncan Dana. His Eli counterpart was a scrappy junior from Hotchkiss named Archie MacLeish.

This rivalry was perhaps the first in which one legitimately could apply the phrase, "You can throw out the record books." Moreover, Yale could take some comfort in various "nevers." Harvard *never* had beaten

Yale's estimable fullback Otis Guernsey. In the 1913 Game, the Bulldogs banked on Guernsey to match Crimson kickers Eddie Mahan and Charlie Brickley. *Prints and Photographs Division, Library of Congress, LC-DIG-ggbain-10969.*

Yale at the Stadium. Harvard *never* had scored a touchdown against Yale at the Stadium. Harvard *never* had beaten Yale two years in a row. The *nevers* kept Crimsonians young and old tossing and turning during the lengthening late-autumn nights.

On the warm, sunny afternoon of November 22, 1913, these lingering doubts swirled about Soldiers Field. Temporary steel stands at the open end swelled the capacity to the limit. The packed-in blocks of humanity were testament to what Harvard graduate manager Fred W. Moore had said: "The whole trouble in a nutshell is that we need 150,000 seats, and we have less than 40,000."[24]

As the crowd jostled and settled, the teams took the field, and Brickley entertained with his virtuoso pregame kicking exhibition, which was meant to shock and awe the Elis, much in the manner of Babe Ruth or Mark McGwire taking batting practice. He was wearing his square toe. During the game, he could slip it on as needed. The cynosure of all eyes was characteristically cool. "I have often been asked what my sensations are just before attempting a dropkick in a big game," he wrote two years later in a series on kicking published in the *Globe*. "My sensations are nil. I feel no more nervousness or concern than if I were eating dinner."[25]

At 2 p.m., the ever-reliable Langford summoned the captains for the coin toss. Harvard's Bob Storer won it and took the south goal at the Stadium's closed end—meaning, in the first quarter, the wind would be at the Crimson's back and the sun would be in Yale's eyes. As per the custom of the day, Yale chose to make the opening kickoff rather than receive. The teams took the field. Langford gestured to each side. "Are you ready, Harvard? Are you ready, Yale?" He blew his whistle.

Mahan ran the kickoff out to the 19. Before the game, he and Logan had decided that on the first play from scrimmage, they would run right at Yale left tackle Talbott. When the Crimson broke the huddle, they began in punt formation with Mahan back, then shifted to the tandem run formation. The ball was snapped to Logan, who pitched back to Mahan, who headed right.

In 1926, a *Boston Herald* story finished the play.

"Tacks [*sic*] Hardwick did his work well," said Logan, "charging Talbott out of the hole the play was to go through, and with Brickley and Bradlee preceding Mahan, it looked like a good gain and maybe a long run. But just as Mahan was going through the line, the Yale left end—Avery, I think his name was—in charging laterally along the line of scrimmage, found himself all snarled up with Talbott, Brickley, Hardwick, and Bradlee. In trying to twist himself loose from the mix-up he swung one of his powerful arms around, and the back of his hand caught the leaping Mahan squarely on the nose. The blow stopped him; he was quickly tackled; the ball was down, and we lined up for the next play.

"Mahan again went back to the kicker's position," Logan continued. "I turned to give the signals. His nose was a mess. My expression was such that it caused him to look directly at me, and the same thought flashed through both our minds. A week's preparation of that first play had brought nothing but Mahan's bloody nose. And the humor of the thing struck him so that he grinned."[26]

Mahan was not the only Crimson back to emerge scathed. Early on, depending on accounts, either a cleat or a fingernail scraped Brickley in the eye. Wrote Bill Cunningham in the *Boston Herald* in 1947 (he ascribed to the cleat theory), "His vision was clouded, and it kept getting worse, until he could scarcely see as far as the goalposts."[27] If he left the game, he would be unable to return until the next quarter. So, Brickley persevered as a punting duel began between Mahan and Yale's Guernsey—a battle that Mahan, with deep and high drives, was winning. He also showed himself a clever directional kicker. When he saw Yale was dropping only one receiver back—quarterback Wilson—Mahan aimed his boots diagonally away from the Elis, making Wilson (who, unaccountably, was the sole man posted to receive the kick) chase the ball, crippling his return chances.

Gradually, the exchanges of punts helped Harvard advance deep into Yale territory. At the Yale 30, Brickley assumed dropkick position. But, of course, in the Haughton attack, that could mean anything. Brickley carried out his bluff—and the ball was snapped directly to Bradlee, who barreled for 13 yards and a first down. "When the . . . attack stalled on the 14," wrote Arthur Daley in the *Times* in 1948, "Brickley, the mechanical man, faded back to the 26 for a dropkick. His eyes were constantly welling with tears as nature fought against the scratches. He stood there, poised and unconcerned, only his blinking eyes betraying him."[28]

W. D. Sullivan, writing in the *Globe* the day after the game, thought he discerned a grin through the tears. "You could see the greatest dropkicker of the age smiling as Trumbull shot him the ball," claimed Sullivan.[29]

Grin or grimace? The result was the same. "The ball spun back," continued Daley. "The ball spun forward—as gracefully easy as a pitcher whipping over a strike. Harvard led, 3 to 0."[30] And Brickley had field goal number one.

Yale got the first real break. When its ensuing kickoff struck the goalposts, Harvard's Frank O'Brien carried the ball back into the end zone, thinking he had earned a touchback. It would have been—had it been a punt or a free-kick field-goal try. But on a kickoff, the ball was live. When O'Brien downed it past the goal line it was a safety, and the score was a baseballesque 3–2. The miscue capped a tough week for O'Brien, who earlier had fallen down the stairs in his dorm. Nor would his miseries end there: Yale would vote O'Brien his "Y," claiming he was the only Harvard man ever to score for Yale. (The following year the rule would be changed so that a ball striking the goalpost on a kickoff was an automatic touchback.)

The half proceeded, and so did Mahan's punting cannonade. Packy blasted a 75-yarder. The feeble riposte was fair-caught by Logan on the Yale 42. The Crimson was entitled to a free kick. Brickley chose to try a placement, with Logan the holder. "It was interesting to note," wrote Sullivan, "with what perfect confidence the Harvard multitude watched the preparation for the kick."[31]

Little did they suspect that their hero could not make out the goalposts. "As blinded as he was," wrote Daley, "he still needed only the direction pointed out to him."[32] So directed, he stepped back, then forward. Thump! The ball sailed end over end, up and up, comfortably clearing the crossbar and finally landing in the seats of the bowl, perhaps 25 yards in back of the goal line. Field goal number two for Brickley. Harvard 6, Yale 2.

Yale answered. Mahan boomed another punt, but this time he outkicked his coverage. Wilson caught it and charged straight upfield. Now, from the Harvard 36, it was Otis Guernsey's turn. His boot hung in the air, then descended, nearly grazing the crossbar. But clear the bar it did. Harvard 6, Yale 5.

And then, to the dismay of the Crimson crowd, the Elis threatened again. Harvard was hoisted on its own petard: Carroll Knowles of Yale went back to punt. Hardwick of Harvard rushed from his end to block it. Knowles drew the ball down. Fake! Knowles easily skirted Hardwick and headed upfield. Brickley finally hauled him down at midfield. With the half drawing to a close, Guernsey was able to try another field goal. As the ball hung in the air, so did all the *nevers*. The kick missed—barely. The score remained Harvard 6, Yale 5. As they headed for the locker room, both sides seemed used up.

The Harvard players had to guide Brickley to his spot. All the while, Brick rubbed his eyes in hopes of clearing his vision. Wrote Cunningham, "Harvard's team physician, Dr. Nichols, spotted the trouble, examined Brickley . . . and told Haughton he ought to be out of the game."[33]

Haughton, said Daley's account,

> asked the doctor only one question: "It won't make him blind, will it?" The team physician shook his head. "There's no fear of permanent injury," he said. "His vision will get increasingly blurred today, but his eyesight will be perfect again in a few days." Haughton grunted. "He doesn't have to see," responded this hard-bitten realist who coached the Harvard football team. "Charlie Brickley can kick field goals with his eyes shut."[34]

As the second half began, Yale kept the pressure on. Knowles took the ball at his own 29 and made a brilliant run all the way to the Harvard 37. He was taken down by O'Brien, who was hurt on the play. The injury was unfortunate—and fortuitous. In trotted his replacement: Duncan Dana. There Harvard held, and Guernsey tried another field goal, from midfield. It was way short, and the ball rolled over the goal line for a touchback.

For the Elis, that would be the high-water mark. From here on, the Haughton Machine took over. Perhaps the insight Reggie Brown had provided was the key, but in any event, Yale's vaunted cross-blocking was no match for the quickness and power of Pennock, Storer, Trumbull, Hitchcock, and Gilman on Harvard's interior. On offense, the Crimson's formations revealed little of what was in store. Trick plays alternated with straight rushes. In the first half, Yale outrushed Harvard 79 yards to 68. In the second half, Harvard gained 148, Yale 78—and precious little after Knowles's run. Above all, Logan's play-calling had Yale off balance. True, Yale did keep Harvard from crossing the goal line, but the Crimson had the ultimate answer: Brickley.

After Guernsey's failed field goal, Mahan spurted for 21 yards past midfield. The hour had rung for Duncan Dana. The sub end swung around, took a pitch from Logan, and, "sweeping inside the interference,"[35] dashed for nine crucial yards. The jaunt set up Brickley perfectly. His dropkick from 36 sailed through. Harvard 9, Yale 5. Field goal number three for Brickley.

Now it was Brickley's turn to carry the freight. From Harvard's 32, he bolted up the middle through a hole that a Pierce-Arrow could have gone through. Brick veered for the sideline. Some 35 yards later, Alex Wilson knocked him to the turf, but Brickley, not ruled down, kept going. Finally, Avery and a host of tacklers slammed him into the hay on the sideline on the Yale 24, whereupon Avery was replaced by Archie MacLeish, later better known as Archibald MacLeish, Pulitzer Prize-winning playwright and Librarian of Congress. Three plays later, Brickley stepped back to the 30. Again, Trumbull spun the ball back. From a slight angle, the dropkick split the uprights. Harvard 12, Yale 5. Field goal number four for Brickley.

The fourth period began. For Yale, behind by a touchdown and an extra point, and showing little ability to move the ball, desperation time was at hand. Guernsey flung a pass 25 yards downfield. The intended receiver, Maurice Brann, slipped. Running full tilt in coverage, Brickley picked it off on the Harvard 30. Mahan blasted a 55-yard punt, with no return. A Yale punt only brought the ball back to the Elis 44.

Harvard set about putting the final nail in the coffin. An eight-play march, highlighted by another run by Dana, this time for 10 yards, placed the ball at the Yale 11. Brickley dropped back two yards deeper than normal, to the 21. Again, the ball was hiked back. Again, he kicked. From that distance, automatic. Harvard 15, Yale 5. An astonishing five field goals for Charles E. Brickley.

He would get a chance at another, from 45 yards out, after a Mahan fair catch, but the try dribbled to the goalpost. On the day, Brickley was 5-for-7. Of those he made, wrote Daley, "every shot split the posts cleanly and at dead center. Not one wavered in its flight."[36] Without being able to see the goalposts cleanly, how did Brickley do it? Summed up Cunningham, "His answer was, 'Mostly by instinct.' He knew the distance and the angle, and such was his precision, and such had been his ceaseless practice that he knew just how much power to apply."[37]

For the first time—in football, anyway—Harvard fans experienced a new emotion: smugness. "To the credit of the multitude supporting Yale," chided the *Harvard Alumni Bulletin* afterward, "it must . . . be said that their cheers and songs in the final period were like nothing so much as the playing of the ship's band on the sinking *Titanic*."[38]

Brickley was at the Yale 42, lining up for a potential sixth field goal, when the timekeeper blew the whistle. Harvard 15, Yale 5.

More precisely, Brickley 15, Yale 5.

✿ ✿ ✿

Fair Harvard went fairly bonkers. "Harvard had defeated Yale . . . for the first time in the Stadium, and Brickley's right toe had scored every point," wrote Cunningham, who added,

> There has never been such a scene in all Stadium history. The crowd hoisted Haughton and all the Harvard players they could reach to their shoulders and snake-danced entirely around the Stadium. Brickley's uniform was practically torn off him by people trying to shake his hand or slap his back.[39]

Emulating their hero, Crimson fans tossed their hats over the goalposts. Described the *Chicago Tribune*,

> The crowd of crazy students and graduates wearing Harvard colors turned upon coach Percy Haughton and quickly raised him off the ground. Haughton was literally carried off the field, with thousands of happy Harvard men and women wildly cheering the man who has made the Crimson invincible on the football field.[40]

As news of Brickley's big day spread, the reaction was no less giddy. "We today can hardly comprehend the impact of that feat around the nation," wrote Clark Shaughnessy in 1943. Shaughnessy continued,

> In small Midwestern towns, schoolboys to whom Brickley was a hero gloated over it and practiced dropkicks—pretending they were Brickleys. Garrulous farmers passing on the dirt roads, having heard of it from far away like the presidential election returns, checked their teams to comment on the hardy muscular feat reminiscent of the sporting contests of the old pioneer days. Strangers in city crowds

Brickley's five-field goal day was headline news, and not just in Boston. "We today can hardly comprehend the impact of that feat around the nation," wrote famed football coach Clark Shaughnessy in 1943. *Boston Globe.*

used it as an introduction, and friends employed it in passing the time of day instead of remarking on the weather. Everyone gloried in it; everyone felt vicariously the thrill of it. Everyone had a part in it, shared in it, grew close to Brickley, became a friend of his. [41]

Obscured in the Brickley frenzy were the stalwart performance of Harvard's line, the vital bit role of unheralded Duncan Dana, and, above all, the contribution of Mahan. By positioning Brickley, his punting did as much to win the game as Brick's kicks. Mahan punted 13 times for a 42-yard average, with only 33 yards in returns. Yale's punts averaged but 34 yards. The ultimate accolade came from W. D. Sullivan: Mahan's punting was "right up in the class with Felton and Haughton." [42]

The Elis were so disgusted by the perceived incompetence of referee Langford they vowed never to have him officiate another of their games.

Alexander McKinlock was not one of the eight Crimson substitutes inserted by Haughton. Thus, he did not get his "H"—not this year. He was only a sophomore, so presumably he would have two other chances.

That evening, the Harvard squad was the toast of the town. "Brickley and Harvard Team Theatre Idols" headlined the *Boston Herald* the next day.

> After their strenuous afternoon, the Harvard players went to the Colonial Theatre last night to see Montgomery & Stone and Elsie Janis [who during World War I would achieve further fame as "the sweetheart of the AEF"], and to forget their bruises, for even they had received a few. . . . When the players appeared in autos they were cheered collectively and individually. . . . All the first-tier boxes and the first few rows of the orchestra were reserved for "Bob" Storer's heroes. . . . Coach Haughton was cheered, Capt. Storer was cheered, Mal Logan was cheered and—they were all cheered. . . . An added attraction at the theater was Mayor Fitzgerald and a party of friends. . . . In his party were Mr. and Mrs. William Randolph Hearst. . . . By special arrangements, many of the stage characters wore red, with the exception of Don, the dog. He wore a huge blue bow and growled at the Harvard men in the boxes. . . . The house went into uproar in the second act when Elsie Janis threw a football into the box at Mal Logan and he crudely fumbled it.

The Elis went out on the town, too. "Down Tremont Street, at the Shubert Theatre, the Yale players were watching Al Jolson in 'The Honeymoon Express,'" wrote the *Herald*. "Al Jolson was encored time after time, and his cheery little remarks addressed to the players, as for instance, 'Never mind today, remember 1909,' brought forth howls of approval."[43]

Again, Harvard was acclaimed national champion, although there were worthy alternatives in Chicago and Notre Dame (both 7–0), among others. James Vautravers of Tiptop25.com gives the nod to the Crimson, partly because Harvard was the defending champ and was not knocked off. "Is domination in the previous year a valid argument?" asks Vautravers. He continues,

> Well, that's up for debate, but the previous year's showing has driven plenty of "national championship" races in college football history, and it's about all Oklahoma had going for them in 1956. . . . Similarly,

Harvard dominated their schedule this year, and they were not threatened in any game, even the 3–0 win at Princeton. These teams performed pretty similarly (Chicago had one more close game, but one of those came against a top 10 opponent, which Harvard did not play), but Harvard had a slight scoring edge against both "unrated" and "rated" opponents. . . . They were also a far deeper team than Chicago, who often had to weather fourth-quarter fatigue this season. I would probably rate Chicago number one myself, due to that big win at Minnesota, but I am fairly certain that Harvard was the better team, and either is an option at number one. The two teams definitely merit a share of the mythical national championship regardless of which you want to place at number one.

As for the Fighting Irish, Vautravers notes they had a common foe with the Crimson—Penn State: "Notre Dame followed up their most impressive outing [against Army] with their least impressive, winning just 14–7 at 2–6 Penn State. According to newspaper accounts, PSU outplayed Notre Dame for 50 of the game's 60 minutes."[44] Harvard had thumped the Nittanys, 29–0. Still, who knows what role travel-induced fatigue played. And it's tantalizing to imagine how many fans and reporters would have crammed into the Stadium had Rockne and Dorais brought their aerial show to Cambridge, intent on snapping Haughton's winning streak, now standing at 20.

It was a good month for anyone associated with Percy D. Haughton. On November 18, the *Boston Advertiser* had reported, "Mrs. Percy D. Haughton . . . receives $380,000 from the estate of her first husband, the late Rev. Dr. Richard L. Howell, according to a transfer tax report filed here today. Dr. Howell, who was known as one of the wealthiest clergymen in America, died Feb. 1, 1910."[45]

For a few weeks, Charlie Brickley arguably was the most famous athlete—and maybe the most famous man—in the United States. In early December, the *New York Times* did a feature on his flat-toe attachment.[46] The paper noted that Brickley's five field goals gave him 11 on the season and 24 in his two years of varsity play. It also reminded readers that the five field goals were not a record for a game; Jim Thorpe and Chicago's Walter Eckersall each had booted seven in an afternoon. But Brickley, of course, had accomplished his feat of feet against Yale. Had there been a Heisman, Brickley would have won in a walk.

Other Harvard players received their share of ink. Hitchcock, Mahan, and Pennock joined Brickley as consensus All-Americas. But in what today would be called crossover coverage, the big news was the engagement of Tack Hardwick. His affianced, Miss Margaret Stone of 149 Buckminster Road in Brookline, was the daughter of Galen L. Stone, cofounder of the brokerage firm of Hayden, Stone & Co., at 87 Milk Street. "She attended a Boston private school and graduated from Bryn Mawr College this year," noted the *Globe*, adding, "She is an expert horsewoman and motorist."[47]

The couple would wed in July 1915, a month after Tack graduated. The ceremony—the "most sumptuous bridal that ever graced the Buzzards Bay shore,"[48] according to newspaper accounts—took place, as the *Globe* breathlessly reported, "in the presence of almost 1,000 guests . . . at Great Hill [in Marion, Massachusetts], the beautiful summer home of the bride's parents." Almost 500 guests arrived on a special train from Boston. The ushers included Hardwick's classmates and football teammates, "Walter 'Wallie' Trumbull, acting captain last year of the Harvard varsity 11," and "Fred T. Bradlee, halfback on the same team. . . . While at Harvard," concluded the account, "Mr. Hardwick won the unusual distinction of being captain of the varsity baseball team, All-American football end, shot-putter, and the strongest man in college for two years."[49]

8

THE FOOTBALL–INDUSTRIAL COMPLEX

Spanning the Charles River from Boylston Street to the entrance of Soldiers Field, the Larz Anderson Bridge opened in time for the 1913 season. Supplanting a narrow, rickety wooden drawbridge that had been a choked, dust-kicking trial on game days, the sturdy, paved structure made the march from Harvard Square to the Stadium more tolerable, especially for the multitudes who trekked across and back for the big games and championship games. Its very solidity and permanence also symbolized that the relationship—perhaps unholy—between colleges and sports was now set in stone.

Beginning as early as the 1880s, Harvard, Princeton, and Yale had decided it was part of their mission, educational or not, to provide sporting entertainment for the masses. In the 1890s, Harvard president Charles W. Eliot decreed that his school would no longer play major football games at neutral sites, but on campus only. Within 20 years, the Big Three would have colossal stadiums, and game day had become a ritual, complete with spectacle, song, and spirit. For good or for ill, these institutions set the pattern that has been followed and refined by universities to this day.

There were many carpers, at Harvard and elsewhere. Muckraker Henry Beach Needham, in his 1905 *McClure's* expose, had put his finger on the win-at-all-costs mentality and the creeping realization that the cart was pulling the horse: "The physical development of the student body is neglected, that 11 men of the university may perform for the benefit of the public."[1] The disdain for the immersion into the muck of so-called big-time college sport drips from the comments of eminent historian Samuel Eliot Morison, Harvard class of 1908, in *Three Centuries of Harvard*, his official history published for the university's tricentennial in 1936. These included a swipe at another son of Harvard, Percy Duncan Haughton. "Haughton was the first of the modern 'big-time coaches,' and he certainly 'delivered the goods,'" sniffs Morison, "but it may be questioned whether his talent for picturesque profanity made the game more enjoyable, or whether his strategical and tactical developments turned football in the right direction." Give the man his "H"—for Harrumph!

Morison did concede a positive aspect:

> The growth of athletics tended to integrate college life in the [Charles W.] Eliot era; participation in them, both as players and as managers, brought together men of the widest social origins, and victory over Yale in the four "major" sports of football, baseball, rowing, and track was something that the entire college prayed for.[2]

Those who deplored what football had wrought were bowled over like a would-be tackler in the way of Haughton's gang of interferers. The athletic horse had left the athletic barn; although it would be reined in some after World War II, the rest of the United States took note, especially of the financial windfalls a mighty team could generate. The school had become dependent on ever-burgeoning football receipts to fund its entire athletic program. In 1917, according to documents in the Harvard University Archives, receipts for the school's athletic events would be $155,608.72, against expenses of $117,306.08. Of that total, football accounted for $143,147.19 in receipts and $36,458.85 in expenses, for a net of $106,688.34. In other words, football delivered all but $12,461.53 of the receipts. Rental of the lawn tennis courts was the only other athletic endeavor in this report to operate in the black: $3,907.95 in receipts, $2,171.51 in expenses. (Some years, baseball and crew also made a profit.)[3]

Thus, football was funneling more than six figures in profit to the athletic association. The gridiron was keeping the rest of the department afloat. True, the school could have raised money for individual sports by other means—tuition increases or endowments, or student fees—but then as now, Harvard ran on the principle of "every tub on its own bottom."

In a rare (for Harvard) instance of organized school spirit, handkerchief-bearing students formed an "H" at the Yale Bowl in 1914, while singing "The Marseillaise." *HUPSF Football (259), olvwork376389. Harvard University Archives.*

Even amid unparalleled success on the field and at the gate, Harvard's leaders—including those who championed the Crimson teams—acknowledged unease. Foremost was the president, A. Lawrence Lowell, Eliot's successor, who accurately identified the emerging self-aggrandizing sports apparatuses. (Today, the self-perpetuating athletic department expansion is labeled the "gold-plating of college sports.") "The vast scale of the public games has brought its problems," declared Lowell in his annual report for 1912. He added,

> They have long ceased to be an undergraduate diversion, managed entirely by the students, and maintained by their subscriptions. They have become great spectacles supported by the sale of tickets to thousands of people. . . . Money comes easily and is easily spent under the spur of intense public interest in the result of the major contests, and a little laxity quickly leads to grave abuse. Extravagance

still exists, and vigilant supervision is required to reduce it. Graduates, who form public opinion on these matters, must realize that intercollegiate victories are not the most important objects of college education. Nor must they forget the need of physical training for the mass of students by neglecting to encourage the efforts recently made to cultivate healthful sports among men who have no prospect of playing on the college teams.[4]

(This has echoes of President Dwight D. Eisenhower's eerie warning in 1960 about the military–industrial complex.)

Many within the Harvard community complained that academically, many of the star athletes were unworthy. These were not the functional illiterates who festoon too many college rosters today. The Crimson players had passed the entrance exam . . . most had, anyway. Many were admitted "with conditions." (And as we will see with the case of future Hall of Famer Fritz Pollard, sometimes they were all but waved through.) But would they have been dozing through classes in Sever Hall if not for their ability to punt or carry a football?

The schizophrenia was illustrated by the *Harvard Alumni Bulletin*. (It eventually morphed into what today is *Harvard Magazine*, for which the author serves as a contributing editor.) At the same time that it was breathlessly printing play-by-play of the football games (complete with photos and diagrams), the publication also could be a stern moralizing voice. In early 1913—after Haughton's men had clobbered Yale, 20–0—the *Bulletin* played spoilsport. "Are our colleges and universities being injured or aided by the recruiting of boys who are brought to them because they are athletes, but who otherwise would not go to college at all?" it editorialized, continuing,

> We believe that this type of undergraduate is often an evil to the college which he joins. He may be in every way a sound and wholesome person, and on the way to become a useful, and perhaps a leading, citizen; but if the college attracts him chiefly as an athletic club and a place to earn a sweater decorated with a precious letter, his path to usefulness should not lie through the college. . . . The fact is that, driven on by the enterprise of our sporting editors, we are, as a people, losing our balance in the matter of athletics.[5]

Then as now, some were indignant about the "almost scandalous" amounts spent to equip footballers. Proclaimed the *Bulletin* in 1911—

right after the Crimson had been declared national champion, and shortly after Dean LeBaron R. Briggs had issued a report criticizing the athletic department's management:

> Some months ago the *Bulletin* asked why it cost $1,000 per man to put a football squad through a seven-weeks season when that amount is more than it takes to carry the average student through an entire year. . . . Wastefulness, and a disregard of everyday business: These are the things that explain the paradox, and explain it fully. . . . Why should not the accounts of the athletic organizations be made public in detail? . . . We daresay there would no longer be large items of expenditure for "taxicabs as the sole means of getting about, and for costly dinners with wines and cigars."[6]

Others were aghast at the coarsening of spirit engendered by the desperation to beat Yale. The keening and barking of the stadium crowds was perhaps fine for the working classes watching the Red Sox at Fenway Park, but they were unworthy of Harvard men. It is almost comical to read the editorials and letters in the *Bulletin* as writers fall all over themselves preaching gentlemanliness and sportsmanship. After Charlie Brickley dropkicked the Elis into submission in 1913, one correspondent, calling himself "Sporticus Antiquus," was concerned about . . . the tone:

> In view of the "era of good feeling," which has happily been inaugurated in athletics between Harvard and Yale, may it not be in order to suggest to our "friend, the enemy," that it is time to give up the concerted efforts to "rattle" our players? Whenever Harvard had the ball on the Yale side of the field during the recent game in the Stadium, the Yale crowd set up a great noise, in order to drown, if possible, the signals given to the Harvard men. So also, whenever Brickley prepared to make a drop or placekick, the Yale "rooters" burst forth in shouts and catcalls in their effort to "rattle" him. . . . Of course, this is not sport; its proper designation would be unpleasant for a Harvard man to write. If the practice, though wholly unjustifiable, helped Yale teams to win, it would seem like "squealing" for a Harvard man to suggest that it be discontinued. In view of the fact, however, that during the last six years Harvard has beaten Yale three times and tied her twice at football, and has won four out of the last seven annual series in baseball, and six races in succession at New

London, it is evident that "rattling tactics" have not produced the effect desired at New Haven. Not only Harvard men, but [also] neutrals who belong to neither university, and a saving remnant of Yale men themselves, deprecate a practice which mars the pleasure of witnessing athletic contests.[7]

Well, then. Was stooping to conquer worthy of Harvard men? In a refrain that resounds through the decades among all who cherish braggin' rights, Harvard Athletic Association graduate treasurer Fred Moore had the last word. In his report for the fiscal year ending on July 31, 1915 (and thus encompassing the 1914 Yale game), Moore wrote, "When the score is 36 to 0, and the receipts from the game are $138,000.00, it is rather difficult for the manager to refuse the team and coaches anything in reason they may desire."[8]

* * *

The football–industrial complex had a multiplier effect. In 1916–1917, expenses for training were $2,424.30, for doctors $2,791.66, for "rubbing" (masseurs—we hope) $1,318.25, and for travel $6,477.66. The coaching staff got $9,630.00. Expense of games came to $16,603.93, a figure swelled by "expense of large games" (some of which was shared by the visitors).[9] Eight undergraduates were required to look after the business part of the enterprise—a manager (a post that could be lucrative through the sale of program ads and hence was much coveted), a first assistant manager, and six assistant managers.

In 1911, the *Boston Globe* noted,

> There are little sidelights to a big football game that are interesting. There were 276 student ushers at the Carlisle game, and there will be 300 or more at the Dartmouth and Yale games. There are also required 100 or more policemen. Lunch is served for these 400 men at 12 o'clock in the baseball cage. The details of management of a big football game are certainly considerable.[10]

Ticket prices ranged from 50 cents to $3.00 (for a season ticket that did not include the Yale game) to $5.00 (for a pass admitting the holder to all Harvard athletic events). For the major games, scalping was a huge problem, and beginning in 1913, Harvard tried to forestall it, at least among undergrads and alumni. "This year for the first time the name and address of each successful applicant for the Yale game will be indelibly embossed across the stub of his tickets, and any attempt to alter or deface this stamp will cause the tickets to be refused at the gate,"[11] the athletic department decreed. Worse yet, those found in violation would be blacklisted indefinitely—a stern threat for those whose autumns revolved around afternoons at the Stadium.

Most spectators traveled to the Stadium on foot or by streetcar, but with such a well-heeled (and well-wheeled) clientele, parking at Soldiers Field also became a thriving enterprise. According to U.S. Census estimates from 1914, there were 1.7 million motor vehicles in the United States;[12] on a late November Saturday in Cambridge, it seemed that most of them were outside Harvard Stadium. In 1913, for the early season games, a parking (or "checking") space cost 25 cents; for Brown and Yale, the cost was a half-dollar. For the latter game, a ticket admitted an automobile with its entire party to the parking space, which was enclosed by heavy wire.

The economic effect extended well beyond the Stadium. For those shut out of the arena, Boston music halls offered scoreboards, running play-by-play and even live entertainment. On weekends when major games were played, hotels were booked months in advance, and the music halls featured big-name stars.

The spectators were just as glittering. As the *New York Times* reported the day after the 1910 Game at Yale,

> Special trains, private cars, and automobiles began rolling into New Haven by 9 o'clock this morning, and the entry of fashionable folk from New York and Boston kept up a steady procession. . . . There were 35 specials in all. . . . The women were bundled up in furs. But that did not keep them from wearing flowers, and large bunches of violets, clusters of carnations, and red roses added considerable color to the feminine throngs whose costumes were hidden by furs.[13]

Among the notables were "Mrs. W. K. Vanderbilt Jr. . . . Mrs. E. H. Harriman [whose son Averell was a freshman that year at Yale] . . . Harry Payne Whitney."[14] From Boston came Mayor John "Honey Fitz" Fitzgerald, among whose party was daughter Rose, who four autumns later would wed Joseph P. Kennedy, Harvard class of 1912.

Like other sports with mass appeal, for example, baseball, horse racing, and boxing, football was producing its mandarin class of scribes. For the "championship" games, as many as 150 reporters crammed the press box. They included the big names of the day: Rice, Runyon, Lardner, Heywood Broun (Harvard class of 1910), Herbert Reed (known as "Right Wing") of the *New York Tribune*, Harry Cross of the *Times*, and George Trevor of the *New York Sun*, plus correspondents from such major magazines as *Collier's* (which published Walter Camp's All-America team) and *Harper's Weekly*. During the week before the game, column inch after column inch was devoted to analyses, predictions, lineups, statistics, and features. The game itself got page-one treatment. In 1911, the *Boston Globe* "Sportsman" declared, "180 football writers and 50 operators will work in the press stand at the Harvard–Yale game Saturday. . . . The only event in sport exceeding the Harvard–Yale game in its demand for wire service is the World's [*sic*] Series in baseball, and that is in a class by itself."[15]

Already, a few writers were going beyond play-by-play and glib commentary and, like Haughton, beginning to break down the game. In 1913, Herbert Reed published *Football for Public and Player*. Like a few of his press-box brethren, Reed had played the game—in his case, at Cornell, under Pop Warner. In the era before players and modes of attack and defense could readily be identified, and at a time when the game was in flux, he explicated the action and what lay underneath in sensible language, with illustrative photos and x's-and-o's diagrams. It was Reed who, invoking the dictum of Gen. William Tecumseh Sherman about an army, propagated the notion that a team needed a "soul" to be successful. "There was a 'soul'—call it a personality if you prefer—in the Harvard 11 of 1912, and Captain Wendell made the most of it," Reed declared.[16] Like most of his colleagues, Reed was an unapologetic proselytizer of the sport. "If football is a game . . . and not so serious a business as many of its opponents believe," he wrote in the opening chapter of his book, "it is, nevertheless, the most important game we have, the sport that makes the heaviest demand upon every fine quality of the best possible athlete." He continued, "It is the crucible in which character is molded at an age when character is in the process of formation—it is, to change the simile, the white light that beats upon a young man's actions and ideals."[17]

In contrast to the nationally known names who descended on Cambridge for the big games were the journeymen reporters for the Boston dailies, of which there were a half-dozen in 1913. Since Haughton was so press-averse, they had to rely on other sources and their own powers of observation. George Carens of the Brahmin-oriented *Boston Transcript* had an in: It was his analysis and his paper's photos that Haughton had his team scrutinize during Monday practice. But the true fixture was the *Boston Globe*'s Melville E. Webb Jr., whom we often quote in these pages.

Born in 1876, Webb grew up in Boston's West End the son of a doctor. At age 14 and as a student at Boston English High, Mel saw his first Harvard game. He went to work for the *Globe* four years later and, flitting between the Huntington Avenue baseball grounds, Fenway Park, Braves Field, and Harvard Stadium, would fashion an enviable career. (Disdaining the newfangled typewriter, he composed his stories in longhand with stubby pencils.) In the warmer months, he covered the Red Sox and the Braves, and in 1908 Webb was one of the charter members of the Baseball Writers' Association of America. In the autumn, he devoted himself to Crimson football. In the 1910s, Webb thus spent his year covering the four-time World Series champion Red Sox and their sensational young lefty, Babe Ruth, and the equally dominant Haughton 11. It was a tough job, but someone had to do it.

Eventually, Webb (who lived until 1961) would attend 50 Harvard–Yale games. Soon after the Stadium opened, with his fellow writers grousing about their substandard accommodations, Webb helped graduate athletics manager Fred Moore design the press box at the rim of the amphitheater. Webb made sure to give his colleagues special work areas and writing tables. His efforts were so successful that when Yale and Princeton opened their stadiums in 1914, they consulted with him on the construction of their press accommodations, which, in turn, influenced later press-box design. [18]

Webb was not a colorful or vivid writer in the mold of Grantland Rice or Ring Lardner. But for the daily and Sunday *Globe* reader in those preradio and pretelevision days, he performed two bread-and-butter functions. First, he gave a detailed account of the game that unsparingly noted strengths and weaknesses (including those of the Crimson). He also deployed statistics as well as one could during those imprecise days. Second, during the week and in postseason summaries, he was most alert to trends. Webb saw through the big crowds to posit that the sport would lose popularity if it did not make it easier to score points. As the rules changed, he noted that bulk and mass, formerly the most important attributes of a powerful team, would need to be supplemented if not supplanted by athletic ability, speed, and versatility. Somewhat in the manner that no one can envision his parents having sex, the modern reader is constantly surprised by the sophistication of Webb and his fellow scribes of the early days.

For the undergrads, the *Crimson* and *Yale Daily News* also were exhaustive, if exhortatory and not always authoritative. Chiming in were the "special numbers" of undergraduate publications, for instance, the humor magazine the *Harvard Lampoon*, which, of course, twitted the other side sophomorically. (Sample: In 1915, in prose and cartoons, the publication skewered Yale's defeated 1914 coach Frank Hinkey as "Coach Dinkey.")[19]

Once inside the amphitheater, spectators were treated to not only a football game, but also grand theater. First came the riot of hues. "It was a gold mine for the hawkers," reported the *Times* of the scene in New Haven in 1910. "'Get your colors,' they yelled until they were hoarse. The flower vendors, with just the kind of flower every girl should wear. . . . Souvenirs of every kind were on tap—little yellow leather footballs pinned on blue and crimson ribbons and large colored letters which could be pinned on the lapel of your coat."[20] Programs cost 50 cents and were in the shape of a football; the contents were loaded with ads for cruises, stylish men and women's "furnishings," and luxury goods and hotels.

Marching bands would not arrive until after World War I; Harvard's would be formed in 1919. Instead, the undergraduate sections offered organized cheers and sang school songs. In 1910, when singing "The Marseillaise" (not the French national anthem, but a beloved fight song), the Harvard section, in a precursor of the latter-day "card sections," caused a sensation by forming, at a signal, a white "H."

The programs printed the more popular songs, some of which had been passed down throughout the years, while others were the product of recent competitions. The 1912 edition contains a few that still are sung: Harvard's "Our Director" ("Three cheers for Harvard! And down with Yale! RAH! RAH! RAH!") and Yale's "Boola, Boola," "Bright College Years" ("For God, for Country, and for Yale") and "Undertaker

Song" ("Oh! More work for the undertaker/Another job for the casket maker; In the local cemetery they are very, very busy on a brand-new grave. No hope for Harvard"). But in the Great Sing-off of 1912, Yale had the composing equivalent of Charlie Brickley in its head cheerleader: one C. A. Porter, '13. Cole Porter composed the new ditty "Bingo Eli Yale":

> Bingo, Bingo, Bingo, that's the Lingo!
> Eli is bound to win.
> There's to be a victory,
> So watch the team begin.
> Bingo, Bingo, Harvard's team can aught avail;
> Fight! Fight! Fight with all your might!
> For Bingo, Bingo, Eli Yale!

In 1914, the Crimson riposted with the rousing "Ten Thousand Men of Harvard," written by Alfred Putnam, '18 (grandfather of a classmate of the author). If not exactly accurate concerning undergraduate manpower—at any given moment, there might be 3,000 in the college, and today there are about 6,000, half of them women—it became the signature fight song, with its foregone conclusion:

> Ten thousand men of Harvard
> want vict'ry today,
> For they know that o'er old Eli
> Fair Harvard holds sway.
> So then we'll conquer old Eli's men,
> and when the game ends, we'll sing again:
> Ten thousand men of Harvard
> gained vict'ry today!

There were many, both on campus and off, who debated whether the energy the young men at these citadels of learning were devoting to sweat, songs, cheers, and sophomoric scribbling was properly directed. They occasionally sermonized. "'If Jesus Had Gone to the Yale–Harvard Football Game' was the subject on which Rev. Albert R. Williams, pastor of the Maverick Congregational Church, East Boston, spoke last night," reported the *Globe* in 1911. Quoth the Rev. Williams:

> If Jesus had gone to the Yale–Harvard game, I think He would have much admired the Spartan courage of these men. He would have been glad to find that the players were not all tutti-frutti, chocolate

eclair, champagne Charlie boys. He would have been glad to find
that they were not the up-all-night-and-in-all-day kind. . . .

If Jesus had gone to the game, He would have enjoyed the enthusiastic cheering which came crashing down across the arena, but He
would have asked, "Is there as much enthusiasm for My work?"[21]

9

"YALE SUPPLIED THE BOWL . . . BUT HARVARD HAD THE PUNCH"

Never was college so exciting, or drunks so drunken, or the generous feelings of ardent youth so exalted, as in those last golden years before World War I.—Samuel Eliot Morison, *Three Centuries of Harvard*

In 1914, the Yale Bowl was dedicated with The Game. To commemorate the occasion—and, he was confident, a victory—Elis coach Frank Hinkey decided to have the contest filmed. The footage has come down to us today (you can see snippets on YouTube, at the beginning of "Football at Yale: The Story of a Tradition, Part 2")[1]. It would be better for the Blue had this horror movie been destroyed. Amazingly, the Harvard blowout could have been even more emphatic had the already power-packed Crimson backfield retained the services of a runner who sat on their bench during the opener: a young African American from Chicago named Fritz Pollard.

☼ ☼ ☼

On Tuesday, September 15, 1914, the *Boston Globe* headlined on page six, "Harvard Starts Football Campaign with Squad of 68."[2] Pictured were coach Percy Haughton, dapper in a seersucker suit and straw hat, strolling with team captain Charlie Brickley, togged out in sweats. The 1914 season loomed as a grand tour that would cap Brickley's career, perhaps the greatest football yet had known. Substitute back Alexander

McKinlock was also shown, "getting points in dropkicking from Capt. Brickley." Reassuringly, another Stadium season was at hand.

On page one, however, the headlines were of more distant battles. "Germans Turn and Fight" roared the large, boldface type. Elaborated the subhead, "Right Wing Rallies on Line of Aisne River to Stop Allies' Crossing, after Battle—French Force Passage at Compiegne and Soissons." Six weeks before, the Great War had begun. Before it would end, it would involve, sometimes tragically, the men who "spent an hour on strenuous evolutions" on Soldiers Field.

Speaking at a reception for freshmen, college president A. Lawrence Lowell grimly sounded an alarm. "Allusion has been made to the terrific conflict going on in Europe, a conflict of dimensions such as the world has never seen, a conflict of a magnitude such that we in this room would merely make food for a few shrapnel shells shot casually in battle," Lowell said. "And a few moments of machine-gun fire would lay every one of us on the field."[3] Vivid as Lowell's remarks were, the conflict literally seemed far away. For P. D. and his troops, it was business as usual.

Perhaps the undergraduate view also was insular because it was an exciting time to be at Harvard, athletically and otherwise. In the spring of 1914, the varsity crew had rowed gallantly before losing (by inches) a memorable race with Yale (already the 53rd edition of the nation's oldest collegiate athletic rivalry). On the Fourth of July, the Harvard second crew, featuring a future U.S. senator, Leverett Saltonstall (coach of the football second team), and a future congressman, Laurence Curtis (also a football end), symbolically punctuated a golden age when it won the Grand Challenge Cup at Henley—the last regatta until war's end. (At their 50th reunion, all nine members of the boat not only were alive but also went out for a row.) Tennis's national champion, Richard Williams—a *Titanic* survivor—was a member of the class of 1916.

The football stars were nationally known and acclaimed. During their senior year, backs Fred "Peebo" Bradlee and Charlie Brickley, along with linemen Stan Pennock and Wally Trumbull, lived in the same Harvard dorm, giving Mathews Hall more All-Americas than any college in the nation.

As Trumbull, first marshal of the class of 1915, would write in his class's album,

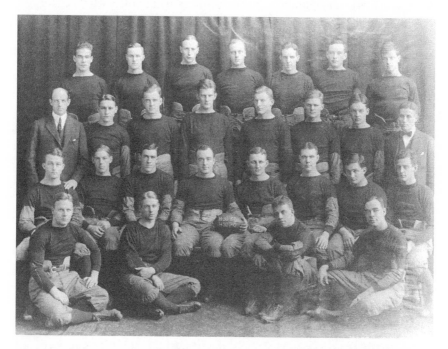

Harvard's 1914 team, considered Haughton's most talented. Bottom (left to right): Atkinson, Swigert, King, Watson. Second row: Bradlee, Hardwick, Mahan, Brickley (Capt.), Trumbull, Logan, Pennock, T. J. Coolidge. Third row: Coach Haughton, Soucy, Parson, Weston, Withington, Francke, Curtis, Richards (Mgr.). Top row: McKinlock, Weatherhead, Smith, Bigelow, Wallace, Underwood, C. A. Coolidge. *Harvard University Sports Information.*

Perhaps no other class has seen such a tremendous enlargement of the university. During our senior year, we have seen the erection of the Anderson Bridge, the three freshman dormitories, the Widener Memorial Library, the two T. Jefferson Coolidge Chemical Laboratories [named for the late father of end Jeff Coolidge], the Cruft Electrical Laboratory, and the new music building. The class at the same time has grown in strength. We have risen in scholarship standing during the last year. We have lived in an era of great athletic prosperity, to which we have substantially contributed.[4]

Of the 25 players to win their "H" (awarded to those who played against Yale) during the 1914 season, 14 came from the class of '15.

Today, Harvard's ongoing 20-game unbeaten (and 18-game winning) streak would be buzzed about in headlines and on *SportsCenter* reports and talk radio. Back then, it was mentioned, but in passing. The

Boston papers had plenty of other athletic achievements to cover. As Grantland Rice would note in 1915,

> Last season Boston was the sporting capital of America. This eminent citadel of culture and clout—of wisdom and the wallop—maintained the World's Series champions in baseball [the Braves], the football championship with Harvard, and the golf championship with [Francis] Ouimet.[5]

By season's end Boston no longer would be home to the grandest college football edifice. An early stadium arms race was being contested in earnest: In 1914, Princeton and Yale opened new arenas, Palmer Stadium (seating 40,000) and the Yale Bowl (housing a titanic 70,000, including standees). To a degree, they owed their construction to former Harvard president Charles W. Eliot's decree that his school must play on campus sites only. But their existence also was testimony to the surging demand for and financial riches found in big-time college football.

The game itself also finally was beginning to resemble, if only in a rudimentary way, the one we see today. An experiment in numbering of players for the Cornell–Brown game—kind of a Numbers 1.0—was a hit. But the ever-secretive Haughton did not want numbers. (At Harvard Stadium, the scoreboard did list the names of the players.)

The season of 1914 was the year the forward pass really began to take hold. This is reflected in many of the rules changes enacted before play began. Two of the most important prohibited roughing the passer and intentional grounding.

There was one other edict: In an attempt to keep the game in the hands of the players, coaches were not permitted to walk along the sidelines. Haughton and his counterparts no doubt found ways around the restriction.

Those coaches also were coming to the realization that the aerial game gave a physically weaker team a way to play with, if not to beat, the big boys. To deal with Harvard, Springfield used what the *Globe* called a "far-flung formation"[6] —which must have been an early version of the spread—from which it tried an astonishing 35 passes, completing 11. (Alas, five others went into Crimson hands.) The result was a more open and crowd-pleasing game, featuring more scoring.

Another modification decreed, "Teams will no longer be allowed to encroach upon the neutral zone in making shift plays. As soon as either team is lined up on the offensive any shift must be made without a player passing into this neutral zone under a penalty of five yards."

If the measure was aimed at Harvard's vaunted wheel shift, Haughton could sneer at this feeble slap. It appeared as if he could simply turn his team loose and let it ramble: The Crimson was *loaded*. Another unbeaten, untied season was a realistic prospect. There would be only one road game: dedicating the Bowl at New Haven.

The entire 1913 national championship backfield—Brickley, Bradlee, quarterback Mal Logan, and halfback Eddie Mahan—had returned. To the dismay of opponents, there also were solid backups, particularly senior fullback Hugo Francke, from Cambridge's Browne & Nichols. Francke was a former soccer captain who had been forced to sit out the previous two seasons with a heart ailment. His father, Kuno, was a distinguished professor of Germanic studies at Harvard. His heritage would necessitate Hugo's making a difficult choice in 1917. But now, with the war strictly a European concern, he was known goodnaturedly as the "Big Teuton" or "Hugo, the Frank." Waiting among the scrubs was little junior Richard "Bob" King, a former second-teamer. The Boston Latin product was an anomaly: He was living in Watertown with his wife—and two children. King, McKinlock, and other reserves, including quarterbacks Ernie Swigert and Don Watson, would work hard in practice and hope for a rout in the Yale game that would allow them to get in and win their "H."

Entering its climactic season, the Group of Seven was unbeaten and untied. Its members now were known, at school, if not in the wider world, for their distinct personalities and talents: Captain Brickley was the showman; Bradlee the reliable one; Pennock the mighty bulwark; Logan the pepper pot and heady field general; Trumbull the inspirational sparkplug whose enthusiasm threatened to burn him out; and Coolidge the brainy one, skilled, if fragile.

But the most feared player in all of football was Huntington Reed Hardwick. As Grantland Rice would put it after his death, "If football had a weakness for Hardwick, it was that the game was not quite rough enough."[7] Tack was the school's strongest man, as confirmed by tests conducted at Hemenway Gym. The average score for all students was 630, for athletes 750. Hardwick registered 1,381.[8] He was a shot-putter on the track team and captain of the baseball team, for which his tape-measure homers resounded. As a hard hitter on the gridiron, Hardwick was an early-day Ronnie Lott. At 6-foot-1, Tack weighed but 171 pounds, but it was all sinew. He had excelled as a back but found his true métier as an end and interferer, chopping foes down with ferocity and relish.

He described his technique as follows:

> When you have carried out the assignment and have blocked the tackle, the tendency is to self-complacently pat yourself on the back. Why, your work has just started! Go down the field, take out a defensive back, then another, and so on until the whistle blows. I have known players to get four men on one long dodging run. When the play is on the other side, cut down and take out a defensive back. This is dirty but fascinating work. .... Eight or nine times you fail, but the 10th time you go down with the same speed and determination, this time your runner is clear, the defensive back has his eyes glued on the approaching ball, your opportunity has arrived. Crash! Down he goes, and the long run is assured. There's the original "grand and glorious feeling." And furthermore, the nine failures are essential to the 10th success. You've got to play it your hardest every time, as you never know when the big moment will arrive.[9]

Hardwick was hardly all brawn. From ends coach Leo Leary, he learned caginess. "'Cagey' play is foxy—such as never getting in the same position on every play, moving about, doing the unexpected," Hardwick explained. "If you wish to put your tackle out, play outside him, and draw him out, and then at the last moment hop in close to your own tackle, and then charge your opponent. The reverse is true as well. The unexpected and unusual make up 'cagey' play."[10]

Haughton had taught his fellow Grotonian well. Later, Grantland Rice would label Tack "dynamite on the football field" and the "top man in the matter of flaming spirit," while grouping him with Ty Cobb, Jack Dempsey, and Walter Hagen among the greatest competitors he had ever seen.[11]

✴ ✴ ✴

The first two games went according to form and provided Haughton with a chance to give the scrubs some work. Bates and Springfield were rolled over by identical 44–0 scores. But looking back, what is most noteworthy about the opener is a player—possibly the best in the stadium that day—who was sitting on the Harvard bench in his street clothes.

Frederick Douglass Pollard—known even then as "Fritz"—was an African American from Chicago, where he had made a reputation as a running back and track star at Lane Technical High. His brother Leslie already had played football at Dartmouth, so although Fritz was not academically motivated, he had every expectation of being able to matriculate somewhere. As author John M. Carroll related in his biography *Fritz Pollard: Pioneer in Racial Advancement*, the aspiring scholar began something of a tramp athlete's tour, alighting variously at Northwestern, Brown, Columbia, and Dartmouth (and, oh, by the way, playing semipro ball in his hometown against George Halas). Having to overcome racial prejudice, Pollard also was variously waylaid by academic and administrative obstacles. Later, Carroll noted, Pollard would reflect, "In my young life I'd had more experience with deans than most men my age."

After Pollard left Dartmouth, he went to Boston. There, on the advice of Leslie, he went straight to the office of William Henry Lewis, one of the nation's most prominent African American attorneys. More to the point, Lewis also had been an All-America center for Harvard and was a sometime Crimson coach. Realizing what he had in front of him, Lewis sprang into action the way he had when he had a Yale ballcarrier in his sights. That same day, Pollard found himself talking to a member of the admissions committee. Twenty-four hours later, on a Friday morning, Frederick Douglas Pollard was a member of the Harvard class of 1918, with the "condition" that he would make up his Spanish requirement the following summer.

The next day was the opener against Bates. Cordially, captain Charlie Brickley arranged for Pollard to have a seat on the Crimson sideline. What Pollard remembered was the mob scene, with perhaps 100 players dressed. "I took a seat way down at the end of the bench," he said. "Six inches more to my left and I'd have been in one of the water buckets." He watched as Brickley scored four touchdowns against the hapless Mules. As the score mounted, Haughton was able to shuttle in subs.

After the game, Pollard was walking across the field when he ran into a fellow he had played semipro ball against in Chicago who was now one of Bates' assistant coaches. The man began recruiting him. Did Pollard really think a small African American back would get any playing time in the star-studded Crimson backfield? And at Harvard, he'd really have to buckle down academically, whereas Bates would be much more congenial.

By the end of the discussion, Pollard was headed for Lewiston, Maine. He would spend a miserable autumn there and eventually return to Brown.[12] The next time he was at Harvard Stadium, it was as a member of the Bruins, for whom he later would play in a Rose Bowl. Eventually, along with his old rival Halas, he would be one of the seminal figures of the National Football League.

For the moment, however, it looked as if Harvard wouldn't miss Fritz Pollard.

❊ ❊ ❊

Brickley continued his rampage against pass-happy Springfield, making one of the five Crimson interceptions, scoring two touchdowns, kicking two extra points, and dropkicking a field goal. No one envisioned they were the last points he would score in his illustrious career, save an indelible one. The following Friday night, the Harvard captain awoke with stomach pains. At 4 p.m. on Saturday—almost precisely the time the game against Washington & Jefferson was being decided—he was in the infirmary undergoing an appendectomy. For all intents and purposes, his season—his career—was over.

Now, Haughton was going to have to do some coaching. Mahan and Logan were injured and also unavailable for the Presidents. This was not a typical early-season cupcake, but a reputable team coached by shrewd Bob Folwell that had held Yale to a scoreless tie the year before. Hardwick was shifted back to the backfield, and he, along with Bradlee and McKinlock, picked up the slack in a 10–9, come-from-behind squeaker that pushed the unbeaten streak to 23. Faced with a dangerous opponent whose attack was replete with "forward passes, double passes, [and] crisscross passing by the backs," Haughton made an adjustment at halftime: Keep the ball on the ground and hammer away while eating up the clock. Tack scored all the Crimson points, booting a first-quarter field goal following a fair catch, then capping a fourth-quarter drive with a five-yard sweep around left end, "protected from [W & J's] alert McCreight by the efficient interference of Bradlee,"[13] wrote the *Globe*. Smartly, Hardwick then touched the ball down directly in front of the goalposts, which allowed him to make an easier straight-ahead kick for the decisive extra point.

Again, a foe had shown Harvard the possibilities of the pass. The Presidents had seven completions, and "beauties they were,"[14] Mel Webb added, including a touchdown toss caught in the end zone—a novelty. Even with its absences, the Crimson was saved by its wealth of material, which allowed it to grind down a thinner squad.

That also proved true the next week in the rain and muck against Tufts, whom Harvard beat only 13–6. The Jumbos from nearby Medford threw 19 passes but, partly because of the conditions, completed only two. "Harvard diagnosed the passes and defended against them much better than against W & J a week before," said the *Globe*. Tufts used a wing split formation with a direct snap to the runner. Said the newspaper, "It worked like a German siege gun battering down defenses"[15] —that is, until Harvard tackle Donald Wallace figured out how to stop it by coming in behind the play. Tufts had 17 first downs to Harvard's 13, but turnovers—two interceptions—led to the two Crimson touchdowns, both of which were scored by the emerging Bradlee, who had half the Harvard rushing attempts.

With October past its midpoint, another preliminary season was over. The leaves were falling, and so was the presumed hegemony of the Big Three. The plain fact was, because of the way the game was changing, Harvard and the other traditional powers no longer could afford to take anyone lightly. But that's just what Haughton did against Penn State. He went to New Haven to scout Yale and sent Logan and the still-injured Mahan to get a look at Princeton. Pennock and Trumbull were held out as well. This partly may have been a result of a report that he got from one of Reggie Brown's network of scouts, in this case former Harvard player Charles Hann Jr. After traveling to State College, Pennsylvania, to watch the Nittany Lions beat Gettysburg, 13–0, he sent along a batch of plays and wrote Haughton: "Penn State will give you a game about like the substitutes against the varsity."[16]

Instead, what occurred was nearly a rerun of the Carlisle game three years before. In front of 20,000 at the Stadium, the Nittany Lions took advantage of the depleted lineup and held a 13–6 lead with minutes to play. The streak was within snapping distance, and the Nittanys even were talking a little trash. "Did you ever see the like of the [*sic*] Penn State for 'yapping' on the field?" wrote the *Globe* the following Monday. "No college ball team ever had anything on this fine football 11 for continuous chatter."[17]

Many in the crowd already had left, disconsolate, when Penn State muffed a Francke punt and Harvard's Dick Curtis fell on it. Acting coach Leo Leary inserted into the lineup at halfback a little-used sub, Westmore "Willie" Willcox, who was also a renowned quarter-miler. With Harvard on the Penn State 45, Willcox took a well-disguised pitch, turned the left end, and sprinted downfield before the Nittany Lions defenders figured out he had the ball. He was hauled down by two tacklers at the five, but the trio slid across the goal line. With the bitter-enders holding their breath, Ted Withington fussed and fiddled with his placement, then booted the ball through the uprights. The winning streak was gone, but the unbeaten streak—now at 25—was saved. When the whistle sounded, Leary gave the game ball to Penn State's captain.[18]

There was no time for anyone to catch his breath. Next up in the Stadium: *Michigan*. This was a long-awaited matchup between perennial powers of the East and West, and two of the acknowledged coaching maestros, Haughton and Michigan's Fielding H. "Hurry-Up" Yost. (Today, think Nick Saban versus Jim Harbaugh.) It also was a meeting of two of the marquee brand names of American education, private and public, and football-wise was posited as a clash of styles: the more button-down establishment East versus the upstart, wide-open West. To travel east, Michigan got a $12,000 guarantee.[19]

This was not a vintage Wolverines squad: It would finish 6–3, had already lost to Syracuse, and would lose its finale to Cornell. As his notebook shows, Reggie Brown had scouted the Wolverines thoroughly. He had praise for shifty 155-pound back Johnny Maulbetsch: "Runs like Brickley though not as fast, and drops tacklers—a good hard runner." But overall he saw many weaknesses: "Interference poor. . . . Kickoffs weak. . . . Ends slow down under punts and easily blocked."[20] Of course, Harvard did not have Brickley or Mahan, whose injured leg kept him out. But that didn't quiet the buzz. Even Notre Dame's Knute Rockne, now an assistant coach for the Irish, got into the act. "Many veterans have been looking forward this year to prove the superiority of Western over Eastern football," declared the Rock, whose team was coming off a 28–0 loss to Yale. He added,

> I do not think that we or any other Western team could win from Yale, even later in the season. The Eastern teams get more seasoned men for football through the large preparatory schools and in this way have an advantage over the universities of the West. . . . I do not look to Michigan to defeat Harvard, despite the latter's handicap from injuries. . . . Yale is very dangerous with the double passing game, and it is going to be difficult for Harvard and Princeton to meet it after Yale had spent the whole season perfecting it.[21]

Perhaps the best indicator of the game's frisson was the press coverage. Some 60 reporters were allocated space in the press stand, a large number for a midseason game, as symbolized by Ring Lardner's picking up the Wolverines in Ann Arbor and accompanying them on their trip east. "'The greatest team ever developed in the West' is on its way to Cambridge," reported Lardner with his trademark deadpan humor. Lardner continued,

> "The greatest team ever developed in the West" is what this year's Michigan bunch was called in a Boston paper which was circulating round Ann Arbor before Yost and his young men left there this afternoon. That the Boston writer was perfectly accurate in so styling the Wolverines is the firm conviction of everybody excepting the entire population of the United States and Canada.[22]

As the party prepared to depart, Lardner wrote,

> Tomorrow's train will consist of one car of alumni from Chicago, one of students and scrubs from Ann Arbor, two of graduates from Detroit, one each of alumni now resident of Grand Rapids and Toledo, and one containing the university band. The band has 41 members, and as they are slated to travel in one Pullman, it is expected that some of them will have to sleep in the horns or on the bass drum.

Among the members was a 16-year-old from Portland, Oregon, named George Fischer—the first official drum major of the Michigan marching band. Upon arrival, the band marched through downtown Boston blaring "The Victors."

The gate was impressive and showed the appeal and possibilities of big-time intersectional football. According to Harvard Athletic Association records, 15,165 single-game tickets were sold. (Two weeks later, longtime and nearby rival Brown would attract only 5,421.) Almost 12,000 of these were premium reserved seats at $2 each; Michigan sold 1,805. The attendance came to 22,297, and the gross was $32,831.43. Expenses totaled $4,383.74, leaving a net of $28,447.69, which the schools split evenly. Yost and his crew walked away with a dandy $14,223.85, outkicking their guarantee by $2,223.85.[23]

They did not depart with a victory. The Crimson prevailed, 7–0, in a game that, although lacking fireworks, had "hard and sometimes fierce" football that Mel Webb deemed "interesting all the way through." As predicted, Yost and Haughton were like chess masters. The Michigan coach tried to throw off the Crimson with all manner of wing shifts, direct snaps to the runner, and unbalanced formations, including one in which the nominal center positioned himself at the end of the line to snap the ball. For his part, Haughton employed kicking formations and worked draw plays and delays in an attempt to keep the Michigan defense off balance. The Wolverines, with Maulbetsch carrying the load (as foreseen by Reggie Brown), outgained the Crimson on the ground, 210 to 140, but they blew two golden scoring opportunities, once through confusion near the Harvard goal line and another time when they were stopped by the Crimson's bend-but-don't-break defense; Harvard "became a wall," reported the *Globe*.[24]

Mahan, still nursing his injured leg, again sat out. The ever-versatile Hardwick took his place and had a hand in the game's only score. It came in the second period. Logan caught a Wolverine punt at midfield. With the ball at the 30, Hardwick surprised the Wolverines with the game's first pass, which senior Henry St. John Smith hauled in at the 18. Then it was Big Teuton time: Francke carried five straight times to the five. From there, Tack plunged for the touchdown.

Only five passes were thrown, the one attempted by Michigan ending up in the hands of Harvard's Mal Logan. Hardwick completed three of his four, and his final heave, late in the game from the Michigan 30 in lieu of a punt, landed near but not over the sideline at the Wolverines' seven, giving Michigan the ball on downs at the original line of scrimmage. Had it hit past the sideline, Michigan, according to the rules, would have been pinned in the shadow of its goal line.

Following Haughton's pattern, Harvard got stronger as the game went on. At the finish, the play was almost entirely in Wolverine territory. All in all, noted Webb,

> The intersectional idea was not there at all. There was none of the wild Western flinging expected by those who expected to see the Wolverines lob the ball out on all parts of the field; and if there was anything very radical in the game of either team, Harvard was the team that showed it, not Michigan.

Perhaps the most novel moment of the game came at halftime: "The Wolverines had their band with them, and between the halves there was a parade down on the field, the musicians forming in a huge letter 'M' and tramping about in this formation."[25]

As it turned out, the game against the rugged Westerners would prove perfect preparation for "real football": Princeton and Yale, sandwiched around Brown. Harvard, Princeton, and Yale were still the sport's biggest names, but Haughton was about to expose his rivals as frauds. Princeton came to the Stadium with a 5–0–1 record, and even a 7–7 tie with Williams did not dampen the enthusiasm of first-year coach Wilder Penfield. "If we ever get possession of the ball inside Harvard's territory, we have 'punch' to score," he told a Boston gathering of Princeton men. "If we ever get the ball at Harvard's 20-yard-line at any stage of the contest, a Princeton touchdown, or at least a goal, will develop."[26]

Penfield was destined to be a last-year coach after his Tigers slunk away from Cambridge, having been hammered, 20–0. The 32,000 at the Stadium might have seen a larger margin; Mahan missed four field-goal tries in addition to the two he made. (Imagine if Brickley had been available.) Bradlee culminated two drives with short touchdown plunges that had been set up by the bulldozing of Francke and, on the end-around (in those days called the "end-around-end"), Hardwick.

Princeton was dominated physically, but it also was bamboozled. "Harvard Had Tigers Fooled, Often All at Sea as to Who Had the Ball," headlined the *Globe*. Explained former Harvard player Dudley Dean,

The Princeton backs lined up in formation about as did Harvard. But that was the only resemblance between the two scrimmage attacks. When [Princeton's] Driggs or Law fell back it was a punt to a moral certainty. When Mahan fell back it was any old thing. . . . The deception in handling the ball on Harvard's part was excellent, and the backs carried out their assignments splendidly. Players like Wilbur Shenk were repeatedly fooled as to what Harvard player in reality was carrying the ball, and Bradlee more than once dashed through Shenk's position after standing stock still for a couple of seconds holding the ball, while the Princeton line was pursuing the wrong Crimsonite.[27]

In other words, Haughton had drawn up a primordial halfback delay. The newspaper's W. D. Sullivan added,

Harvard' s most effective plays developed out of a formation in which the ball would be passed to a halfback starting in one direction, to be met by Hardwick, crossing at full speed in the other direction. Sometimes the halfback would tuck the ball into Tack Hardwick's arms and sometimes he wouldn't, but would turn and dart ahead through the line, which had by this time become opened up because the Tigers could never quite tell whether Hardwick had the ball as he kept on his mad rush about the field, or whether the halfback who sprinted through the line had it.[28]

The Tigers' task was further complicated by Harvard's "gentle art of bluffing." As Sullivan described it, "To add to the general confusion of Princeton forwards, the halfback who first received the ball would very cleverly hold it in one hand and make a bluff as though to throw a forward pass. Of course, the success of this series of plays all depended upon the perfect smoothness with which Hardwick, Bradlee, and Francke executed them. They did their work so well that time and again, the Princeton team would be split in halves, leaving a tremendous hole in the middle through which the man with the ball would tear along for a good gain. . . . Bradlee, who has this season developed into one of the most remarkable line breakers the game has known, fought so hard that in one of his desperate rushes he had his jersey completely torn off his back."

Summed up Webb, "A shiftier, more puzzling form of attack was probably never produced."[29]

In a newspaper column, Haughton was unsparing about the Tigers and effusive about his quarterback. "I believe Princeton's defense was at fault in theory and in its execution, and its inherent weakness was greatly magnified by the choice of plays which Logan, the Harvard quarterback, directed against it,"[30] Haughton wrote.

The following week, there was no question Harvard was looking past Brown to Yale. Haughton, most of his assistants, and almost the entire starting team traveled to Princeton's just-dedicated Palmer Stadium to scout the Elis, who withstood a Tigers rally to win, 19–14. Not only were the 40,000 who packed Palmer riveted by the action, but also the 15,000 at Harvard, who were kept abreast of the score of the game by the Stadium scoreboard. Harvard played almost all reserves and settled for a scoreless tie that at least kept intact the unbeaten streak, now at 28 games.

It was time to visit a new colossus.

✿ ✿ ✿

In 1914, reflecting their desperation, the Elis had installed as coach one of their greatest players, Frank Hinkey, All-America from 1891 to '94. As an end, he was so fierce it was said no ballcarrier ever turned him. Hinkey purged many of the old guard—even the venerated Walter Camp was not welcome at practices—and set about designing a new-fangled triple-option offense essentially built on rugby-style laterals engineered by quarterback Alex Wilson and halfback Harry LeGore. When executed properly, it had been a scourge, seemingly unstoppable, as Yale rolled to seven wins against one defeat, a 13–7 loss to Washington & Jefferson.

For The Game, the Blue's strategy was truly novel in a defensive-minded era: outscore the Crimson in a shootout. (An analogy today would be Rich Rodriguez's high-octane approach at Michigan.) Hinkey also had the revolutionary notion to use motion pictures as a practice aid. By contrast, the ever-paranoid Haughton wanted no filmed records that opponents might get their hands on.

As Mel Webb reported,

> Yale's adoption of these new offensive wrinkles has kept the coaches worrying all season at Cambridge to produce a defense adequate to

stop them. Early in the fall they imported some Canadian players from across the border, in order to see at first hand the working of the thing. In addition, the Yale games have never been played without one or more Harvard men present, taking keen note of all that went in. . . . Washington & Jefferson stopped Yale's new plays by closing in on them from the ends before the play could develop. The end either tackled the man with the ball before he could get rid of it or else got between the man with the ball and anyone to whom he could pass it, in order to intercept the pass and chase the carrier into the arms of the secondary defense. If the play continued outside the end, then the defensive backs closed in and either caught the runner or forced him to the sidelines. If the play develops into a forward pass, the defense will fall on the backfield; if there is a mere feint at a side play, and a line plunge is the reality, it will have to be stopped by the forwards.[31]

Throughout the season, sitting quietly through games and practices at New Haven, Reggie Brown assiduously had been mapping Yale. In his notebooks, he doodled formations, labeled "shown" (meaning, actual) and "possible." One variation he dubbed the Harvard 10 defense—a zone scheme, with only five men on the defensive line instead of the normal seven. The right tackle and center-rush were dropped back and responsible for a back or a receiver—"spying," as it is called today. Brown noted that his notion "has some weaknesses." If the Crimson overshifted to stop Yale's plays to the weak (left) side, then the strong side would be left entirely to a lone defensive back.[32]

As it turned out, Haughton, Brown, and the rest of the staff took Brown's concept even further. They would go with three men on the defensive line and position the rest of the defenders across the field—a spread defense for a spread offense. In essence, they were daring Yale to eschew the pitch and beat them with runs up the middle.

Yale's front seven was slightly heavier on average than Harvard's, 187 pounds to 183. This, and the magic of the Yale football brand, limited Harvard to being a mere 10–9 favorite.

Yale had an intangible, and it literally was a big one. The Game would christen the Yale Bowl, which, built at a cost of $450,000, was the Cowboys Stadium of its day and would serve as the template for huge campus stadiums. Writer Albert Barclay described how a group of Yale graduates arranged to cover the exorbitant $450,000 cost: "After the committee had tried every other scheme to raise money, they adopted a plan of selling privileges to subscribe to seats for the Bowl, which will guarantee the holder seats for a period of 15 years. Subscription for a single seat costs $200."[33] (Hmmm . . . personal seat licenses . . . what a concept.)

Architecturally, the Bowl literally broke new ground by scooping a giant hole and putting half its seats below ground, with the remainder resting on the embankment made by the excavation from the lower half. That did away with the need for steel or reinforced concrete. "The arrangement of the seats brings the spectator remarkably near to the playing field," Barclay reported. "Equally remarkable is the fact that this great structure can be filled or emptied in eight minutes. . . . This . . . is made possible by 30 underground portals which land the spectators halfway up each section of 2,000 seats."[34] The Bowl would be the model for the Rose Bowl, as well as Michigan's Big House, Georgia's Sanford Stadium, and other campus arenas.

The *Harvard Alumni Bulletin* predicted that on Saturday, November 21, New Haven would see "probably the greatest volume of passen-

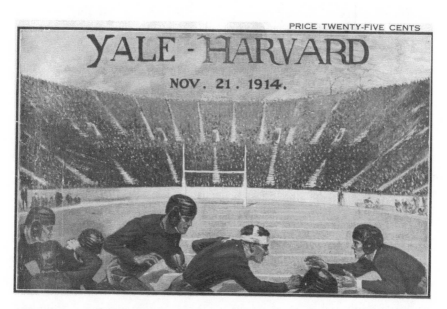

As the game program advertised, the dedication of the colossal Yale Bowl in 1914 would be as grand a spectacle—artistic, as well as sporting—as the United States ever had witnessed. *Yale University Sports Information.*

ger traffic to and from a single point, within a few hours, ever handled by any railroad in the country."[35] Moreover, reported the *New York Times*, "It is also expected that automobile traffic will be greater than any city has ever handled in one day, and special arrangements have been made for the parking of the machines in the open meadows around Yale Bowl."[36] The *Globe* reported that newlyweds Alice Reid and Daniel McCrossan (he Harvard 1907, Harvard Med 1910) were attending The Game for their honeymoon.[37] After all, there was nothing—nothing!—that could top what Mel Webb termed in his preview the "most spectacular event in the history of American sport."

When the receipts were toted up, the records of the Harvard Athletic Association put the crowd at 68,042, paying face value of $2 a ticket for a colossal gate of $136,084. (Harvard sold 24,119 tickets.)[38]

What transpired that afternoon would turn on its head every notion fostered by previous Harvard–Yale games. In the previous 22 games, the largest margin of victory had been 28 points (Yale's shutout in 1900)—which also was the most points scored by the two teams combined. Now Harvard alone was about to blow right through that total. In this mostly closely watched of all football rivalries, the scoring potency of the Crimson would herald a watershed for the sport.

To great roars, the teams emerged through the tunnels onto the floor of the Bowl. The temperature was chilly and the skies overcast as the players' cleats trod the turf, which had been softened from rain earlier in the week. There was a great buzz when the spectators looked toward the Harvard sideline. There stood Charlie Brickley—in uniform. In recent weeks, Brick had done some scrimmaging, but he was still not fully recovered from his appendectomy. There had been a rumor, however, that he might see action, and, in fact, Brickley had passed word to the Yale captain, Bud Talbott, that if he did take the field, the Elis were not to go easy on him.

Just before 2 p.m., referee Nate Tufts, a Brown alum who had supplanted longtime Game official William Langford, called the players to the field. Soon after Mahan kicked off, Harvard lost little time asserting itself.

Early in the first period, Mahan took a 45-yard punt from Yale's Foggy Ainsworth and, following his interference, weaved his way 50 yards downfield. The Crimson began hammering at the Yale line and reached the three. There, on third down, Mahan took the snap and dropped back. Every Eli defender charged at him and paid no attention to Hardwick, who had slipped behind them and into the end zone. Mahan coolly drew his right arm back and flipped him the ball. Touchdown! Harvard led, 6–0.

Yale's feared lateral attack was not igniting. In the second quarter, Harvard drove 65 yards. Haughton had found a weak spot around Yale's right flank. Mahan went for 18 yards in that direction, and Hardwick worked the end-around-end for 22. With Mahan, Francke, and Bradlee banging away at the same spot, the ball went to the Yale seven. Mahan again swung around left end but fumbled over the goal line—whereupon, after a scramble, the Big Teuton recovered it for the second Crimson touchdown.

Now, with the score 12–0 against them, the Blue got in gear. LeGore returned a punt 30 yards, and Ainsworth tossed downfield a prehistoric alley-oop, which his end, Maurice Brann, leaped up and snared in front of Bradlee. Yale was on the move, and throughout the mammoth Bowl its fans were serenading the Elis with choruses of "Bingo, Bingo!" Soon the ball was down to the Crimson four.

In many football games, there is a reversal of fortune that serves as a dagger through the heart of the loser—the blow from which it is impossible to recover. This was that moment, a play that symbolized the opposite directions of these two powers. Carroll Knowles attempted a plunge—but lost the ball. Harvard's alert Jeff Coolidge grabbed it and headed in the opposite direction, convoyed by Bradlee, a streaking bolt of Crimson. "Never did a man with a football tucked under his arm run so fast," said the *Times*.[39] Ninety-eight yards later, Coolidge touched the ball down on the goal line. Hardwick kicked the extra point. Harvard 19, Yale 0.

That was the backbreaker. Mahan added a field goal at the end of the half. In the third quarter, Harvard blocked a punt and set up on the Yale 30. Mahan ran 22 yards to the Yale one, where Francke took it over. Hardwick again booted the extra point: 29–0.

"As the third period came to an end, the Yale team was a pitiable wreck," said the *Times* the next day. His grand strategy throttled by Harvard's quickness and alertness, the "glum and silent Hinkey sat on the sidelines with his black velour hat pulled down over his eyes as he held his long black cigar between his clenched teeth."[40]

This afternoon would mark the final appearance in a Harvard jersey of the illustrious and unvanquished Group of Seven. Haughton ceremoniously pulled them. "As each old player came out," wrote the *Globe*'s W. D. Sullivan, "the great Crimson bank rose to receive him with a cheer."[41] Happily, subs streamed in to win the coveted "H," among them Alexander McKinlock.

Then came an even louder roar. With the ball on the Yale 15, in trotted a familiar figure: captain Charlie Brickley. Was he recovered enough to try a dropkick? Could he throw a pass? Or even run from scrimmage?

On the first snap, Brickley stepped back as if he were going to kick, but the ball went to Mahan, who barreled to the four. Five plays later (and after a penalty had negated a touchdown), Brickley again stepped back. But the ball was snapped to Watson, who spun a pass to the corner of the end zone, where Hardwick gathered it in. 35–0.

As Brickley told Arthur Daley of the *Times* in 1948,

> The inherent decency of intercollegiate sport was beautifully exemplified in that game . . . Yale could have crucified me because I didn't wear pads, and was very vulnerable from my operation. But as soon as I reported, Bud Talbott, the Yale captain, gathered his players around him and ordered them not to lay a hand on me. It was a sporting gesture that I'll appreciate to my dying day.

Now for the extra point. Brickley stood on the 15. "It was the only occasion when he was nervous or unsure of himself," Daley related. "He juggled the pass from center and booted a wobbly dropkick that barely cleared the crosspiece and barely stayed inside the uprights."[42] Referee Tufts raised his arm, signaling that the kick was good. Harvard 36, Yale 0. It was Brickley's 215th point for the Crimson, a school record that would not be exceeded for 91 years.

After the game, the common gibe was that "Yale supplied the Bowl, but Harvard had the punch." The margin was incomprehensible to longtime observers and captured in the florid tones of the day. Wrote the *Times* in its front-page story by Harry Cross,

> Harvard's overpowering football team carried its merciless warfare, undaunted, into the new Yale Bowl on this fair November afternoon and left a mark of dedication which is stamped more indelibly on the

minds of the sons of Yale than if it was chiseled yards high on the cold concrete walls of old Eli's massive amphitheater. . . . When the men of Yale in the four corners of the globe hear the score, they won't believe it. And yet Harvard smashed, bruised, and jostled Frank Hinkey's team, the great hope of a Yale football revival, over the soft verdant turf until they had crushed them, without pity, under a 36 to 0 score.

Moreover, the paper declared, "New Haven was as quiet tonight as Wappingers Falls on a rainy day."[43]

Quiet, that is, except for the raucous Crimson victory party at New Haven's two-year-old Hotel Taft. "Saturday night after the game the Harvard players had some amusing stories to tell," wrote Mel Webb. He continued,

> One of these drew a general laugh and is worth repeating. Late in the game and when Harvard had secured all its points, the Yale team, in putting on all it had in its effort to get a touchdown, was none too keen on signals. This exasperated Capt. Talbott, who "went after" one of his linemen—the Harvard men think either Conroy, White, or Betts. "What's the matter?" called Talbott, "can't you remember those signals?" And then the reply came back: "How do you think I can keep track of the signals when I can't even count the touchdowns?"[44]

What Harvard could not celebrate is a third-straight mythical national championship. James Vautravers of Tiptop25.com sums up the weakness of the Crimson's case:

> There can be little doubt that Harvard's starting lineup was the most powerful football team in America. Problem is, Harvard's starting lineup only actually started the first two games, against patsies. After that, almost every starter was lost to injury, and Harvard ended up suffering two upset ties, finishing 7–0–2. That left the door open for 7–0 Illinois and 9–0 Army to be selected as 1914 national champions decades later.

He adds,

> Harvard was healthy for [Brown] but chose to play nothing but substitutes so as to ensure the health of their starters for Yale. Basically,

Harvard just didn't care if they beat Brown or not. So does that mean the tie doesn't count? Several of the better-known Eastern writers of the time thought so. And I can see their point. Harvard's regulars didn't play against Brown, so in a way it's like Harvard's "JV" team was taking them on rather than Harvard's varsity team. But to me it says a lot about Harvard coach Percy Haughton's competitive fire. I cannot imagine Fielding Yost, Bear Bryant, or Bobby Bowden, as examples, *ever* conceding a loss or tie for any reason. Certainly not so they could increase their chances in a following rivalry game by a couple of percentage points. These guys played to win—*every game.* That's what champions do. And if Harvard wanted to concede a tie to a mediocre Brown team, hey, that's their decision, but to me it is not the decision of a champion. It's just the decision of a "Big Three" champion.[45]

Touché. On the other hand, as Fred Moore had noted, when the score is 36 to 0 against Yale, the season is a smashing success. National championship or no, this might have been Haughton's best coaching job to date. He lost one superstar, Brickley, for most of the season, and another, Mahan, for significant portions. Yet, his System ensured that Bradlee, Hardwick, Pennock, and Trumbull were able to carry the load. These four, with Mahan, were named to Walter Camp's All-America team. Writing in the *ESPN College Football Encyclopedia*, published in 2005, esteemed sportswriter Dan Jenkins claimed that had there been a Heisman Trophy in 1914, Mahan would have won it. But the versatile Tack probably was Harvard's MVP, and he was deservedly a consensus All-America.

Some 700 alumni crammed into the banquet room of Boston's Copley Square Hotel to fete the team. Brickley and Trumbull spoke. But as the *Alumni Bulletin* reported, the house was brought down "by a visitor who was introduced as Professor Chang Loy Soong of the Imperial University." Added the *Bulletin*,

He spoke at some length in Chinese, and his remarks were "interpreted" by R. C. Benchley, '12. No one in the room understood what the distinguished visitor said, and it may be assumed that he did not know what Mr. Benchley said. Some parts of the latter's "interpretation" were astonishing.[46]

Soon, Robert Benchley would be entertaining larger audiences as one of America's premier humorists.

* * *

Charlie Brickley was not done with Yale. In June, on Soldiers Field, in the annual best-of-three baseball series, his ninth-inning double brought home the tying run; then he scored the series-winner on a single. Recounted the *Bulletin*, "Memorable was the sight of Brickley, the idol of this moment, as of many others, squatting as complacent as a Buddha on second base while the spectators shouted themselves hoarse and waved themselves lame."[47]

The members of the class of '15 would be graduated in June with a 25–0–2 varsity record. At commencement, Jeff Coolidge, the end who had broken Yale's back, was recognized as a member of Phi Beta Kappa with an A.B. in mathematics, magna cum laude. One of the addresses was given by still-capitalizing graduating senior E. E. Cummings, who spoke on "The New Art."

On the frontispiece of the athletics section in the class of 1915 album, there are verses by another 1915 commencement speaker, class poet Lionel de Jersey "Johnny" Harvard, an English lad who had attended the college on scholarship and was, in fact, the first man with the surname Harvard to matriculate at the school. They read,

> These thy sons who fearless
> side by side
> Gave of their best to bring
> fair Harvard fame,
> Nor thought of self, nor
> counted e'er the cost
> In eager race or game.[48]

Less than three years later, Johnny Harvard, a lieutenant commanding a British company, would be mortally wounded opposing the German spring offensive at Arras.

10

POOR ELI'S HOPES WE ARE DASHING

The torch now was Eddie Mahan's to carry.

"Football times . . . have changed," wrote Mel Webb of the *Boston Globe*. He continued,

> The requisites for a successful team no longer are power and weight, but the presence on the 11s of real athletic types of college manhood; men who are agile, quick of action, intelligent, and fellows who can comprehend and then put on a brand of football the basis of which is shiftiness rather than an old-time ability to beat down an opponent by means of a trip-hammer attack. [1]

In essence, during the span of a half-dozen years, the ideal player had evolved from the bull-like Percy Wendell to the speedy, elusive, and multiskilled Mahan. As long as Harvard had Eddie, it was a threat to win any game.

In October, Grantland Rice would indicate Mahan's place in the pantheon. "A football camp follower from Pittsburgh desires to know the name of the greatest all-around football player that ever lived," wrote Rice. "It sounds simple enough, but take it home and try it on your harmonica. There is Ted Coy, and there is Jim Thorpe. They are close enough together to split the vote. And there is Mahan and there is Brickley." [2]

But who would block for Ned? To whom could he throw his halfback pass? He'd be a marked man for every opponent thirsting to smack him to the turf and end that unbeaten streak, now at 29 games. Sure, he's

A Walter Camp All-America halfback in each of his three seasons, elusive Eddie Mahan had to carry the load after the Group of Seven graduated. Mahan was such a powerful and precise punter that even the notoriously meddlesome Haughton chose not to mess with his style. *Harvard University Sports Information.*

great, they sneered, but let's see how he does without Brick, Tack, and Peebo. The foes who could stop Mahan also would humble the oh-so-arrogant Percy D. Haughton and wipe the grins off the smug, self-important Crimson faces.

System? Bah!

❖ ❖ ❖

Although still distant, the drums of war were pulsing ever louder as Haughton, captain Mahan, and the rest of the Harvard football squad assembled on Soldiers Field on Monday, September 13, for the first practice of the 1915 season. The United States had stayed out of the Great War, and President Woodrow Wilson had asked Americans to be "neutral in thought, as well as deed," but most sympathized with the Allies, particularly after a German U-boat had torpedoed the British liner *Lusitania* in May.

"Not for a moment was the Harvard community neutral in thought or deed," wrote history professor and future university historian Samuel Eliot Morison. Returning from a year at the University of California, he noted that at Berkeley, the war "had seemed to the average student as unreal as the Wars of the Roses." In Cambridge, by contrast, "one was on the outskirts of the battle."[3]

This feeling had been heightened in the summer of 1915, when many from the university attended a military preparedness camp in Plattsburg, New York. The bivouac for reserve officer trainees, which stretched from August 10 to September 6, was the brainchild of U.S. Army major general Leonard Wood (Harvard M.D., 1884), who was advised in the endeavor by Harvard president A. Lawrence Lowell and former president Theodore Roosevelt, now a member of the university's Board of Overseers. Of the 1,600 encamped—most drawn from the upper reaches of society—more than 500 had a Harvard affiliation, including Haughton, who was shown in the August 15 *Boston Globe* wearing khaki and a campaign hat,[4] and who was in the machine-gun squad with former players Hamilton Fish and Dick Wigglesworth. There also were 84 undergraduates, among them varsity quarterback Don Watson. That fall, Lowell induced Wood to teach a class in military science, in which some 560 enrolled.

Martial fervor, however, had not yet eclipsed football fever—or pennant fever, for that matter. In the fall of 1915, rookie southpaw Babe Ruth was finishing a season in which he would go 18–8, with a 2.44 ERA, for the Red Sox, winners of the World Series in five games over Grover Cleveland Alexander and the Philadelphia Phillies. But for the first time in three seasons, there was trepidation. Harvard's unbeaten streak seemed eminently snappable. The varsity was larded with untested material. Graduation had essentially cost two-thirds of an All-America team: Fred Bradlee, Charlie Brickley (who was coaching Johns Hopkins and bylining a syndicated newspaper column), Jeff Coolidge, Hugo Francke, Tack Hardwick (an assistant coach at Navy), Stan Pennock, Wally Trumbull, and Mal Logan. Moreover, trusted ends coach Leo Leary had decided not to return. Of those who had started against Yale at the Bowl, only Mahan and two fellow seniors, tackle Ken Parson and center-rush Don Wallace, were back, although Wallace's scholastic eligibility was in question.

This being Harvard, Haughton had players on his assembly line who were familiar with the system. In the backfield were the ponies, seniors Alexander McKinlock, Bob King, and Wink Rollins. Up from the freshmen team came a number of candidates, most prominently halfback Tommy Enwright, an Exeter product alleged to have vaguely Wendel-lesque punch. The quarterback situation was unsettled: Dumpy Watson (so nicknamed for his physique), who had been Logan's principal backup in '14, was in a duel with the hero of the Penn State game, speed merchant Willie Willcox. Still another hopeful was senior Jack Doherty, another Boston Latin lad. Like several other seniors, Doherty might finally win his "H" if The Game was another blowout.

One consolation for Haughton was that however unformed his roster was, his Big Three rivals had bigger problems. At New Haven, Frank Hinkey was back as coach, still smarting over the defeat in the Bowl. Worse, there were rumblings that he might lose his best player, halfback Harry LeGore, over allegations that LeGore had received money for playing summer baseball. (Eventually LeGore was ruled ineligible.) At Princeton, the Tigers had turned to John "Speedy" Rush, their fifth coach in six seasons (and their first ever to be paid), to try to right the ship.

For the first time in many years, rules changes were at a minimum. A forward pass thrown out of bounds was now an incompletion, and the ball was brought back to the line of scrimmage; it could no longer be used as a de facto punt. In essence, players, coaches, and fans were satisfied with what the game had become.

Now if only someone could knock the cocksure Crimson off its perch.

✧ ✧ ✧

As usual, the first four weeks offered little hope for Harvard haters.

The opener on September 25, against overmatched Colby and played in front of 8,000 at the Stadium, went according to preliminary-game form. In the 39–6 victory, the Harvard regulars played the first half only but still gained 240 yards on 28 snaps. "Delayed pass plays . . . foxed" the Mules, reported the *Globe*.[5] Mahan scored twice and kicked two extra points; he also busted loose for runs of 31 and 41 yards, the latter from kick formation. Colby's long passes mostly fizzled, but it was seen as ominous that the Mules actually scored (albeit against the subs) and made 10 first downs.

The next week, a one–two punch of the weather and the Massachusetts Aggies (today the University of Massachusetts Minutemen) almost broke the streak. Fifteen hundred hardy souls took refuge in the covered colonnade section and watched the teams wallow in the rain and muck. Remarkably, there were no fumbles. Mahan sat out with a strained ligament. Crimson quarterback Dumpy Watson essayed nothing fancy. Harvard made only five first downs and gained 96 yards total. As the game neared its end, Willie Willcox tried the same kind of dash that had salvaged the Penn State game the year before, but he was bogged down. "The Harvard players had plenty of experience Saturday as mud horses,"[6] Webb wrote. With a tie (and a moral victory) in the bag, Palmer, the Aggies' quarterback, tried a pass. Harassed by senior end Ernie Soucy, Palmer threw it into the arms of the Crimson's Dick Harte, who sloshed the 30 yards for the score, providing a typically Haughtonesque 7–0 win, one born of waiting for a break and capitalizing. The streak was at 31.

Meanwhile, in New Haven: Yale was losing to lightly regarded Virginia, 10–0—heretofore an almost unimaginable defeat. In the following week, there were rumors that Hinkey would resign. "This fall the undergraduates have already begun to protest," said the *Globe*, which added, "Ex-president Taft's [younger] son [Charles, a sophomore] has been tried several times this week in the backfield."[7]

With Carlisle coming to town, there were lineup shuffles in Cambridge, too. Most significant was the switch at quarterback, to Willcox. "Willcox and Mahan a speed combination which cannot be overlooked," noted the *Globe*.[8] At running back, sophomore Enwright moved in for McKinlock—then promptly blew out a knee in practice. Veterans Parson and Harte were also displaced. Possibly, Haughton saw complacency creeping in and wanted to eradicate it. He was right to be worried. The next two games loomed as traps: Carlisle, the last team to have beaten the Crimson, and Virginia, conqueror of Yale.

The Indians, however, were not the same juggernaut that had outplayed Harvard in 1911. They lacked two main ingredients from that Stadium shocker: Jim Thorpe, who was now playing pro baseball, and Pop Warner, now coaching Pitt. (The new Carlisle coach was Texan V. M. Kelly.) This time they were dispatched rather handily, 29–7. Harvard scored the first 23 points. "The Indians did not display the craft that they had when they were under Glenn Warner even though their only score did result from a deceitful double pass," reported the *Globe*. (The details shared front-page space with the account of the Red Sox's 2–1 victory in Game 2 of the World Series in Philadelphia, a contest witnessed by President Wilson and his new bride, Edith Bolling Galt.) Mahan scored the first Crimson touchdown on a 35-yard punt return, on which he daringly took the ball on the fly. McKinlock scored another on an 80-yard interception return. "The interference of the Harvard men prevented the Indians from catching him," said the *Globe*.[9] The streak was at 32.

The next week, more than 14,000 showed up at the Stadium to see if the Cavaliers would take down another Big Three member. Once again, they did not allow a touchdown. But the Harvard defense was even more dominant, holding Virginia to one first down. Mahan booted three field goals, which stood up for a 9–0 victory. "Ned Mahan . . . surely stood as Harvard's lifesaver against Virginia," wrote Mel Webb, who then conferred the ultimate accolade:

> With him in the game there is no need to mourn for Brickley; for Mahan is as accurate as Brickley was and is a much surer shot at distances farther from the goal than 35 yards. Mahan's three goals all were clean against the Southerners, and his longest, that of 41 yards,

would have scored had the Harvard leader been stationed 12 yards
farther back.[10]

Webb went on to extol Mahan's "remarkable" punting:

> On Saturday it was so good as to demand more than a passing note.
> While he played, Mahan made 10 punts, and his kicks covered a total
> of 417 yards. This is an average of nearly 42 yards. His punts, in
> order, were for 37, 45, 38, 40, 38, 35, 51, 43, 42, and 48 yards.
> Mahan's ends held every inch of distance on three of the kicks,
> including the one he made 40 yards down the field while standing far
> back of his goal line. There were runbacks of two and three yards,
> one of five yards, three of seven yards, and one of eight yards—39
> yards in all—making Mahan's final [net] average on his 10 punts 37
> 8/10th yards . . . while on the 48-yard punt, which was Mahan's last,
> the end rushers were slow in getting down.[11]

Outkicking the coverage was a Haughton shibboleth, but in every other
respect Mahan was performing by the Book According to Percy.

The unbeaten streak had reached 33, but it was hanging there like
an underthrown pass. And Cornell was the perfect team to pluck it.

❁ ❁ ❁

Today, we would say this game had national championship implications.
Like the Crimson, the "Ezrans" (so nicknamed after founder Ezra Cornell) were 4–0, having outscored their foes 134–13. In quarterback
Charley Barrett, Cornell had the one player in the nation who could
match Mahan as a triple threat. Barrett already had scored 10 of Cornell's 20 touchdowns. (Harvard had 11.) Cornell coach Al Sharpe, a
former Yale player, was confident. "It will take all that Harvard has to
beat this team," he told a mass meeting in Ithaca. Added the *Globe*,
"Dr. Sharpe says he saw no reason why Cornell should not tally one or
two touchdowns, or maybe a field goal or two."[12] Sharpe should have
put money on that prediction. Perhaps he did. Harvard men were giving odds of 5 to 3, but Cornellians were holding out for 2 to 1.

Traveling with the Cornell party to Cambridge would be their mas-
cot, a bear named Touchdown, who would appear on the sidelines with
his keepers.

A crowd of 25,000 turned out. As the game began, Touchdown the Bear was nowhere to be seen. Apparently, he had been kidnapped. Harvard had its own concerns. Early in the first period, Mahan, trying to get the Crimson out of a hole, fumbled on his 25. Murray Shelton, Cornell's All-America end, pounced on the ball. Six plays later, behind an unbalanced line, Barrett barreled over the left side from the three for a touchdown, then booted the extra point.

Thereafter, the teams traded blown opportunities. On Mahan's returns, Cornell kept him in the middle of the field. Thrice more he fumbled, leading to two Cornell recoveries. In the third quarter, he threw an interception. On one of his runs, he collided with Barrett, who was knocked out of the game. But this smashup, or others, also may have made Mahan wobbly enough to cause his turnovers.

The third quarter saw a signature exchange. Punting with the wind, Mahan plastered one that ended up 70 yards downfield. Cornell's kicker, halfback Fritz Shiverick, had a low, boring trajectory on his boots. Standing on his three, he unleashed a punt that ended up on the Crimson 14—some 83 yards downfield. Then, early in the fourth quarter, Cornell worked the ball to the Harvard 30. On fourth down, Shiverick dropped back to the 38 to try a field goal from a difficult angle. If he made it, the game, and the streak, would be as good as over.

The ball was snapped. "The Harvard rushers . . . were where it would seem certain that they would beat the ball down as it left the kicker's boot," said the *Globe*.[13] But they didn't. To the delight of the Ezrans, the ball sailed through the uprights. That was the clincher. Cornell 10, Harvard 0.

Touchdown had shown up in time to see the denouement. "According to all accounts, some detective work on the part of the Cornell football supporters resulted in the discovery of the bear's place of imprisonment"—the Harvard baseball cage—"and his rescue was affected early enough for his appearance in the Stadium during the game," said the *Globe*.[14]

For the first time in 1,442 days, the Crimson had lost. Live by the breaks, die by the breaks. "The thousands in the Stadium yesterday received one very distinct shock," wrote Webb. "This was to see Ned Mahan, rated as the country's very best football player, plunge into the midst of what was a prize package in the way of an off day."[15] Grantland Rice was philosophical. "Harvard was merely due," he wrote, adding,

Within the long span of five and a half seasons, the Crimson banner had come down but twice. Through this period Harvard's reign had been as complete as Yale's used to be in the old days of Yale glory. The wonder is not that Harvard was at last stopped, but that she was able to show such mastery for so long a time.[16]

In tears, Mahan apologized to Haughton for his subpar effort. According to Mahan's 1975 obituary in the *Boston Globe*, the coach put his hand on his star's shoulder. "Mahan," said P. D., "you are the greatest football player God ever made."[17]

According to Mahan, this was little solace. "I was feeling pretty blue until the Monday after the game, when the coaches picked 11 men as the varsity team," he told author William Edwards for the 1916 book *Football Days*. Said Mahan,

Just as soon as they sent these 11 men to a section of the field to get acquainted with each other—that was the beginning of team work. From the way those fellows went at it that day, and from the spirit they showed, we felt that no team could ever lick us again, neither Princeton nor Yale. The Cornell game acted like a tonic on the whole crowd. Instead of disheartening the team, it instilled in us determination. We said, "We know what it is to be licked, and we'll be damned if we'll be licked again."[18]

* * *

Speaking of Yale, that Saturday, as big a story as Cornell's snapping the streak was, Yale's 16–7 loss to Washington & Jefferson was perhaps bigger. The Elis now were 3–2, and everyone was trying to explain the "Blue Slump." Rice quoted Haughton:

"We have been beating Yale by using stuff that she had forgotten." By this Haughton meant certain fundamentals that were always a big part of the old Yale system. Yale's victories in the past were mainly due to the fact that she could block, tackle, and charge better than any rival. In these more than important fundamentals, Yale is weaker than even the average 11 that isn't supposed to carry any unusual class.[19]

The next day, Rice unsheathed an analogy made for Prof. Copeland's English class: "Yale still has a chance to attain the hights [*sic*] by beating Colgate, Princeton, and Harvard. And we have a chance to attain fair literary renown by writing better verse than Byron and better prose than Thackeray."[20]

With October fading into the twilight, Haughton could not worry about Yale's deficiencies. P. D. had to regroup and prepare his own team for the second half of the season. On October 30, in front of 15,000 at the Stadium, Penn State was handled rather routinely, 13–0. Again, however, the larger headline came out of New Haven—and it was on page one of the entire paper. Yale had lost to Colgate, 15–0. Quarterback Alex Wilson "asserted the traditional prerogative of Yale captains, namely that, 'the captain is king'" and "deposed" Hinkey as coach, reported the *Globe*.[21] (Author Mark Bernstein has written that Hinkey was "forced out because his smoking, foul language, and heavy drinking offended [Walter] Camp.")[22]

While Yale stewed, Haughton was cooking up something for the Crimson's only road game, at Princeton. If any contest during his tenure contained at least a little of every element of Haughton's genius and forethought, this would be it. The coach was determined that the Crimson would not be beaten by straight-ahead power football. What P. D. came up with would be celebrated in a report in *Harper's Weekly* by erudite correspondent Herbert Reed. Its title was "Harvard: Gridiron Deceiver."

As Reed explained, Haughton had tinkered with a new wrinkle for the forward pass: the timing pattern.

> Harvard's was the first system, if memory serves, to decide that the ball should be thrown not to a man, but to a spot at which a man, generally an end, but sometimes a back, was due to arrive. There was a controversy over the danger of the play at the time, but since the crossing end generally took the ball in front of a wall of Crimson players coming down the field, the danger of a runback was not great, even were the pass to be intercepted. Further, it was harder for the defense to cover the man taking the pass, because it also had to judge the direction and speed of the ball, as well as the man. Harvard's great deception lay in working up this pass in private to a remarkable degree of mechanical excellence, and using it in public very sparingly.[23]

On the first Saturday in November, a packed house of 35,000 showed up for the Crimson's first visit to two-year-old Palmer Stadium. So far, to open his tenure, Tigers coach Speedy Rush had been as good as his preseason word. His team was 6–0; had outscored foes, 123–10; and had thumped Dartmouth, 30–7. A victory over Harvard would leave only Yale in Princeton's way for the national title.

In the early going, the teams felt each other out. After six interchanges of punts, Harvard had first down on Princeton's 40-yard line. That's when Haughton and quarterback Dumpy Watson sprung their quick strike. A century later, what is notable is the sophistication and complexity of the thought and execution.

Recounted Reed,

> This time, Watson waited until third down, first fussing the Tiger defense with [runs by sophomore Billy] Boles and Mahan, and then protecting the pass as he had previously protected the kicker with a wheeling line to the kicker's right side. It looked like a kick or a run but turned out to be a pass. Watson had mixed up his downs perfectly, with the result that Harte, a tall end with a long reach, snatched the ball for a long gain.

In fact, Watson had tossed it to the prearranged spot at which he assumed Harte, crossing the field from the right end, would arrive. A photo of the play shows Harte "well in the clear," as the caption put it. The advance was 20 yards.

"With only 25 yards to go Harvard started to turn on power," continued Reed. "One play failed, and then Mahan stepped back to kicking position to draw the attention of the Orange and Black." Harte swung by as if on an end-around, but the "ball was slipped to King." He faked a toss to Harte, then "set sail for Princeton's weak left side." Reed added,

> McLean, the tackle, slipped as he met the play, King shot past him, and the ultimate defense was [Dave] Tibbott. This good player slowed up, however, thinking the play stopped, and the hard-running Harvard back went over the line for a touchdown, from which a goal was promptly kicked. The quarter was perfectly handled by Watson, who showed not merely orthodoxy, but *finesse* in his generalship.

As the November 10 installment of the *Harvard Alumni Bulletin* summed up in its account, "The suddenness of the [score], made in the three plays from the center of the field, astonished both spectators and players."[24]

In the second period, after a fair catch by Watson on the Princeton 41, Mahan booted a field goal from placement. Princeton rallied in the second half with two Tibbott field goals, but the 10–6 score held up. At game's end, Mahan felt he had redeemed the loss to Cornell. Reported the *Globe* later,

> When the whistle blew, it was some seconds before the Harvard captain realized that the game was over. Then his face lighted up [*sic*] with the happiness he felt, and, throwing up both hands, he exclaimed, so that he was heard on the front seats of the Palmer Stadium, "There goes the whistle, and the game is ours!"[25]

Said Haughton proudly, "Harvard today defeated the best team she has played against since I have been coaching at Cambridge."[26]

Reed was even more admiring. "Harvard, the deceiver, outkicked and outgeneraled one of the best 11s the Tigers have ever turned out, and furthermore did not fumble," he wrote. "You cannot make mistakes, both of the head and the hand, and hope to beat the Crimson."[27]

Again, a Harvard victory had to share headlines with a Yale defeat. Brown beat the Elis, 3–0. The Bulldogs now handed over the coaching reins to another of their immortals, hard-driving Tom Shevlin, who from 1902 to '05 had made All-America at end every season. He also had been involved in a controversy when, in the '05 Game, he leveled a Harvard punt returner who had signaled for a fair catch; the incident remained fresh in memory. Now, with alma mater calling, Shevlin hightailed it to New Haven from his Minnesota lumber business. The hope was that, along with installing his "Minnesota shift," he would at least instill some fight for the game with heavily favored Princeton at the Bowl.

Harvard, of course, was looking to Yale, and thus looking past Brown, its next foe. The Bruins were headed to the Rose Bowl (they would lose in Pasadena to Washington State, 14–0) and featured two players who would loom large in football history. One was guard Wallace Wade, later a Hall of Fame coach of national champions at Alabama. The other was former Crimson-for-a-day Fritz Pollard. Already, the 155-pound Pollard had shown flashes of greatness and earned the nickname the "Bronze Mahan." Playing against the subs, Pollard put on a show for the 30,000 in attendance at the Stadium. "Pollard was whirl-wind on the offense," wrote the *Globe*. "He gathered momentum so quickly that by the time he hit the line he was moving so fast that he slipped from the grasp of the Harvard tacklers."[28] But he also was a bit of a goat when his fumble set up the first Harvard touchdown in a 16–7 Crimson victory.

Meanwhile, in New Haven, Haughton and many of his starters were among the 57,000 in the Bowl witnessing a "Shevlinized" Yale team shock Princeton, 13–7. Yale won on breaks; the Elis offense was never past the Princeton 40. The Tigers outgained Yale, 238 to 112, with 187 yards on the ground and 51 through the air (on 5-for-18 passing). No doubt Haughton took keen note of this disparity.

The victory brought Yale to .500, but, more importantly, it put The Game in an entirely new light. Shevlin was openly disdainful of Haughton's System, sneering, "What is a football system? It is nothing. The Haughton System is one year older than last year, but you can't say the Harvard team is as good a team as that of last year. . . . What is needed is football men, real ones. It's the men, the real football men, that count."[29] Above all, he believed he had resuscitated the vaunted "Yale Spirit" that had frustrated so many Crimson teams in the past. "Watch us against Harvard, boy, watch us!" Shevlin enthused in the flush of the victory over Princeton.[30]

Shevlin sounded suspiciously like France's Marshal Joffre referring to the élan vital of his poilus. In fact, even "Over There" Harvard men working with the American Ambulance Field Service were co-opting battlefield strategy for football. The *Harvard Alumni Bulletin* printed a letter from Stephen Galatti, '10 (and backup quarterback during the '09 season):

> The "Harvard Club of Alsace Reconquise" [associated with the American Ambulance Field Service] came into being on the night before the Yale football game and [sent] a telegram to Percy Haughton advising him how to beat Yale by Joffre tactics. The [telegram] was censored by unsympathetic officials.[31]

The Harvard team appeared above the fray. On the Thursday before The Game, after running through a signal drill at the Stadium in front of 1,500 cheering undergraduates led by track star and class of 1916 first marshal William J. Bingham (a future Harvard athletic director),

the squad and coaches repaired to the Vesper Country Club in Tyngs-
boro, Massachusetts. "Golf will hold a more prominent part in the exer-
cise today than football," reported the *Globe* on Friday. "Many of the
men left Cambridge with golf bags, and even before departing many
games were arranged between some of the men."[32]

The links were an oasis from the madhouse that was Cambridge.

* * *

On Game day, all 47,997 tickets (the official count), priced at $2, had
long since been sold out; graduate manager Fred Moore said he could
have sold 200,000. "Such tickets as have reached the 'specs' [specula-
tors] are commanding almost unheard-of prices," reported the *Globe*.

> Yesterday two seats in the wooden bleachers at the open end of the
> Stadium were sold for $38, and seats in the "horseshoe" brought $33
> and $35 a pair. The more choice seats upon either side of the field
> sold like hot cakes and usually brought from $40 to $50 a pair. One
> dealer in tickets paid $8 for two seats on the 35-yard line and sold
> them for $50, while another, who paid $20 for a brace of seats be-
> tween the 45-yard line and the middle of the field, refused $60 for
> them, saying he had been requested to reserve them until this fore-
> noon, when the prospective purchaser will part with $75 for them.[33]

While there would be 173 extra parlor cars ascending from New
York to Cambridge, the automobile was coming to the fore. The pregame estimate was that 12,000 fans would be transported by more than
3,000 motor vehicles, about 1,000 more than had assembled on Soldiers
Field two years before.[34] At 2 p.m. on Saturday, November 20, as the
spectators filed into the Stadium, they were asked to contribute to a
collection for European war relief.[35]

It had rained earlier in the week, giving Yale hope that a soggy
Stadium turf might slow Harvard down. Now it was sunny but cold—
Crimson weather. But the *Yale Daily News* sounded a hopeful note: "In
kicking, Yale should be fully equal to Harvard. . . . The Harvard rush
line from tackle to tackle averages 192 pounds and includes four veteran players. The Yale line averages 191 pounds, so there is little to
choose in this respect."[36]

"It is Mahan's last game for Harvard," Charlie Brickley had written in his syndicated column, "and I predict it will be his best."[37] Harvard quarterback Dumpy Watson was more succinct. Anticipating Joe Namath by a little more than 53 years, he told friends at his home in Milton that the Crimson would run rings around the Elis.[38]

It did not start out that way, although Mahan won the toss and took the wind. Early in the first quarter, during an exchange of kicks, Yale dropped Otis Guernsey back into punt formation. The Crimson charged to block him. But the ball was slipped instead to halfback Alex Wilson, who dashed 33 yards to the Crimson 25. Was Shevlin, Shift, and Spirit to be the formula? No.

On the next play, Yale's Bob Bingham—brother of Harvard first marshal Bill—coughed up the ball. Little Bob King pounced on it. On Harvard's first down, Watson called out the signals, and Yale expected a run. But reversing Yale's strategy, Don Wallace snapped the ball to Mahan, who blasted a long, high boot. It was, as former Yale star Billy Bull termed it, one of Mahan's "famous twisters"—particularly hard to handle. Wilson had left only quarterback Howell Van Nostrand deep enough to receive it. Trying to keep an eye on the hurtling Crimson coverage, as well as the ball, Van Nostrand hesitated. The ball glanced off his hands, took a bounce, then another—into the mitts of the on-rushing Dick Harte. Convoyed by Ernie Soucy and Joe Gilman, Harte sped into the end zone. It was the first touchdown scored by Harvard against Yale in seven Games at the Stadium.

"Up rose the great Crimson bank on the west side, and such a shriek of exultant cheering was never before heard at the Stadium," wrote W. D. Sullivan of the *Globe*.[39]

Mahan missed the extra point. It was only 6–0, and there were more than 50 minutes to play, but postgame observers would claim that Yale's back already was broken. The reversal of fortune was deemed the "psychological blow."

What ensued was the most astonishing beatdown achieved to date in a "championship game." (In later football terms, it is comparable to the Chicago Bears' 73–0 slaughter of the Washington Redskins in the 1940 NFL Championship Game.) Later in the period, Harvard got the ball at its 43 and drove in nine plays for a touchdown. Haughton's viewing of the Yale–Princeton game had shown him one of the Bulldogs' main weaknesses: In attempting to "follow the ball," the Elis were vulnerable to being mousetrapped. They also were confused by Harvard's offensive-line "wheel shift," which might indicate the direction the play was going—or might not. And the clever Watson mixed up his plays, first probing the right side, then the left, then feinting. Finally, from the one, Mahan followed the right side of the line and banged over. This time he kicked the point. Harvard 13, Yale 0.

The Elis hoped that getting the wind in the second quarter might turn things around, but they were not to cross midfield. That's where Harvard began another drive. It bogged down at the 15, and the Crimson assumed a dropkick formation, with Mahan appearing ready to add three more points. Instead, the ball was snapped to Watson. He faked to each of the other backs, King and sophomore Ralph Horween. Who had the ball? The Yale players did not know, but they scattered to cover the flanks. Watson then tucked the ball into Mahan's gut. He blasted right through the wide-open goal line, bowling over the last Eli defender. Most of the spectators did not realize it was a touchdown; they thought Mahan was part of the interference. Mahan added the point. 20–0.

Four minutes later, from the Harvard 43, after Watson executed yet another series of hidden-ball fakes, "little black-haired King" found a gaping hole in the middle, then cut to the right. "Down went one blue-stockinged player after another," wrote Sullivan, "bowled over by the charging boys in the Crimson jerseys, and on sped King down the sidelines. He ran 57 yards and scored." Mahan again sent the ball through the uprights. 27–0.

At halftime, the buzz in the stands was not only Harvard's intelligent attack, but also the way the Crimson line was manhandling the Blue's, blowing open huge holes and, on defense, stopping the shift plays cold. No Yale team had been so completely whipped. "Between the halves on the Harvard side they discussed the size of the score, and some bets were made that it would exceed the score of a year ago. . . . Over in the Yale banks of seats they could only sit quietly and wait for the slaughter."[40]

It continued in the third quarter. Harvard sub end Charlie Coolidge (repeating the feat of cousin Jeff the year before) recovered a fumble. Watson completed two passes to take the Crimson to the Yale five. Three plays later, Mahan scored again and added the point. 34–0.

How snakebitten was Yale? Wilson took a pass and ran 35 yards for a score, which was called back by an offside penalty. In the fourth quarter, the Elis drove to the Crimson five, where Harvard stiffened. On fourth down, Yale's Joseph Neville attempted to at least break the shutout by trying a field goal. Wide left.

As the coup de grace, a Yale pass fell into the hands of Wink Rollins, who returned it 35 yards, setting up a completed pass, some rushing by McKinlock, and one more—one last—touchdown run and conversion by Mahan. He had scored 29 points on the day.

It was 41–0. If a bettor had taken the "over" on topping the '14 margin, he had won. Haughton mercifully cleared his bench, allowing such faithful scrubs as McKinlock, Jack Doherty, and Harry Atkinson to make an appearance and earn their H's. (On the day, 23 players won a letter.) When the keeper called time, reported Sullivan, "victors and vanquished cheered each other. The two captains shook hands heartily, for they are warm personal friends, having spent all last summer in the same camp at Gales Ferry." Head Harvard cheerleader Bill Bingham, ever solicitous of his brother, urged the Crimson fans not to gloat. After all, they were all gentlemen.

❀ ❀ ❀

At the Harvard locker building, the crowd demanded a curtain call from Haughton. He appeared, reported the *Globe*, "wearing his happiest and broadest 1915 smile." P. D. declared,

> "Well, just now I haven't much to say, except that this is the happiest moment of my life, and that as I haven't had a chance to congratulate Eddie Mahan yet, I think I'll hurry right in and do so." . . . Inside Haughton went directly to the shower baths, where his able pupils were removing the grime of the contest. Without thought of the widely spraying showers, Haughton boyishly rushed in and grabbed Mahan by the hand. . . . That handshake and smile from Haughton was Mahan's honorable discharge from the service. Percy Haughton's smile and grip is the Iron Cross in Harvard football. In this incident lies a hint of Haughton's ability to handle his men and the wonderful hold he gets on their respect and affections.[41]

In four years' worth of victories, Harvard had humiliated Yale, 112–5. Haughton had seen superstars and vaunted role players depart, and simply had developed men, many with less physical talent, to replace them, all while keeping the Crimson one step ahead of the pack. In the riotous Harvard dressing room, Mahan acknowledged as much in an oration, saying, "Fellows, Percy Haughton told you that the team had 'guts,' and today the team proved that statement. But let me tell you that it was Haughton that gave the team the guts. Let's give three cheers for him." On hand to provide affirmation were many stalwarts from the great run: Percy Wendell, Wally Trumbull, Frank O'Brien, Fred Bradlee, and Tommy Campbell, plus those who had assisted Haughton: Derry Parmenter, Stan Pennock, Bob Storer, Mal Logan, and Dick Wigglesworth.[42]

That evening, once again, the Crimson was the toast of Boston. At the Colonial Theatre, the Haughtons, the team, and 1850 undergrads and their friends sang, and some even went on stage, during a dozen encores as the stars of *Watch Your Step*, Miss Elizabeth Brice and Charles King, performed the number "Settle Down in a One-Horse Town" and improvised a verse:

> Harvard won today,
> so this we want to say.
> They are the greatest team by far. . . .
> Their rushing and kicking was supreme.
> And with such men as young Eddie Mahan.
> They had Yale licked, man for man.
> Three cheers for Harvard's team.[43]

Tom Shevlin was left to ponder a conundrum that had mystified coaches before and has since. Asked by a writer how his team could look so good on one Saturday and so terrible the next, Shevlin had a tart answer. "Very easy," he said. "You can't make two lemonades out of one lemon."[44]

Shevlin left Cambridge with larger troubles. He was suffering from a terrible cold he had picked up while coaching. A stay in California improved his health, but upon his return to Minneapolis, he contracted pneumonia. On December 29, he died, leaving a widow, celebrated Kentucky beauty Elizabeth Sherley, and two children.

Aside from Mahan (a consensus choice), Dick Harte and Bob King were named to Walter Camp's All-America team. The latter had capped a rise from runty second-teamer. There was no question of Harvard's being named national champion; its conqueror, Cornell, had run the table. In his mythical top 25, James Vautravers of Tiptop25.com does place the Crimson at number two, over unbeatens Pittsburgh, Nebraska, and Washington State.[45] Even if the parochial Northeast didn't always acknowledge it, there was worthy football being played everywhere.

✹ ✹ ✹

At commencement the following June, second marshal Edward P. Mahan could guffaw along with the rest of the '16ers as class orator Evan Howell Foreman intoned,

> Our class has now seen four successive football victories over Yale and Princeton, and—as you all know—for four successive years the captain of our chess team has checkmated Yale's king. In other sports we are now beating Yale simply from force of habit. The latest beating we administered was so severe that since last November, the Elis have been unable to sit on the old Yale fence.[46]

The 1916 class album contains photos of the Harvard Regiment crossing Soldiers Field and on its first practice march. By the next year, the marches would be for keeps.

11

FROM SOLDIERS FIELD TO FLANDERS FIELD, AND BEYOND

In *The Great Gatsby*, F. Scott Fitzgerald etches the character of Daisy Buchanan's husband, Tom: "He had been one of the most powerful ends that ever played football at New Haven," Fitzgerald wrote, "a national figure in a way, one of those men who reach such an acute limited excellence at 21 that everything afterward savors of anticlimax."

For many of the players from those Crimson autumns, life would be that anticlimax.

"It must be a queer feeling to have as valuable and as educated a Big Toe as Mahan has," wrote Grantland Rice on the day of the 1915 Harvard–Yale game, "and then have nothing to use it for after the last Yale game for the rest of his natural existence."[1] The storied sportswriter thus captured the plight of the star college football players of that era. In their athletic prime, there was nowhere to market their skills, save for the few coaching jobs available and for which their aptitude might be limited. The National Football League wouldn't come into existence until 1920, and would be low-rent at least until the later 1920s.

Eddie Mahan harbored hopes of becoming a big-league baseball player. "I had a chance first to go with the Boston Red Sox when I was in my senior year at Harvard," he said, continuing,

> They said to name my price, and I named $6,500. They thought it was too much. Then the Detroit club made an offer to me, but they too thought I had a gold-brick scheme. The Chicago White Sox were willing to give me a good contract with a bonus if I made good, but

Two of the most accomplished dropkickers in football history, good friends Charlie Brickley (left) and Jim Thorpe held a kicking contest at the Polo Grounds in 1921. The boot-off was meant to promote the New York Brickley Giants, the former Harvard star's franchise in the nascent National Football League. *George Rinhart/Corbis Historical/Getty Images.*

the risk was not worth the undertaking. I considered the [Boston] Braves more seriously than any other team, but my negotiations there too were not satisfactory.[2]

Unlike most of his teammates and opponents, Mahan did not come from money. For many of this class, a lifetime would be spent seeking the same outlet they had found on the gridiron, on the diamond, or in the shell. Of course, they would incessantly attempt to recreate the competition, accomplishment, and camaraderie. Some would find these on the battlefield, some in club and society life, a few in politics. Many tried to replicate them in finance. As had been expected from birth, a few would become stewards of their generation.

They were aided immensely by their connections and the exclusivity dictated by their social class. Novelist John P. Marquand, Harvard class of 1915 (and also an alumnus of the *Lampoon*), many of whose fictional protagonists were men of this social stratum, wrote in his 1948 best seller *Point of No Return* from the perspective of Charles Gray, a Dartmouth man,

> Football men and crew men were somehow the most desirable material at [the financial firm] E. P. Rush & Company, and it seemed to Charles that all of the team came from what were known as the final clubs at Harvard. He only learned these facts gradually, but later he realized that they were important in a business way and he faced them without rancor. . . . His position on the team reminded him of the story of the man who maintained that the Harvard crew was democratic because after three years everyone in the boat spoke to him except number seven.[3]

* * *

Percy Haughton spent one more season coaching Harvard. P. D. had stayed too long at the fair: The 1916 record was 6–3. At New Haven in the finale, played days after Woodrow Wilson had been reelected under the slogan "He kept us out of war," Haughton finally met his match in the tough-minded, organized T. A. D. Jones, Yale 1908. "Gentlemen," Jones informed his Elis before they took the field in front of 70,000 at the Bowl, "you are now going to play football against Harvard. Never again in your whole life will you do anything so important."[4] His players took Jones's message to heart. Harvard scored first on a field goal. The Bulldogs pushed over a touchdown and held on for the 6–3 win, which, remarkably, was Yale's first victory over Harvard in seven years. Haughton swallowed whatever disappointment he must have felt and composed the following letter to Walter Camp:

> Dear Walter:
> For the past few years it has been my privilege to receive from you congratulations upon a Harvard victory over Yale. Times have changed, and as I have been told that you had a great deal to do with Yale's splendid victory over us this year, I want in turn to give you personally my heartiest congratulations. I have always maintained that Harvard's victories in recent years were due to a great measure to Yale's unsound methods. But this year it was Greek meeting Greek—and the "Big Fellow" won.
> Perhaps someday I can lessen the smart of defeat by wresting some golf honors from you, and then again perhaps not. At any rate, as far as football goes, you did a splendid job, and I wanted you to know my appreciation of it.
>
> Sincerely yours,
> Percy D. Haughton[5]

* * *

Sad as the defeat was, it would pale in sorrow next to the real tragedy that occurred scarcely one week later. Stan Pennock, who had graduated in 1915 with honors in chemistry, was killed in an explosion at the Aromatic Chemical Plant in Newark, New Jersey. "Mr. Pennock was a partner in the concern," reported the *Boston Globe*. "The explosion injured another partner, Chauncey Loomis of New York City, killed two workmen, and wrecked the plant. It occurred during a test."[6] In a letter to the *Harvard Alumni Bulletin*, Loomis wrote,

> For the past six months, [Pennock] had been working on the development of a new process for chlorination, one of the most widely used and important reactions in organic chemistry. . . . He was working without a guiding hand in the no-man's-land of science and industry; he had to overcome difficulties which no one had ever en-

countered before; he met phenomena which had never been met before, and which carried with them the forces of sudden death and destruction.[7]

In his class's *25th Anniversary Report*, Loomis amplified,

> To all lovers of football the name Stan Pennock will long be dear. His powerful physique and unusual skill made him one of the greatest guards of all time, and his contribution to the successful football record of the class of 1915 can hardly be overestimated. Probably no other football player of his ability figured in so few spectacular plays. During his three years on the team, he was almost universally selected each year as All-American guard, yet anyone who did not understand football and watch the game closely would hardly notice him on the field. It is as a big, simple, genial soul, strong in whatever purpose it followed, yet never seeking recognition, that Stan Pennock will be remembered by his classmates; more even than as a great football player. His football merely revealed the spirit.[8]

A year before Pennock's death, his roommate, Brickley, had unwittingly composed a pithier epitaph in his syndicated newspaper column: "Pennock, All-American guard for three years, could not be surpassed in opening holes or on defense."[9]

* * *

Some of the players from the glory years went into coaching, if only as a way station before they could figure out what would come next. Thus, a Haughton coaching tree began to branch out. Bob Fisher stayed in Cambridge as one of Haughton's lieutenants. Much sought after, Brickley coached successfully at Johns Hopkins and Boston College. Tommy Campbell went to Bowdoin and North Carolina, Paul Withington to Wisconsin, and Percy Wendell and Reggie Brown (in the 1920s) to Boston University. Brown later went on to the NFL.

But even as his disciples spread his System, Haughton decided to step away. He turned to his lifelong passion, baseball. (Seventy years later, another immortal football coach, Michigan's Bo Schembechler, would pursue the same path when he became president of the Detroit Tigers.) In early 1916, Haughton put together a syndicate of bankers that purchased the Boston Braves. Since it had won the 1914 World

Series, the club had remained respectable, finishing second in the National League in 1915, a year in which Braves Field opened in midseason.

Just short of his 40th birthday, Haughton remained lean and athletic, and was photographed at 1916 spring training taking part in drills with his players.[10] According to Harold Kaese in his 1948 team history, Haughton's main contribution, possibly with a more refined fan base in mind, was an attempt to inculcate some patrician polish into his hardscrabble charges. "Percy Haughton lectured the players on the evils of profanity, a subject in which the former Harvard coach was well versed," wrote Kaese, noting the irony. He added,

> "Instead of swearing when something goes wrong," he told the gaping players, "say something else, like 'good' or 'nice.' It sounds a lot better and has the same result." In an exhibition game that same afternoon, a ball took a bad bounce over Sherwood Magee's head at first base, giving the Giants a lucky run. "Good!" shouted Magee. "Good, good, good!" When he came into the bench still saying, "Good!" [manager George] Stallings exploded, calling Magee everything but good, and thus ended forever Haughton's ban on profanity.[11]

The Braves contended again in 1916, but finished third and drew a disappointing 4,019 fans per game in their first full season at Braves Field. Before the next Opening Day, however, baseball was pushed to the back burner, for Haughton and the entire nation.

* * *

On April 2, 1917, in the wake of the Zimmermann Telegram and despite President Woodrow Wilson's previous vow to keep the country out of the European conflict, Congress acted on the president's wish and declared war on Germany. More than 11,000 current or former Harvard students enlisted in the armed forces of the United States or her associates; 375 died.

Haughton and virtually all the men who had played under him mobilized. Because of their educational (and, indeed, social) background, most of them were viewed as officer material. The coach became a major in the Chemical Corps. According to assistant Harry von Kersburg, Haughton's defensive signals also went to war. "Hanford MacNider [Harvard class of 1911] learned the signals from Perry Smith, substitute fullback on the 1908 team," said von Kersburg, who continued,

> MacNider was one of the officers of the army training schools in France. They were working out the new open order infantry formations under artillery fire, and they had to invent new arm signals to cover the new formations. MacNider gave them the Harvard signals, and General Pershing made them a part of the new Infantry Drill Regulations.[12]

Percy Wendell enlisted as a private in the 102nd Field Artillery but eventually went overseas as a second lieutenant with that outfit. After the Battle of Seicheprey, he was commissioned a first lieutenant and returned to the United States as an instructor at Camp McClellan. Charlie Brickley and Eddie Mahan became naval officers. Tack Hardwick went to France as a captain in a trench mortar unit. Former quarterback Dick Wigglesworth served as commanding officer, First Battalion, 353rd Field Artillery, 76th Division.

Among this youthful, red-blooded cohort, health permitting, service was enthusiastically embraced, in some cases as an antidote to humdrum postcollege jobs. As such authors as Hemingway, Fitzgerald, and Dos Passos memorably captured, it was this generation's grand adventure. Writing in 1920, in the class of 1913's *Third Report*, punter Sam Felton said of his service in France as a captain, "In every place I visited and in every outfit I came in contact with, there was at least one Harvard man. I am convinced that Harvard won the war."[13]

Some men served with distinction and lived to tell about it. The redoubtable Ham Fish became a captain in the celebrated 369th Infantry Regiment, a unit whose enlisted men were African American; the outfit became known as the "Harlem Hellfighters." The 369th spent 191 days at the front, the most of any American unit, and was the first U.S. regiment to reach the Rhine. For his service, Fish later was inducted into the French Legion of Honor.

Others returned home maimed and scarred, physically, emotionally, or both. Rugged, handsome Harvey Rexford "Rex" Hitchcock, a tackle on the 1912 and '13 teams, pitcher on the baseball team, and class president as a junior, went overseas as a first lieutenant and artillery instructor. In the class's *15th Anniversary Report*, his address was listed as St. Elizabeth's Hospital, Washington, D.C.[14] The class's *50th Anniversary Report* elaborated: "He had been ill for many years, his health having been shattered during his action as a field artilleryman."[15] Hitchcock died in 1958 at the age of 66.

The lists of the dead in Europe included the names of several who had been Harvard's most honored foes. Princeton lost two All-Americas, Hobey Baker and Arthur Bluethenthal. Yale quarterback Alex Wilson perished, as did Charley Barrett, the crack Cornell back who had ended Harvard's streak.

Four from the Haughton teams did not return. Substitute quarterback Jack Doherty, who had been Paul Withington's backfield coach at Wisconsin in 1916, was in action as a first lieutenant during some of the American forces' most notable battles, at Cantigny, Chateau-Thierry, and in the Noyon-Montdidier offensive. He was killed near Soissons sometime between July 18 and 24, 1918.

Harry Atkinson, who had won his "H" by entering the 1914 blowout in the Bowl as a substitute center, died in Angers, France, on November 2, 1918, of pneumonia, during the influenza epidemic. He had just achieved the rank of captain; the commission reached him on the morning of the day he died.

Eric Lingard, a backup running back in 1912, became a navy flyer and chased German U-boats along the Massachusetts coast. He died of exposure in October 1918 after his plane crashed into the sea.[16]

If there was a precise American counterpart to the European flower of a generation that had been mown down in the early years of the war, he was Alexander McKinlock. In the class of 1916's fifth reunion book, he is pictured in uniform: handsome, smiling, jaunty, a young Lochinvar. His story is told in various class reunion books, in a volume called *Memoirs of the Harvard Dead in the War against Germany* (one of the saddest works you ever will read), and in James Carl Nelson's 2012 work *Five Lieutenants: The Heartbreaking Story of Five Harvard Men Who Led America to Victory in World War I.*

"Physically, he was a perfect specimen of manhood and possessed strength unusual for a boy his age," reads McKinlock's entry in his 25th reunion book. It continues,

> In his last year he was made a monitor, a position of great importance in the traditions of St. Mark's. . . . [After being commissioned

Lt. George Alexander McKinlock, product of Chicago's tony North Shore, St. Mark's School, and Percy Haughton's Harvard juggernauts. In 1918, as a forward artillery observer, McKinlock would go missing during the Cantigny offensive. A hall at Harvard's Leverett House is dedicated to McKinlock and the remainder of the 25 members of the class of 1916 who lost their lives in World War I. *St. Mark's School archive.*

as a lieutenant in World War I], he was transferred to the headquarters of the Second Infantry Brigade, First Division, for duty as intelligence officer on the staff of Brigadier General B. B. Buck. He took part in the Cantigny, Marne-Aisne offensive. He was awarded the Croix de Guerre (General Order of the Army) and the Distinguished Service Cross. In the midst of terrific fighting he was dispatched on a dangerous mission (as a forward observer), from which he failed to return.

Apparently, he was cut down by a German sniper. "Six months later he was officially reported as killed in action." Alexander McKinlock was 25.[17]

The U.S. military was unable to provide McKinlock's parents with the location of his grave. After the war, his mother, Marion, and his football coach at St. Mark's, Daniel Woodhead, traveled to France and searched sites for months before finally finding a grave marked "McKinlow." The helmet hanging on a little cross at the head of the grave was labeled with his correct name inside.[18] Upon visiting the First Division Headquarters after the Armistice, Marion had been told how beloved her son had been. "Well, don't you suppose I knew him too?" she said. "You may have known a wonderful boy," was the reply, "but we knew a wonderful man."[19]

In their son's memory, George and Marion McKinlock donated McKinlock Hall, dedicated in 1927, and today part of Leverett House, one of Harvard's residences for upper-class students. In the lobby is a marble plaque listing the 25 members of the class of 1916 who gave their lives in the service of their country.

❊ ❊ ❊

With the war's end, football returned to normalcy in the 1919 season—which meant Harvard remained a power. Under Haughton disciple Bob Fisher (ably assisted by, among others, Tack Hardwick), the Crimson rolled to a 9–0–1 regular-season record, semi-blotched only by a 10–10 tie at Princeton. The squad then journeyed to Pasadena and, on January 1, 1920, beat Oregon, 7–6, in the Rose Bowl. No doubt this will stand forever as Harvard's only Bowl victory.

Upon his demobilization, Haughton worked on State Street and kibitzed around the Harvard football program. He further demonstrated his involvement with the game in 1922 by publishing his primer, *Football and How to Watch It*. According to his agent, Christy Walsh, Haughton did not use a ghost. In a 1935 *New Yorker* profile of Walsh, author Alva Johnston said, "Not all of Christy Walsh's syndicated literature has been ghost-written. Percy Haughton, for example, would not let a ghost come near him. He would not let a comma of his copy be changed."[20] The next year, P. D. received an offer he couldn't refuse. Columbia, which had resumed football in 1915 after a 10-year hiatus but had competed indifferently, lured Haughton to Morningside Heights with a two-year contract reported to be anywhere from $15,000 to $20,000 a year. For the era, it was staggering.

Haughton immediately began implementing his System. Among his prospective material was a powerfully built junior fullback and punter named Henry Louis Gehrig. Before the 1923 season, however, Lou Gehrig, who was also a first baseman for the Lions, signed with the New York Yankees and left school.

In 1923, Haughton showed signs he would turn around Columbia the way he had his alma mater 15 years earlier, going 4–4–1. In '24, the improvement accelerated. The Lions were 4–1 after thrashing Williams (coached by Haughton's former star Percy Wendell), 27–3, on October 25. (Haughton's old assistant coach, Harry von Kersburg, was one of the officials.) The next day, a Sunday, P. D. played 36 holes of golf at the Meadow Brook Polo Club with Maxwell Stevenson, head of the Columbia Rowing Committee. On Monday, he reported to Baker Field to begin practice for the following Saturday's game. To assistant Paul Withington (who also was an M.D.), he complained he had not slept well the night before and had pain in a band across his chest. Thinking it might be indigestion, Withington gave him two soda tablets and told him to lie down. Haughton sent Withington out to run practice. "Paul, you congratulate the team for me," P. D. said. "Tell them I'm proud of them."

The pain worsened, and Withington eventually prevailed on Haughton to go to St. Luke's Hospital. There, he received a hypodermic injection. "I feel better, but I still don't think much of your medicine," he joked to Withington. Then he said to another physician, Dr. Everett Gould, "I feel so much better that I think I'll be back to work in a day or two." Suddenly he seized up. Within a minute he was dead.[21]

Percy Duncan Haughton was 48. He left behind his wife, two step-daughters, and a daughter, Alison. (Her daughter, Alison Hildreth, is today a noted nature artist in Maine.) Although he appeared robust and had no prior symptoms, Haughton had a family history of cardiac disease, which had claimed his mother and a brother.

Amid nationwide tributes, he was buried, in a simple Episcopalian service, three days after his death, at Mt. Auburn Cemetery in Cambridge, a few booming punts from Harvard Stadium. Fisher and Paul Withington were honorary pallbearers. The six surviving members of the Group of Seven sent a large display of roses.

* * *

In the 1920s, Charles E. Brickley completed a journey from acclaim to disgrace.

It's possible that Charlie Brickley's greatest crime was being born 10 years too early, before newsreels and the newly minted NFL made such college football stars as Red Grange instantly marketable. In 1915, Brickley emerged from his amazing college football career with fame but no easy way to make money from it. Attempting to maintain his status among his privileged peers no doubt amplified certain defects of character that sadly caused him to cut corners, to attempt to gain the same advantages he had achieved with such ease on the football field.

His post-Harvard life had started promisingly enough. After his graduation with the class of 1915 (for which he was elected by classmates to the prestigious position of second marshal, with teammate Wally Trumbull as first), Brickley could not fully capitalize on his fame and skill: The NFL was a half-decade away. He did keep his hand in the sport, bylining a syndicated newspaper column and coaching. First, he was an assistant to Haughton, then he coached John Hopkins for one season and Boston College for two, ending each year 6–2. Upon America's entry into World War I, he served in the U.S. Naval Reserve. After leaving the U.S. Navy, Brickley became backfield coach at Fordham, among whose players was his youngest brother, Arthur. In 1921, he put together a team in the nascent National Football League, the New York Brickley Giants. One Sunday, hoping to goose the gate at the Polo Grounds, he competed in a kicking exhibition against Jim Thorpe. In

1922, he dickered with Northwestern about becoming head coach, but the two sides could not agree on terms.

Married to New York society girl Kathryn E. Taylor and with two young sons, Brickley found his main arena in the financial world. This was a well-worn path for Ivy Leaguers, particularly those with social connections or athletic celebrity that might attract customers. In Brickley's case, Thomas W. Lamont, nephew of J. P. Morgan and a Harvard Overseer, "interested him in Wall Street."[22] He soon was making $500 a week but, in 1920, chose to begin his own firm, Charles E. Brickley & Co.

In this rough-and-tumble environment, Brickley found the going much tougher than he had against Princeton or Yale. He was perpetually in hot water. He bought a seat on the New York Stock Exchange, but in 1921 his firm was dissolved. He and other brokers were defendants in a suit brought by the Back Bay National Bank. They were accused of not repaying a $15,000 loan. Two months after the firm's dissolution, he was sued for not repaying a $10,000 loan given him by one Joseph Jackson. As the *New York Times* put it in a front-page story (albeit burying the juice at the story's bottom), the "action revealed that [Brickley] had been threatened with a horsewhipping in the Harvard Club by Mrs. Miriam Reinhardt," Jackson's sister, related to the football hero's failure to make good.[23]

Brickley then went to work for the Bigelow Hartford Carpet Company (along with Archie and Theodore Roosevelt Jr., sons of the late president and also Harvard alums). In 1923, Brickley was among those indicted in a swindling case involving the company's stock; he had told a fellow employee, W. J. Hines, he was making more money trading stock than he was earning at the mill.[24] The charges involved larceny and forgery of borrowed stock certificates that Brickley had used as collateral for a $10,000 loan from Springfield's Commercial Trust Company. Released on $10,000 bail, he asserted, "I am absolutely innocent of forgery or larceny, and it will be my endeavor to clear my name. I have the utmost confidence that my vindication will be complete."[25]

It would be two years before the case would come to trial. Hines asserted that Brickley induced him to hand over stock certificates by telling him he could buy Bigelow stock lower than at market price if he could prove he already owned some and that Brickley had arranged for signatures on the certificates to be forged so he could use them when applying for his loan. In his testimony, Brickley denied the allegations, claiming he was unaware the signatures were forged. In his closing arguments, Brickley's lawyer, the celebrated Joseph B. Ely (a Harvard Law grad who six years later would become governor of Massachusetts), declared that Brickley was "paying the penalty of reputation" in facing trial. District attorney Charles H. Wright parried that the accused was a "bully" and a "blackmailer." After five hours of deliberations, the 10-man jury declared Brickley not guilty.[26] Not even Tack Hardwick had blocked more effectively for Brick than had Ely.

Would exoneration keep—or, depending on how you look at it, put—Brickley on the straight and narrow? Not according to four indictments (totaling 17 counts) handed down by a Suffolk County Grand Jury on August 5, 1927, charging Brickley with forgery, larceny of stocks and bonds worth $35,588, and, since December 1, 1925, operating a bucket shop (in which stocks were illegally speculated on but not actually traded). Brickley was remanded to Charles Street Jail on $20,000 bail.

The case came to trial the following February. Brickley spent two and a half days on the witness stand. His main defense was that clients of Charles E. Brickley, Inc., at 68 Devonshire Street, had given him money with the understanding he would invest it and retain 25 percent of the profits. Among the complainants was John Shea, whom Brickley had coached at Boston College and who claimed Brickley had bilked him out of $838. (Brickley's defense was that this was merely a margin payment.)[27] He said only one of his 125 clients who had suffered losses was unwilling to take his note, the exception being Patrick Callahan of Boston, who alleged that Brickley had filched $2,195; however, under cross-examination by assistant district attorney Frederick T. Doyle, Brickley revealed his record-keeping was shoddy to nonexistent.[28]

Brickley could not wriggle out of this one as if it were an opposing tackler. On March 1, a jury found him guilty of four counts of the indictment, Patrick Keating, the judge hearing the case, having thrown out many of the others. Remanded on $12,000 bail, he was facing hard time.

On March 22, the day of sentencing, the room at Suffolk Superior Court was Crimson, as the *Globe*'s page-one account noted the next day. Keating was class of '83. Doyle was Harvard Law, class of 1917; the clerk of court who would read the sentences was Walter A. Murray,

Harvard College, class of 1917, Harvard Law, class of 1920. Presenting the closing arguments for Brickley was William H. Lewis, Law School class of '93. As Crimson center "Bill" Lewis (playing while attending law school, when graduate students were permitted to compete), he had been the first African American All-America. Afterward, he was an assistant coach. Later, he was the first of his race to be a member of the American Bar Association and also be named (by old Crimsonian Teddy Roosevelt) U.S. assistant attorney general.

After various witnesses, including his Everett High principal, W. J. Lockwood, testified to Brickley's essentially decent character and pleaded that he not be sent to prison, Brickley made a brief statement. "I am very sorry that anyone lost money through my trading in the stock market," he said, "and if the wheel of fortune ever breaks my way again, I hope to pay back all my obligations."

Then Lewis, known as a spellbinder, came in with the heavy oratorical artillery. His voice breaking, he declared,

> I stand here more as friend of Charlie Brickley than as his counsel. I have known him as a boy and a man. He played the game that only the top-notch can play. I have heard the bands play and have seen the banners wave, and I have seen him borne from the field on the shoulders of those who idolized him. He has not played the game of life quite so successfully. I have told him that the stock market game was not his game and that he better try something else. . . . Let him go out from here to work with a pick and shovel or to drive an ice wagon, but let him start anew. Give him a chance, give him a chance to go out and play a game that he can play. [29]

Doyle adamantly opposed probation. "The trial did not show an isolated case of wrongdoing," he told the court. "It was a bucket shop, with procedure well planned out." [30]

It was now Keating's turn to pronounce. He stated,

> I think this is one of the most unpleasant duties I have ever been called upon to perform, and if I could consistently, with my sense of duty as a justice, grant the request of counsel for the defendant—the request for probation—made in such a touching manner—I would gladly do it. But the defendant has been convicted of three indictments and . . . there are not sufficient reasons advanced to make me feel justified in placing the defendant on probation.

He sentenced Brickley to 15 months in the Charles Street Jail, later shortened to a year.[31]

Various legal maneuverings ensued. At one point, declaring that he and his wife, Kathryn, were living apart, Brickley asked for custody of his two sons, Charles Jr. and John, a futile strategy for a man facing prison. Brickley began his sentence on May 17, and spent the next seven months variously at Charles Street, the Deer Island House of Correction (where he managed the baseball team), and the State Prison Camp at Tewksbury. After an illness, he was paroled just before Christmas.

Charles E. Brickley would live for two more decades. In his lifetime, the wheel of fortune would never break his way again.

✿ ✿ ✿

Being a former Harvard football player provided no shelter when the Depression swamped the United States. Neither education nor accomplishment, celebrity nor wealth (inherited or earned) proved a bulwark. Writing in his *25th Anniversary Report* in 1940, Fred Bradlee recounted, "I . . . worked for Blair & Co., Inc., first as a salesman and then as vice president, in charge of their New England activities. Their pulling in of horns at the start of the Depression did not leave even a prong to hang my hat on."[32] (As he was submitting this entry, his son Benjamin, the future *Washington Post* editor of *All the President's Men* renown, was a student at Harvard in the class of '43.)

The pages of these reunion reports in the 1930s and 1940s drip with disdain for the New Deal promulgated by their fellow alumnus Franklin D. Roosevelt, class of 1904. By and large, Harvard men, like others in society's upper echelon, shared the view that FDR was a traitor to his class. To them, he was a raving socialist, or worse. The most prominent anti-New Dealer was Ham Fish, now an unreconstructed right-wing congressman from Dutchess, Orange, and Putnam counties in New York. As World War II approached, Fish, as House chairman of the Committee on Foreign Affairs, became one of the nation's leading isolationists. After he led an unsuccessful effort to block FDR's policy of Lend-Lease of warships and armaments for Britain, the president would pillory him and two of his colleagues in a memorable 1940 speech that used the mocking refrain "Martin, Barton, and Fish." ("A perfectly beautiful rhythm," chortled FDR.) In 1944, after 12 terms (and being redistricted), Fish was defeated for reelection by a liberal Democrat. Afterward he would say, "It took most of the New Deal administration, half of Moscow, $400,000, and Governor [Thomas E.] Dewey to defeat me."[33]

During the hard times, men looked to find a perch. Wally Trumbull became director of admissions at Middlesex School, his alma mater. "With a sophomore son at Cambridge," he wrote in 1940, "I feel as though I were living my undergraduate years all over again. . . . Not quite the same days as 1911 to 1915—apparently no more Astronomy I courses for sleeping purposes."[34] His classmate John P. Marquand made Trumbull the basis for hyperenthusiastic ex-Crimson jock Bo-Jo Brown in Marquand's best-selling novel *H. M. Pulham, Esq.*[35]

Many who had lost fortunes or jobs pounded the pavement while attempting to maintain appearances. Among these was Eddie Mahan. In his file folder in the Harvard University Archives is a note from the Harvard Alumni Placement Service: an application for employment dated May 10, 1932. The "position desired" was "Financial/Investment Banking," with the notation "Keep Confidential/Does Not Want It Known Out of a Job." The application explained that Mahan had spent his career on Wall Street, variously in "statistical work" and as a bond salesman, "customers' man," in new financing, and from 1927 to '32, at Hornblower & Weeks, most recently as "broker on N.Y. Curb Exchange" at an $8,000 salary, "dropped because of small volume of business." The denouement here, at least, was happy. On December 12, 1932, Mahan notified the Placement Service he had "placed himself at Hill School, teaching science and assisting the coach of the school football team."[36]

* * *

Many of the former gridiron heroes died shockingly early, at least from a 21st-century perspective. Perhaps, as we see with the football players of today, the hard knocks of the game were a contributor or even a cause.

The lifespans of the Group of Seven provide a typical range. Pennock, of course, died in an accident at age 24. Brickley (age 58) and Hardwick (56) each died in 1949. Coolidge was 66 when he died in

1959, and Logan 67 when he died in 1961. Bradlee, who died in 1970, made it to 77, and Trumbull, who died in 1976, to 82.

Perusing reunion reports of these classes, a reader sees that if a man of this era made it to 70, he lived a good, long life. Of course, the war took its early toll. So, too, might have the era's fashionable lifestyle, which often predisposed smoking and drinking. So did the 1918–19 influenza epidemic. So did the relatively primitive state of medicine, which left no defense against the heart attack that killed Haughton or, in those days before antibiotics, pneumonia. Bob King, '16, who had worked his way up from scrub to All-America, succumbed to that disease in 1930, at age 35, in a hospital in Bogota, Colombia, where he had been South American sales representative for the Boston-based Gillette Company.[37]

Bob Fisher, All-America, second marshal, and victorious Rose Bowl coach, died in 1942, at age 53. After that bowl win, the Crimson's football fortunes had declined. As Fisher wrote in his *25th Anniversary Report*, "Those were the days when Harvard was expected to win every game and, in fact, you were rather frowned upon if any other team even crossed the goal line."[38] Fisher became a stockbroker and listed his affiliations as the Harvard Club, the Madison Square Garden Club, and (most august) the Country Club of Brookline. At the time of his death, four of his sons were playing football for Harvard.

His old teammate Percy Wendell's demise had been swifter and less gentle. Despite (or maybe in those days because of) his lackluster academic record, after college he tried medical school for two years. More notably, he had patented noseguards and advertised them in *Spalding's Official Foot Ball Guide for 1914*, in which he was described as "famous line bucker."[39] Following his war service, he went west and worked in the oil fields, until he was lured back to his hometown for what clearly was his calling: coach of Boston University's football team. In 1920, his only season on Commonwealth Avenue, the Terriers went 4–3–1. Wendell then moved to Williams for four happy seasons, going 26–10–4, then to Lehigh for three unhappy ones (5–20–2), during which he encountered, as his *25th Anniversary Report* put it, a "general housecleaning and faculty-frowning on athletics."[40]

In April 1928, Wendell married a widow named Nathalie Fallon; she died in October 1929. As his *25th Anniversary Report* then noted, "The following summer a grave condition developed, which threatened

Percy's sight. As his injury was attributed to war service, he was treated for some months at the Veteran's Hospital in Washington."[41] Given what we are learning 80 years later about the lingering effects of concussions, we have to wonder if Wendell's condition was a result of all the knocks "Bullet" experienced on the football field when he put his head down and bucked the line.

The report continued,

> Percy came out of the hospital in the spring of 1931, and, although far from well, faced his problem with the same spirit he carried onto the Yale field; squared his shoulders and went out to make a magnificent comeback. Fighting against great odds, he was so far recovered that he was able to go back to Harvard in the fall and work with the freshman team, where he endeared himself to the players and his associate coaches. The following March, Percy was stricken with pneumonia and died, a great loss to every member of the class.

✧ ✧ ✧

On December 7, 1941, the players from the Haughton era were in their 40s and 50s. Nonetheless, following the Japanese attack on Pearl Harbor, some thought to join up. Mahan enlisted in the naval reserve. The most intrepid was Tudor Gardiner, whose promising football career had been curtailed by injury. A member of one of Maine's oldest families (his hometown was Gardiner in the southern part of the state), Gardiner had received his degree from Harvard Law in 1917. After World War I, he embarked on a political career in his state, serving as speaker of the House of Representatives and Republican governor from 1928 to 1932. At the time of Pearl Harbor, he was a wealthy businessman with four children and, more to the point, almost 50 years old. Nevertheless, he joined the U.S. Army Air Forces, which is how, on September 7, 1943, Col. William T. Gardiner happened to be on the Italian corvette *Ibis* with Brig. Gen. Maxwell Taylor, commander of the 82nd Airborne's artillery.

The two men had embarked from Sicily on a secret mission to Rome, in which they hoped to seal a deal (codenamed Giant II) where the Italians would turn against the occupying Germans and aid a paratroop attack that would kick off the imminent Allied invasion of Italy.

The men were familiar with the details. "If you get captured," they were told, "put your forgetters to work."[42] As related in Rick Atkinson's 2007 best seller *The Day of Battle*, the two officers were picked up, put in an Italian staff car, and, posing as prisoners, spirited to the Palazzo Caprera in central Rome. There, while waiting to parley with the temporizing Italian high command, they dined on consomme, veal cutlets, and crepes. They met first with General Giacomo Carboni, then with the nation's military leader, Marshal Pietro Badoglio. The Italians told Taylor and Gardiner that assistance was impossible and they were reneging on their deal, at which point Taylor told them the Allies would begin by bombing the city. Taylor then sent an encrypted cable to the Allied command: "GIANT TWO is impossible."

As Atkinson related, "Badoglio and Carboni stood and snapped to attention with a sharp clicking of heels. 'We returned the gesture,' Gardiner recalled, 'endeavoring to click our heels as loudly as the Italians. There was quite a contest.'"

The Americans returned to the Palazzo Cabrera, "disheartened and exhausted," wrote Atkinson. "Pacing back and forth in what they called 'our hideout,' the two men considered taking a stroll outside but could not find a civilian jacket big enough for the burly Gardiner"—who obviously retained the silhouette from his days as a Crimson tackle. Then they heard bombs beginning to fall. They got into a waiting ambulance, which took them to an airfield, and hightailed it to North Africa in an Italian plane. When they landed, they heard that Badoglio had reversed course yet again, declaring for the Allies and enraging German field marshal Albert Kesselring.[43] For his efforts, Gardiner was awarded the Legion of Merit.[44]

⁂ ⁂ ⁂

The year 1949 saw the deaths of two of the Group of Seven. When they died, they were on opposite shores of social esteem.

Tack Hardwick had prospered in the advertising business in Boston and helped spearhead the construction of the Boston Garden, which opened in 1929. There was one major public bump: his messy 1933 divorce from Margaret, in which Tack claimed, according to newspaper accounts, he was "entirely at fault."[45] In 1947, Margaret died and left her entire estate—valued at $2,799,342—to their daughter, Mrs. Margaret Hardwick Simmons . . . and Tack. In September 1948, Hardwick married Manuela de Zanone-Poma, daughter of Mr. and Mrs. Pane de Zanone-Poma, formerly of Barcelona and Cannes.[46]

Above all, he had remained an unreconstructed jock. "After he had finished football, I caught up with him one late afternoon in Boston," wrote Grantland Rice, who remained close with Hardwick after his playing days. Rice continued,

> Here had been his schedule—boxing 10 rounds with two pro heavy-weights—wrestling an hour with two pro wrestlers—playing with Harvard's scrub team against the varsity in an hour's scrimmage. There were knots and cuts on his head and face. He had a bad ankle and a bad shoulder, not being in training at the time. And he was still looking for more action. "Your heart can't take that much," I told him. "It can for a few years," he said. "After that—who cares?"[47]

On June 26, 1949, Hardwick was on Cuttyhunk Island, clamming with his old teammate Ernie Soucy, when Tack suddenly toppled over. He was dead of a heart attack. Tack Hardwick, the indomitable Harvard strongman, was 56.[48]

✿ ✿ ✿

Six months later, on December 14, Charlie Brickley and his older son, 30-year-old Charlie Jr. ("Chick"), were at Reuben's Restaurant at 6 East 48th Street in Manhattan. Brickley's stock-swindling conviction in the 1920s had left him, in the words of *Boston Herald* columnist Bill Cunningham, "broke, convicted, and shunned by his classmates, and his college, who felt he'd rubbed much luster from his shining shield. And, undoubtedly, he had."[49] His wife, Kathryn, had separated from him, although they remained married. When in desperate financial straits, Brickley would put the arm on some of his teammates for funds.[50]

Brickley had led an itinerant existence. For a time, he managed the health club at the Roosevelt Hotel. Imagine Joe Namath handing out towels at your local gym and you have a notion of how far Brickley had fallen. He always was willing to provide informal kicking exhibitions and coach kickers; Chick, in fact, had inherited the old man's knack and played for, of all schools, Yale. Despite his reduced circumstances and notoriety, Charlie Brickley remained a celebrity; gold-plated square toe and all, he showed up at the 1939 World's Fair in New York City at an exhibit celebrating America's football heroes.

After Pearl Harbor, in his early 50s, Brickley had tried to reenlist in the U.S. Navy; at 190 pounds, he said, he was essentially at his playing weight. Not surprisingly, he was turned down because of his age. Thus, he traveled to Wilmington, Delaware, where he became a pipefitter's helper at the shipyard there, earning $48 a week on the 4 p.m.-to-midnight shift. "I've got two kids in the armed forces overseas, and I couldn't sit around doing nothing," he said.[51] After the war, he returned to New York City, where he lived at the unfashionable George Washington Hotel on West 23rd Street and landed a position as an advertising salesman. He also checked into Roosevelt Hospital twice with heart complaints, prompting his family to beg him to slow down.

Now, on this night at Reuben's, another patron recognized Brickley and began to disparage him: "That old bald-headed so-and-so is the great Charlie Brickley?" the fellow sneered. An uncharacteristically puckish account the next day in the *New York Times* reported, "Words were exchanged, blows aimed, glass and crockery tinkled, whistles blew, a blue flying wedge converged on Brickley senior and junior, and [threaded] its unwanted way through the melee, so the preliminary testimony went."[52] According to a later account by sportswriter Red Smith, another patron, one Edward Millstein of Brooklyn, saw the Brickleys being outnumbered and shouted, "Millstein is the name. Is this a private fight or public? If it's public, I'm in."[53] One of the policemen, who clearly could compare notes with Yale tacklers from four decades earlier, said, "It took about 10 of us" to get the two Brickleys into a prowl car for their trip to the West 51st Street station.[54]

At the hearing on December 28, cooler heads and better feelings prevailed. Restaurant owner Arnold Reuben, who said he had known Brickley for 30 years, declined to press charges. Amid handshakes, the judge, Charles F. Murphy, dismissed the case. After Brickley departed the courthouse, he sat for an interview with Smith. He spent much of it deploring the current state of Harvard football. Under coach Art Valpey, the Crimson was coming off a 1–8 season, its worst ever, and there were rumblings that under athletic director (and Brickley's Harvard contemporary) Bill Bingham, the school would seek to leave major college football. Brickley was incensed at the thought.

He said,

They talk about Harvard's glorious past, but Harvard football wasn't terrific before Percy Haughton's day as coach, and it has gone downhill ever since he left. . . . Haughton was an absolute dictator and that's what Harvard needs. . . . Let's have, temporarily at least, a czar of Harvard football to get the sport on a sound basis. I'm thinking of a man like [1930 All-America center] Ben Ticknor or [former star] Chuck Peabody or Eddy Mahan. . . . I'm dead set against Bingham's plan of backing away from big-time football. Harvard is one of the great institutions of the country. If we can't play the best, we'd better abandon the game.[55]

That night at the George Washington Hotel, Brickley's friend Henry Garrity, a Princeton football player in 1920 who lived in the next room, heard groans from Brickley's room. When he investigated and saw Brickley's condition, he summoned Nate Tufts, the hotel manager. This was the same Nate Tufts who had refereed the 1914 Yale game and signaled that Brickley's wobbly final kick was good.[56] Soon, a physician from nearby Bellevue Hospital, Alan Moody, arrived. At 11:15, he pronounced Brickley dead of a heart attack at age 58.

On January 2, 1950, Charlie Brickley's life was celebrated in a solemn high requiem mass at the Immaculate Conception Church in Everett. Shorty's old hometown did its favorite son proud. One thousand mourners thronged the church. Among them were four of Brickley's teammates: Mal Logan, Eddie Mahan, Bob Storer, and Wally Trumbull.[57] Quality, perhaps, if not quantity. Likewise, the *Harvard Crimson* gave his passing but brief notice.[58]

Brickley would have understood. More than most, he had experienced the dual nature of celebrity. As Bill Cunningham wrote, "I have never known a man who shouldered his cross with greater acceptance, or with less complaint."[59]

✳ ✳ ✳

By the early 1950s, several of the figures from the Haughton-era teams were national leaders, as they had expected to be while in school. They were now, at about age 60, elder statesmen. Harvard Law grad Dick Wigglesworth would serve 14 terms as a Republican congressman from eastern Massachusetts. In 1958, Christian Herter, secretary of state (and Harvard class of 1915), would name Wigglesworth ambassador to

Canada, a post in which he would serve until his death in 1960. Former end Laurie Curtis also was a Republican congressman, representing the wealthy west suburban districts of Boston.

After the war, Tudor Gardiner had returned to New England and his many business interests. On August 3, 1953, he and two friends were going home in a plane piloted by Gardiner from a reunion in Shamokin, Pennsylvania, of their World War I regiment. Somewhere above Schnecksville, Pennsylvania, the plane seemed to disintegrate, and all three were killed. William Tudor Gardiner was 61. (His son, Tudor Gardiner, would marry figure-skating champion Tenley Albright.)

* * *

The College Football Hall of Fame opened its doors in 1951. Percy Haughton and Eddie Mahan were in the charter class. In 1954, Hamilton Fish, Tack Hardwick, and Stan Pennock were enshrined. Percy Wendell entered in '72, Bob Fisher in '73.

Conspicuously omitted was Charlie Brickley. Despite his worthy record on the field, he fell afoul of one of the major criteria for admission: While each nominee's football achievements are of prime consideration, his postfootball record as a citizen is also weighed. He must have proven himself worthy as a citizen, carrying the ideals of football forward into his relations with his community and his fellow man, along with love of his country. Nor was Harvard eager to press his cause.

On October 27, 1967, the Harvard Varsity Club inaugurated its own Hall of Fame. The first class was festooned with Haughtonites, including the coach himself, Fish, Hardwick, Mahan, Pennock, and Trumbull.

But no Brickley. ("Guess whose name was missing?" commented the *Globe*).[60] Even 40 years after his conviction, its shame still lingered. In 1970, after a de facto probation period of three years, Brickley was inducted.

During the next four decades, Brickley's name was mentioned fleetingly—most notably, in 2005, when Harvard running back Clifton Dawson broke Brickley's Crimson career scoring record, which had stood for 91 years. Then, in early 2012, a College Football Hall of Famer named Dwayne Nix stopped into a paint store near his Charlottesville, Virginia, home. Nix had been a wide receiver for Texas A&I in the 1960s, playing with quarterback Randy Johnson and guard Gene Upshaw. He had been inducted into the Hall in 2003. (Nix did not play pro football; instead, he had gone on to a career as a navy pilot.) On this day, he was wearing a jacket with a Hall of Fame insignia. The young man behind the counter admired it. Where, he asked Nix, had he gotten it? "Well," answered Nix, "I'm in the Hall." Said the young man, "My family and I think my great-grandfather should be in there too." The young man was Ryan Brickley—a great-grandson of Charlie Brickley. He began telling Nix about his great-granddad.

Intrigued, Nix began Googling Charlie Brickley. He was amazed at his exploits. Despite Brickley's transgressions, he thought, this man belonged in the Hall. After all, others with checkered lives—including Billy Cannon and O. J. Simpson—were enshrined. (Cannon had been expelled but readmitted.) As a Hall of Famer, Nix had the right to nominate Brickley for consideration by the Hall's senior committee. He did so in 2013, and has renominated him annually. As of this writing, Brickley is waiting for induction.

Ironically, enshrinement in a Hall of Fame might have meant less to Brickley than to his relatives and backers. As always, he knew the final score, as he acknowledged at his hearing after the Reuben's dustup. "Fame," said Brickley, "is fleeting."

* * *

In 1961, Reggie Brown died. He had written in his *40th Anniversary Report* in 1938, "Football has taken me to coaching berths at Brown, Boston University, Holy Cross, and the Redskins of the National Professional [*sic*] Football League, assistant and head coaching, radio broadcasting, and as advisor to numerous head coaches, scouting, and mapping offensive and defensive formations."[61]

Ham Fish was the last of the old Haughtonian warriors to pass. In 1976, the year he turned 88, the twice-widowed Fish had married his third wife, Alice Desmond. Eight years later, they divorced. In 1981, he appeared as his crusty self in *Reds*, Warren Beatty's film about Fish's Harvard classmate John Reed. In 1988, the year he turned 100, Fish married Lydia Ambrogio. On December 7, his 100th birthday, he did a phone interview with the *New York Times*. He reminisced about his old adversary FDR: "I know he hated me, but I really don't believe in hate. So now I don't hate Roosevelt—but frankly I despise him."[62]

His death on January 18, 1991—six weeks after his 102nd birthday—
severed a link to football's glorious past, and not only Harvard's. Hamilton Fish was the last surviving Walter Camp All-America.

❋ ❋ ❋

The legacy of these Harvard teams is powerful but obscure. Yes, they
were lords of their realm. But the realm was comparatively small, con-
fined largely to the East and the Big Ten, and exclusive. The players the
Crimson suited up and the ones it competed against came largely from
a select group: WASP preppies indoctrinated in the sport since boy-
hood at prep schools.

Because of its prominence and location, when Harvard did have a
dominant team, it received the approbation of the Eastern press and
football inner circle, which had the influence to declare a national
champion. There were no polls. (These did not originate until 1935.)
When Harvard was undefeated, the Crimson might have been the nation's best—and it might not have been. When Harvard ventured outside of its peer group, the results were mixed: beaten by Thorpe and
Carlisle, victorious over Michigan, another perennial power, during a
down season for the Wolverines.

After World War I, the hegemony of the Eastern private universities
gradually ended as schools in other regions—seeing the potential to
enhance brands and enlarge coffers—took up the game in a major way.
Drawing on a more heterogeneous population, they soon caught up to
and passed Harvard and its brethren on the gridiron. Moreover, the
sport developed a more modern feel, which made the pre–World War I
brand seem a relic.

To some degree, that's what it remains. Newspaper accounts of early
games, even big ones, can be wildly divergent. Statistics were haphaz-
ardly compiled and unsophisticated. Few, if any, motion pictures exist
of games before World War I, so we don't even have a full sense of
Mahan's running, Hardwick's blocking, or Brickley's kicking (or Jim
Thorpe's, for that matter). By the 1920s, by contrast, the newsreels
were faithfully displaying Red Grange's gallops, which are vivid to everyone who sees them, even today.

So why celebrate these teams? Primarily because they produced
four individuals who would have stood out in any era.

Percy Haughton was a contemporary of John Heisman, Amos Alonzo Stagg, and Pop Warner. All are renowned for their innovations. Heisman has his name on the sport's most celebrated trophy, Stagg's is on a bowl game that decides the Division III championship, Warner's is on the game's most important association for boys. Yet another contemporary, Fielding H. Yost, has one of the game's most illustrious nicknames: Hurry-Up.

These men are justifiably remembered, while Percy Haughton is not. He should be: He literally wrote the book on modern football—a best seller, no less. By making his Harvard machine his most magnificent experiment, he rethought the sport. His reputation is secure, but it would have been even greater had he lived to complete the turnaround at Columbia during the so-called Golden Age of Sport. What if it had been Haughton (who would have been 57 years old), and not Lou Little, who had engineered the Lions' Rose Bowl victory in 1934? With the coverage he'd have received from the New York City press, he might today be hallowed, along with Rockne, Leahy, or Bryant. Likewise, he'd perhaps still be a household name if Harvard, along with the other Ivy schools, had not deemphasized football after World War II.

Of Haughton's players, Eddie Mahan, by contemporary accounts, ranked near Grange as an open-field runner; he also was a superb punter for distance and direction, a lethal quick-kicker and enough of a passer with the squashy ball to keep defenses honest.

Tack Hardwick, the blueblood strong boy, was one of early football's most punishing hitters. He was the spearhead of Haughton's interference. Hardwick also proved his versatility by shuffling uncomplainingly between the line and the backfield as needed—and performing brilliantly wherever he was placed.

Charlie Brickley is among the greatest kickers in football history and the greatest dropkicker, period. Once the shape and consistency of the ball changed from an oval to a bullet, dropkicking became the sport's horse-and-buggy. But that should not minimize Brickley's prowess. (After all, he also could bang 'em through on placements.) And he showed up when it counted, becoming the Mr. Clutch of his day. Brickley's kicking alone might have made him immortal, but (using that Olympian body) he was also one of his era's best runners and defensive backs. Above all, he had a sense of showmanship that captivated the nation. Even three decades after his career and two decades after his legal troubles, his was the first name mentioned when it came to field-goal kicking, and he was kept in the news by sportswriters with long memories. It's intriguing to ponder: If Brickley had stayed out of trouble, would the award that annually is handed out to the best college field-goal kicker be named not the Lou Groza Award, but the Charlie Brickley Award?

✻ ✻ ✻

For a generation after these men played their last, they remained among the most renowned and recognizable names in football. In 1943, Clark Shaughnessy, who as coach at Stanford and with Chicago Bears had popularized the modern T formation, placed Harvard's 1913 backfield—Brickley, Mahan, Peebo Bradlee, and Mal Logan—as the seventh best all-time.[63] Obviously, this lofty ranking vanished when leather helmets did, but the esteem at such a distance is impressive nevertheless.

There is yet one more reason that the memory of these Crimson teams should be resurrected, and it may be the most significant. Harvard and its future Ivy brethren set the template for major college sport, one that remains largely intact a century later—for better and worse. Stadium arms races, game-day frenzy and sacred rituals, bitter annual rivalries, recruiting excesses, favored treatment for jocks, athletic department power and the overemphasis of sport on campus, the coach as apotheosis, alumni bragging rights, the scheduling of early season cupcakes, the fawning of the mass media: They all took root in this era and at these institutions. (The only things they did not pioneer are halftime pageantry and female cheerleaders.) Because these schools loomed so large in the national landscape and in its literature and imagination, colleges everywhere aped their practices and, indeed, embellished on them to develop what we have today: a Saturday staple that is part of our national fabric, one that is deemed (as it is nowhere else in the world) essential to the educational mission.

On November 19, 1927, a white stone frieze of Percy Haughton was unveiled outside the Locker Building at Soldiers Field. The monument was designed by the Boston firm Walker, Walker and Kingsbury, and sculpted by Mary O. Bowditch. It cost $10,000. The largest tablet featured the coach, in uniform, in a characteristic crouch with one knee on the ground, and beneath it were the words, "In Memory of Percy Duncan Haughton." Today, it is embedded in the stadium entrance. Symbolically, the placement is most appropriate, because P. D. furnished the very foundations of the modern game.

But perhaps the most fitting valedictory for these Crimson autumns had come years before from ancient rival Yale. Three days after Haughton's death, as the Elis played Army in the Yale Bowl, a poem entitled "Percy Haughton" appeared in the *Yale Alumni Weekly*:

> So tense we were, we two,
> Torn between,
> Ancient allegiance to the Army,
> And the Blue
> of Yale. They call
> The half, and all
> The eighty thousand breathless, mute,
> Bare headed, wait the flute.
> Clear silver notes the bugler rings
> In requiem to Haughton,

Never to be forgotten: A frieze dedicated to Percy Haughton is affixed to the cement wall at the open end of Harvard Stadium on the home side. *Dick Friedman.*

Yesterday
At play,
Today
A memory.
To you and me
And eighty thousand, thronged,
The bugler blows a benison of beauty
For Haughton, gone,
And duty—
The game goes on![64]

NOTES

PROLOGUE

1. Neal O'Hara, "28 Years in the Stadium Press Box," *Harvard A.A. News* (Cambridge, Mass.), November 25, 1939, 64.

2. Author interview with Dwayne Nix.

I. P. D. STRANGLES THE BULLDOG

1. For details of Roosevelt's role and its aftermath, see John J. Miller, *The Big Scrum* (New York: HarperCollins, 2012).

2. "Only One Worse Sport, He Says," *Boston Globe*, November 8, 1911.

3. Michael Oriard, *Reading Football: How the Popular Press Created an American Spectacle* (Chapel Hill and London: University of North Carolina Press, 1993), 191.

4. Oriard, *Reading Football*, 229.

5. Morris A. Bealle, *The History of Football at Harvard, 1874–1948* (Washington, D.C.: Columbia, 1948), 425.

6. For an illuminating look at the athletic culture in late 19th- and early 20th-century prep schools, see Axel Bundgaard, *Muscle and Manliness: The Rise of Sport in America's Boarding Schools* (Syracuse, N.Y.: Syracuse University Press, 2005).

7. Tim Cohane, *The Yale Football Story* (New York: G. P. Putnam's Sons, 1951), 108.

8. UAIII 15.88.10, Harvard University Archives.

9. Letter from Charles Daly to Cameron Forbes, January 1950, Harvard University Archives.

10. Melville E. Webb Jr., "Harvard Not Up to Mark," *Boston Globe*, October 22, 1911.

11. UAV.170.270.3, Harvard University Archives.

12. A fascinating look at the pre-Haughton turmoil can be found in *Big Time Football at Harvard, 1905: The Diary of Coach Bill Reid*, by Ronald A. Smith. Reid, who was a teammate of Haughton's at Harvard and starred at fullback, comes across as well-meaning, if a bit high-strung. His 1905 and 1906 teams each lost to Yale, 6–0. During those years, Reid would be a prime actor for rules changes, most notably the establishment of a neutral zone between the offensive and defensive lines.

13. The evolution of the rules is covered thoroughly in David M. Nelson's *The Anatomy of a Game: Football, the Rules, and the Men Who Made the Game* (Newark: University of Delaware Press, 1994).

14. Bealle, *The History of Football at Harvard*, 435.

15. "Harvard's Haughton Had Newsmen Chased," *Boston Globe*, January 11, 1955.

16. Allison Danzig, *The History of American Football: Its Great Teams, Players, and Coaches* (New York: Prentice-Hall, 1956), 194.

17. "Forward Pass Is Worked Out," *Boston Globe*, September 24, 1908.

18. "Harvard Opens with 5-to-0 Win over Bowdoin," *Boston Globe*, October 1, 1908.

19. "Football Teams Showing Ragged," *Boston Globe*, October 5, 1908.

20. "This Time Bates Fails to Score," *Boston Globe*, October 8, 1908.

21. George C. Carens, "Douglas Lawson Says Death Alone Balked at Haughton's Laterals," *Boston Transcript*, October 31, 1927.

22. William H. Edwards, *Football Days: Memories of the Game and the Men behind the Ball* (New York: Moffat, Yard and Company, 1916), 378–80.

23. Bealle, *The History of Football at Harvard*, 180.

24. "Harvard Plays Middies to a Tie," *Boston Globe*, October 25, 1908.

25. Edwards, *Football Days*, 378–80.

26. "Harvard Is a Winner, 6–2," *Boston Globe*, November 1, 1908.

27. "Mass Meeting for the Team," *Boston Globe*, November 6, 1908.

28. Bealle, *The History of Football at Harvard*, 429–31.

29. "Wouldn't Let Indians Start," *Boston Globe*, November 8, 1908.

30. Edwards, *Football Days*, 257–58.

31. "Victory for the Crimson," *Boston Globe*, November 15, 1908.

32. John Glaze, "Harvard Earned Victory," *Boston Globe*, November 15, 1908.

33. Samuel Eliot Morison, *Three Centuries of Harvard* (Cambridge, Mass.: Belknap Press, 1936), 406–7.

34. John A. Blanchard, ed., *The H Book of Harvard Athletics* (Cambridge, Mass.: Harvard Varsity Club, 1923), 420.

35. John E. Owsley to Walter Camp, December 16, 1905, as cited in Miller, *The Big Scrum*, 202–3, footnote 86.

36. Bealle, *The History of Football at Harvard*, 443–44.

37. Danzig, *The History of American Football*, 188.

38. Cohane, *The Yale Football Story*, 174.

39. Edwards, *Football Days*, 255–57.

40. "Winning Team Dissects Game," *Boston Globe*, November 22, 1908.

41. "President Elated," *Boston Globe*, November 22, 1908.

42. "Very Satisfactory, Says President Eliot," *Boston Globe*, November 22, 1908.

43. "Very Satisfactory, Says President Eliot."

44. Melville E. Webb Jr., "Crimson Triumphs," *Boston Globe*, November 22, 1908.

45. Cohane, *The Yale Football Story*, 175.

46. James Vautravers, "1908 College Football National Championship," *Tiptop25.com*, http://tiptop25.com/champ1908.html.

47. "In Honor of the Victorious Eleven," *Boston Globe*, December 3, 1908.

48. "Shoe That Beat Yale Last Year Now Gorgeous Affair," *Boston Globe*, October 29, 1909.

2. DEATH IN THE AFTERNOON

1. "Pres Lowell Inaugurated," *Boston Globe*, October 7, 1909.

2. L. B. R. Briggs, "Athletics and College Loyalty," *Harvard Alumni Bulletin*, November 4, 1908.

3. Henry Aaron Yeomans, *Abbott Lawrence Lowell, 1856–1943* (Cambridge, Mass.: Harvard University Press, 1948), 336, cited in Mark F. Bernstein, *Football: The Ivy League Origins of an American Obsession* (Philadelphia: University of Pennsylvania Press, 2001), 90.

4. Ring W. Lardner, "Michigan Seems in for a Licking," *Boston Globe*, October 31, 1914.

5. Charles E. Brickley student folder, UAIII 15.88.10, 1890–1968, Box 498, Harvard University Archives.

6. Table 4.1, "Number and Percentage of Jewish Students to Total Number of Students Admitted to Various Schools within Harvard University in

Specified Years, 1900–1922." Marcia Graham Synnott, *The Half-Opened Door* (Westport, Conn., and London: Greenwood Press, 1979), 96.

7. "Facts and Figures: Income and Prices, 1900–1999," *U.S. Diplomatic Mission*, https://usa.usembassy.de/etexts/his/e_prices1.htm.

8. *Harvard Class of 1916, Secretary's First Report* (Cambridge, Mass.: Printed for the class, 1917), 26.

9. "Football Men at It," *Boston Globe*, April 6, 1909.

10. "Harvard Has Good Squad," *Boston Globe*, September 19, 1909.

11. The other 1908 end, Charlie Crowley, had academic issues and was forced to leave school. In a late 1960s essay, Hamilton Fish wrote, "Crowley had been scolded by a dean because of subpar marks. Crowley responded by calling the dean a S.O.B. Mr. Crowley was requested to leave Cambridge." He would resurface in 1910, at Notre Dame, where for the next three seasons he started at one end; the other starter was a lad from Chicago named Knute Rockne. (Hamilton Fish, "Old Game vs. Modern Football.")

12. *Harvard College Class of 1912 Album* (Cambridge, Mass.: Crimson Printing Company, 1912), 101–2.

13. "Football Notes," *Boston Globe*, October 4, 1909.

14. "Football Notes," *Boston Globe*, October 19, 1909.

15. W. D. Sullivan, "One Fault of a Great Captain," *Boston Globe*, October 24, 1909.

16. Melville E. Webb Jr., "Cadets Showed Poor Condition," *Boston Globe*, November 1, 1909.

17. "The Deadly Mass Play," *New York Times*, November 2, 1909.

18. "Brutal Football," *New York Times*, November 3, 1909.

19. "Stop the Mass Plays," *New York Times*, November 16, 1909.

20. "Football Is Barbarous," *New York Times*, November 4, 1909.

21. "Rush for Yale–Harvard Tickets," *New York Times*, November 4, 1909.

22. "Harvard Very Fit," *Boston Globe*, November 5, 1909.

23. "Dartmouth's Kicking Game," *Boston Globe*, November 14, 1909.

24. Michael Oriard, *Reading Football: How the Popular Press Created an American Spectacle* (Chapel Hill and London: University of North Carolina Press, 1993), 193.

25. "Unequalled Spectacle," *Boston Globe*, November 21, 1909.

26. "Easy Victory for Everett," *Boston Globe*, November 21, 1909.

27. Thomas G. Bergin, *The Game: The Harvard–Yale Football Rivalry, 1875–1983* (New Haven, Conn.: Yale University Press, 1984), 100–1.

28. "Cocktails and Touchdowns," *Boston Globe*, November 19, 1909.

29. Tim Cohane, *The Yale Football Story* (New York: G. P. Putnam's Sons, 1951), 177.

30. Allison Danzig, *The History of American Football: Its Great Teams, Players, and Coaches* (New York: Prentice-Hall, 1956), 100–101.

31. Melville E. Webb Jr., "Coy's Good Right Leg Gives Yale Win over Harvard, 8–0," *Boston Globe*, November 21, 1909.

32. "Football Notes," *Boston Globe*, November 23, 1909.

33. John McCallum, *Ivy League Football since 1872* (New York: Stein and Day, 1977), 56, as cited in Bernstein, *Football*, 88.

34. Webb, "Coy's Good Right Leg."

35. "Want to Marry Ted Coy," *Boston Globe*, November 23, 1909.

36. Morris A. Bealle, *The History of Football at Harvard, 1874–1948* (Washington, D.C.: Columbia, 1948), 191: "The game . . . was marred by numerous holding penalties against Harvard inflicted by umpire Bill Edwards of Princeton."

37. Webb, "Coy's Good Right Leg."

38. "Harvard under the Right General," *Boston Globe*, November 21, 1909.

39. *Harvard College Class of 1910 Album* (Cambridge, Mass.: Crimson Printing Company, 1910), 52.

3. HAUGHTON CUTS CAMP OFF
AT THE PASS

1. *Boston Globe*, October 23, 1909.

2. Henry Beach Needham, "The College Athlete: How Commercialism Is Making Him a Professional," *McClure's Magazine*, Part I, June 1905: "Recruiting and Subsidizing"; part II, July 1905: "'Summer Ball,' the Gate-Money Evil, and 'Unnecessary Roughness' in Football."

3. Needham, "The College Athlete," Part I.

4. Bob Holmes, "The Options Were Many, But It Was an Easy Play," *Boston Globe*, November 24, 1999.

5. "Somerville on Top by 11 to 10," *Boston Globe*, December 5, 1909.

6. Charles E. Brickley student folder, UAIII 15.88.10, 1890–1968, Box 498, Harvard University Archives.

7. "$15,000 Salary to Mathewson," *Boston Globe*, November 6, 1910.

8. Edward W. Mahan student folder, UAIII 15.88.10, 1890–1968, Box 3219, Harvard University Archives.

9. "Live Tips and Topics," *Boston Globe*, November 16, 1911.

10. Mahan student folder.

11. John Sayle Watterson, *College Football: History, Spectacle, Controversy* (Baltimore, Md., and London: Johns Hopkins University Press, 2000), 127–29.

12. Frank G. Cavanaugh, "Harvard Sprung Surprise," *Boston Globe*, November 19, 1911.

13. Percy Langdon Wendell student folder, UAIII 15.88.10, 1890–1968, Box 5314, Harvard University Archives.

14. *Harvard College Class of 1911 Album* (Boston: Massachusetts Engraving Company, 1911), 84.

15. "Harvard Plays Clever Football," *New York Times*, October 16, 1910.

16. Morris A. Bealle, *The History of Football at Harvard, 1874–1948* (Washington, D.C.: Columbia, 1948), 431–32.

17. "Harvard Crosses Army Goal Line; Withington Rushes for Touchdown," *New York Times*, October 30, 1910.

18. *New York Times*, November 6, 1910.

19. W. S. Barnes Jr., "Harvard Ever Master," *Boston Globe*, November 13, 1910.

20. Bealle, *The History of Football at Harvard*, 402.

21. "Yale Surprises Harvard with Tied No-Score Game," *New York Times*, November 20, 1910.

22. "Yale Surprises Harvard with Tied No-Score Game."

23. "Yale Surprises Harvard with Tied No-Score Game."

24. *Harvard Alumni Bulletin*, December 14, 1911.

25. James Vautravers, "1910 College Football National Championship," *Tiptop25.com*, http://tiptop25.com/champ1910.html.

26. *Harvard College Class of 1911 Album*, 84.

27. "Harvard 11 Lacked Initiative," *New York Times*, November 21, 1910.

4. "HERE IS THE THEORETICAL SUPERPLAYER IN FLESH AND BLOOD"

1. *Boston Herald*, May 16, 1911.

2. "Mr. Haughton's Address to the Football Men," *Harvard Alumni Bulletin*, March 29, 1911.

3. "Scoreboard for Game Today," *Harvard Crimson*, October 7, 1911.

4. Irwin, a dabbler in many side businesses, committed suicide in 1921, by leaping from a steamer, when it was discovered he had two families. "Irwin's Double Life Bared by Suicide," *New York Times*, July 21, 1921.

5. "Roper Developing Fast Open Football," *New York Times*, October 9, 1911.

6. Melville E. Webb Jr., "Better Line Now on Big Elevens," *Boston Globe*, October 6, 1911.

7. Herbert F. Reed, "A Game, Not a Religious Rite," *Boston Globe*, October 18, 1911.

8. Melville E. Webb Jr., "Harvard Winner, 20–6," *Boston Globe*, October 29, 1911.

9. "Football Notes," *Boston Globe*, October 31, 1911.

10. "Auto Routes to Princeton," *Boston Globe*, November 2, 1911.

11. Minutes, Harvard Athletic Association, January 19, 1911, Vol. II, 741–42.

12. "Toss-up, Says Hamilton Fish," *Boston Globe*, November 4, 1911.

13. Mark F. Bernstein, *Princeton Football* (Charleston, S.C.; Chicago; Portsmouth, N.H.; San Francisco, Calif.: Arcadia, 2009), 38.

14. Melville E. Webb Jr., "Tigers Beat Harvard, 8–6," *Boston Globe*, November 5, 1911.

15. Matthew J. Bruccoli, *Some Sort of Epic Grandeur: The Life of F. Scott Fitzgerald* (New York: Harcourt Brace Jovanovich, 1987), 33, cited in Mark F. Bernstein, *Football: The Ivy League Origins of an American Obsession* (Philadelphia: University of Pennsylvania Press, 2001), 99.

16. Bernstein, *Football*, 99.

17. *Harvard College Class of 1912 Album* (Cambridge, Mass.: University Press, 1912), 108–10.

18. Bernstein, *Football*, 99.

19. Morris A. Bealle, *The History of Football at Harvard, 1874–1948* (Washington, D.C.: Columbia, 1948), 384.

20. Harvard Athletic Association, financial statements, "Carlisle–Harvard Football Game, Soldiers Field, November 11, 1911," UAV 170.283, Box 2, Harvard University Archives.

21. "Football Notes," *Boston Globe*, October 27, 1911.

22. Harvard Athletic Association, financial statements, "Carlisle–Harvard Football Game."

23. Melville E. Webb, Jr., "Indians Win in Stadium," *Boston Globe*, November 12, 1911.

24. Webb, "Indians Win in Stadium."

25. Webb, "Indians Win in Stadium."

26. Kate Buford, *Native American Son: The Life and Sporting Legend of Jim Thorpe* (New York: Knopf, 2010), 102.

27. *Boston Globe*, November 12, 1911.

28. Buford, *Native American Son*, 103.

29. "Sorry Finish by Yale, Dean Says," *Boston Globe*, November 26, 1911.

30. W. D. Sullivan, "W. D. Sullivan Describes Game as One of Lost Opportunities," *Boston Globe*, November 26, 1911.

31. Melville E. Webb Jr., "Scoreless Struggle," *Boston Globe*, November 26, 1911.

32. Melville E. Webb Jr., "Football Rules Revising Urged," *Boston Globe*, November 27, 1911.

33. "Freshmen Beat Princeton," *Harvard Crimson*, November 6, 1911.

5. THE DA VINCI OF THE DROPKICK

1. "Politics at Harvard," *Boston Globe*, November 3, 1912.

2. "Turkey Trot Barred at Junior Cotillion," *New York Times*, November 26, 1912.

3. "Golden Secret of Dropkicking," *Boston Globe*, September 26, 1915.

4. Arthur Daley, "More on Charlie Brickley," *New York Times*, April 6, 1948.

5. John W. Heisman, *Collier's*, October 20, 1928, as quoted in Allison Danzig, *The History of American Football: Its Great Teams, Players and Coaches* (New York: Prentice-Hall, 1956), 116.

6. Allison Danzig, *The History of American Football: Its Great Teams, Players, and Coaches* (New York: Prentice-Hall, 1956), 146–47.

7. Danzig, *The History of American Football*, 147.

8. William H. Edwards, *Football Days: Memories of the Game and the Men behind the Ball* (New York: Moffat, Yard and Company, 1916), 146–49.

9. "Kicked Five Field Goals," *Boston Globe*, November 25, 1906.

10. Sol Metzger, "When and How to Kick," *Boy's Life*, November 1931, 28.

11. Brickley's precepts are provided in "The Golden Secret of Dropkicking," *Boston Globe*, September 26, 1915.

12. Various interviews with the author; interviewees asked to remain anonymous.

13. James Vautravers, "1912 College Football National Championship," *Tiptop25.com*, http://tiptop25.com/champ1912.html.

14. *Harvard Alumni Bulletin*, October 2, 1912.

15. *Harvard Alumni Bulletin*, October 9, 1912.

16. Edwards, *Football Days*, 229–30.

17. *Harvard Alumni Bulletin*, October 30, 1912.

18. Herbert, "Harvard Victor in Roaring Battle," *New York Tribune*, November 3, 1912, 10.

19. "How Harvard Lowered Princeton's Colors in a Thrilling Struggle," *New York Tribune*, November 3, 1912, 10.

20. Herbert, "Harvard Victor in Roaring Battle," 10.

21. *Harvard Alumni Bulletin*, November 13, 1912.

22. Arthur Daley, "More on Charlie Brickley," *New York Times*, April 6, 1948.

23. "The Yale Game," *Harvard Crimson*, November 22, 1912.

24. *Harvard College Class of 1913 Album* (Cambridge, Mass.: University Press, 1913), 112–13.

25. "Live Tips and Topics," *Boston Globe*, November 25, 1912.

26. W. D. Sullivan, "Yale Played Off Its Feet by Harvard, Getting Worst Beating in 11 Years, 20–0," *Boston Globe*, November 24, 1912.

27. *Harvard College Class of 1913 Album*, 113.

28. Vautravers, "1912 College Football National Championship."

29. *Harvard Alumni Bulletin*, December 11, 1912.

30. Clipping from indeterminate newspaper, December 18, 1912, Brickley student folder, UAIII 15.88.10, 1890–1968, Box 498, Harvard University Archives.

31. *Harvard Alumni Bulletin*, April 30, 1913.

32. "Felton Weds Miss Nelson," *Boston Globe*, October 22, 1913.

6. THE SYSTEM

1. Morris A. Bealle, *The History of Football at Harvard, 1874–1948* (Washington, D.C.: Columbia, 1948), 429.

2. All quotes from Haughton in this chapter relating to his system come from his book *Football and How to Watch It* (Boston: Marshall Jones Company, 1922), unless otherwise indicated.

3. Bealle, *The History of Football at Harvard*, 433.

4. Bealle, *The History of Football at Harvard*, 433–34.

5. Bealle, *The History of Football at Harvard*, 395.

6. Grantland Rice, "Harvard's Haughton Had Newsmen Chased," *Boston Globe*, January 11, 1955.

7. Bealle, *The History of Football at Harvard*, 432.

8. Rice, "Harvard's Haughton Had Newsmen Chased."

9. "Live Tips and Topics," *Boston Globe*, November 25, 1912.

10. Bealle, *The History of Football at Harvard*, 437.

11. Bealle, *The History of Football at Harvard*, 439.

12. "Dinner to the Football Eleven," *Harvard Alumni Bulletin*, January 5, 1916.

13. *Boston Transcript*, October 28, 1924.

14. Bealle, *The History of Football at Harvard*, 436.

15. "Dinner to the Football Eleven."

16. Bealle, *The History of Football at Harvard*, 434.

17. "Dinner to the Football Eleven."

18. Allison Danzig, *The History of American Football: Its Great Teams, Players, and Coaches* (New York: Prentice-Hall, 1956), 195.

19. Author interviews.

20. Bealle, *The History of Football at Harvard*, 438.

21. *Harvard Alumni Bulletin*, December 11, 1912.

22. William H. Edwards, *Football Days: Memories of the Game and the Men behind the Ball* (New York: Moffat, Yard and Company, 1916), 268.

23. Reggie Brown Notebooks, Number 4, 1911/Harvard Football/Scouting, Rare Books and Special Collections, Series No. FBC905–1-4, Hesburgh Libraries, University of Notre Dame.

24. Edwards, *Football Days*, 268.

25. Bealle, *The History of Football at Harvard*, 445.

26. Danzig, *The History of American Football*, 194.

7. BRICKLEY 15, YALE 5

1. "Boston Bans the Tango," *New York Times*, October 12, 1913.

2. Details of the dropkicking contest are found in Morris A. Bealle, *The History of Football at Harvard, 1874–1948* (Washington, D.C.: Columbia, 1948), 206–7.

3. *New York Times*, November 2, 1913.

4. Clark Shaughnessy, *Football in War and Peace* (Clinton, S.C.: Jacobs Press, 1943), 15.

5. Charles E. Brickley, "Critical Moments in Big Games," *Boston Globe*, October 17, 1915.

6. William H. Edwards, *Football Days: Memories of the Game and the Men behind the Ball* (New York: Moffat, Yard and Company, 1916), 422.

7. Edwards, *Football Days*, 314–19.

8. *Harvard Alumni Bulletin*, October 8, 1913.

9. James Carl Nelson, *Five Lieutenants: The Heartbreaking Story of Five Harvard Men Who Led America to Victory in World War I* (New York: St. Martin's, 2012), 104.

10. "Williams Crumbles under Final Smashing Attack of the Crimson," *Boston Globe*, October 12, 1913.

11. *Harvard Class of 1914, 50th Anniversary Report* (Cambridge, Mass.: Cambridge University, 1964), 206–7.

12. *Harvard Alumni Bulletin*, October 22, 1913.

13. "Harvard Defeats Penn State Easily," *New York Times*, October 26, 1913.

14. *New York Times*, November 2, 1913.

15. Haughton to Langford, September 30, 1913.

16. Langford to Haughton, October 2, 1913.

17. Arthur Daley, "More on Charlie Brickley," *New York Times*, April 6, 1948.

18. "Brickley Thinks Notre Dame Strongest Eleven; Giants Play Thorpe's Tigers Here Dec. 4," *Brooklyn Daily Eagle*, November 25, 1921.

19. "Harvard Beats Princeton, 3–0," *New York Times*, November 9, 1913.

20. "Strategy Aided Harvard to Win," *New York Times*, November 10, 1913.

21. Brickley, "Critical Moments in Big Games."

22. Melville E. Webb Jr., "Harvard Breaks an Old Tradition," *Boston Globe*, November 9, 1913.

23. *"Globe* Sportsman," *Boston Globe*, November 24, 1913.

24. Fred W. Moore, "The Distribution of Yale Football Tickets," *Harvard Alumni Bulletin*, November 5, 1913.

25. "Golden Secret of Dropkicking," *Boston Globe*, September 25, 1915.

26. "Mal Logan Depicts the Real Haughton and His System," *Boston Herald*, October 10, 1926.

27. Bill Cunningham, "Instinct Made Brickley Hero," *Boston Herald*, November 20, 1947.

28. Arthur Daley, "A Visit with Charlie Brickley," *New York Times*, April 4, 1948.

29. W. D. Sullivan, "Yale's Ancient Game Shown Up," *Boston Globe*, November 23, 1913.

30. Daley, "A Visit with Charlie Brickley."

31. Sullivan, "Yale's Ancient Game Shown Up."

32. Daley, "A Visit with Charlie Brickley."

33. Cunningham, "Instinct Made Brickley Hero."

34. Daley, "A Visit with Charlie Brickley."

35. Webb, "Harvard Smashes Two Traditions."

36. Daley, "A Visit with Charlie Brickley."

37. Cunningham, "Instinct Made Brickley Hero."

38. "News and Notes: The Victory," *Harvard Alumni Bulletin*, November 26, 1913.

39. Cunningham, "Instinct Made Brickley Hero."

40. "Brickley Kicks Five Field Goals; Harvard Winner," *Chicago Tribune*, November 23, 1913.

41. Shaughnessy, *Football in War and Peace*, 17.

42. Sullivan, "Yale's Ancient Game Shown Up."

43. "Brickley and Harvard Team Theatre Idols," *Boston Herald*, November 23, 1913.

44. James Vautravers, "1913 College Football National Championship," *Tiptop25.com*, http://tiptop25.com/champ1913.html.

45. "Mrs. Percy Haughton Will Receive $380,000," *Boston Advertiser*, November 18, 1913.

46. "Flat Toe Cap Aids Brickley's Kicking," *New York Times*, December 7, 1913.

47. "Hardwick Engaged to Miss Stone," *Boston Globe*, November 30, 1913.

48. "Tack Hardwick Takes a Bride," *Los Angeles Times*, July 9, 1915.

49. "Nearly 1,000 Guests at Hardwick–Stone Wedding," *Boston Globe*, July 9, 1915.

8. THE FOOTBALL–INDUSTRIAL COMPLEX

1. Henry Beach Needham, "The College Athlete: How Commercialism Is Making Him a Professional," *McClure's Magazine*, Part II, July 1905: "'Summer Ball,' the Gate-Money Evil, and 'Unnecessary Roughness' in Football."

2. Samuel Eliot Morison, *Three Centuries of Harvard* (Cambridge, Mass.: Belknap Press, 1936), 414–15.

3. Harvard Athletic Association, financial statement, 1916–1917, UAV 170.228, Harvard University Archives.

4. "President Lowell's Annual Report," *Harvard Alumni Bulletin*, February 26, 1913.

5. "Opinion and Comment," *Harvard Alumni Bulletin*, February 12, 1913.

6. "Opinion and Comment," *Harvard Alumni Bulletin*, March 1, 1911.

7. "On Sportsmanship," Letters to the Editor, *Harvard Alumni Bulletin*, December 3, 1913.

8. Harvard Athletic Association, "Report of the Graduate Treasurer for the Year Ending July 31, 1915," UAV 170.275, "Receipts and Expenditures, Printed and Typewritten Statements," Box 1, 1889–1905 to July 31, 1921, Harvard University Archives.

9. Harvard Athletic Association, financial statement, varsity football, 1916–1917, UAV 170.228, Harvard University Archives.

10. "Live Tips and Topics," *Boston Globe*, November 4, 1911.

11. "Football Tickets," *Harvard Alumni Bulletin*, September 24, 1913.

12. "Motor Vehicle Registrations," *Allcountries.org*, www.allcountries.org/uscensus/1027_motor_vehicle_registrations.html.

13. "Going to the Game," *New York Times*, November 20, 1910.

14. "Society Folk at Yale Field," *New York Times*, November 20, 1910.

15. "Live Tips and Topics," *Boston Globe*, November 23, 1911.

16. Herbert F. Reed, *Football for Public and Player* (New York: Frederick A. Stokes, 1913), 45.

17. Reed, *Football for Public and Player*, 10.

18. "Mel Webb Dies; Rites on Thursday," *Boston Globe*, October 24, 1961.

19. "How to Play Football, by Coach Dinkey," *Harvard Lampoon*, November 18, 1915, 190–91.

20. "Going to the Game," *New York Times*, November 20, 1910.

21. "Lessons of the Game," *Boston Globe*, November 27, 1911.

9. "YALE SUPPLIED THE BOWL . . . BUT HARVARD HAD THE PUNCH"

1. "Football at Yale: The Story of a Tradition, Part 2," *YouTube*, www.youtube.com/watch?v=wS657MblFkU&t=486s.

2. *Boston Globe*, September 15, 1914.

3. "War and Scholarship," *Harvard Alumni Bulletin*, October 7, 1914.

4. *Harvard College Class of 1915 Album* (Cambridge, Mass.: Andover Press, 1915), 113.

5. Grantland Rice, "The Sport Light," *Boston Globe*, September 16, 1915.

6. "Harvard Beats Springfield, 44–0," *Boston Globe*, October 4, 1914.

7. "Grantland Rice on Tack Hardwick," *Boston Globe*, July 5, 1949.

8. "Lower Strength Tests," *Harvard Alumni Bulletin*, June 23, 1915.

9. Huntington R. Hardwick, "A Few Facts on End Play," in *The Book of Athletics*, edited by Paul Withington, revised by Lothrop Withington (Boston: Lothrop, Lee & Shepard, 1922), 102.

10. William H. Edwards, *Football Days: Memories of the Game and the Men behind the Ball* (New York: Moffat, Yard and Company, 1916), 423.

11. Braven Dyer, "Grantland Rice Tells of Greatest Thrills," *Los Angeles Times*, January 26, 1936.

12. The tale of Pollard's tantalizing matriculation at Harvard is recounted by John M. Carroll in *Fritz Pollard: Pioneer in Racial Advancement* (Champaign: University of Illinois Press, 1992), 52–54.

13. "Harvard Wins by a Point, 10–9," *Boston Globe*, October 11, 1914.

14. Melville E. Webb Jr., "Harvard Unlucky in Loss of Captains," *Boston Globe*, October 12, 1914.

15. "Harvard Has Hands Full, But Wins, 13–6," *Boston Globe*, October 18, 1914.

16. 1914/Reggie Brown Notebooks, Number TK/Harvard Football Scouting, Rare Books and Special Collections, Series No. FBC905–1-4, Hesburgh Libraries, University of Notre Dame.

17. "Live Tips and Topics," *Boston Globe*, October 26, 1914.

18. "Football Notes," *Boston Globe*, October 26, 1914.

19. Harvard Athletic Association, financial statements, varsity football, 1902–1918, Michigan–Harvard football game, Soldiers Field, October 31, 1914, UAV 170.283, Box 2, Harvard University Archives.

20. 1914/Reggie Brown Notebooks, Number TK/Harvard Football Scouting, Rare Books and Special Collections, Series No. FBC905–1-4, Hesburgh Libraries, University of Notre Dame.

21. "Rockne Picks Harvard," *Boston Globe*, October 20, 1914.

22. Ring W. Lardner, "The Greatest Team Ever Developed in the West," *Boston Globe*, October 29, 1914.

23. Harvard Athletic Association financial statements, UAV 170.283, Box 2.

24. Melville E. Webb Jr., "Harvard Has the Punch and Beats Michigan, 7–0," *Boston Globe*, November 1, 1914.

25. Webb, "Harvard Has the Punch."

26. "Fine Forecast for Princeton," *Boston Globe*, November 7, 1914.

27. Dudley S. Dean, "Harvard Had Tigers Fooled," *Boston Globe*, November 8, 1914.

28. W. D. Sullivan, "Vindicates the Rushing Game," *Boston Globe*, November 8, 1914.

29. Melville E. Webb Jr., "Harvard–Yale Game Will Be the Greatest Spectacle in American Sport," *Boston Globe*, November 15, 1914.

30. Percy D. Haughton, "Princeton Play Dodged," *Boston Globe*, November 9, 1914.

31. Webb, "Harvard–Yale Game Will Be the Greatest Spectacle."

32. 1914/Reggie Brown Notebooks, Number TK/Harvard Football Scouting, Rare Books and Special Collections, Series No. FBC905–1-4, Hesburgh Libraries, University of Notre Dame.

33. Albert H. Barclay, "Yale's Great Bowl Ready for the Harvard Game," *Boston Globe*, November 1, 1914.

34. Barclay, "Yale's Great Bowl Ready."

35. "New York Trains to Yale Game," *Harvard Alumni Bulletin*, November 11, 1914.

36. "Harvard and Yale Battle on Gridiron," *New York Times*, November 21, 1914.

37. "Somerville Couple to Attend Football Game on Honeymoon," *Boston Globe*, November 19, 1914.

38. Harvard Athletic Association financial statements, varsity football, 1902–1918, Yale–Harvard football game, Yale Bowl, November 21, 1914, 1902–1918, UAV 170.283, Box 2, Harvard University Archives.

39. Harry Cross, "Harvard Beats Yale by 36 to 0," *New York Times*, November 22, 1914.

40. Cross, "Harvard Beats Yale by 36 to 0."

41. W. D. Sullivan, "Yale's Waterloo," *Boston Globe*, November 22, 1914.

42. Arthur Daley, "More on Charlie Brickley," *New York Times*, April 4, 1948.

43. Cross, "Harvard Beats Yale by 36 to 0."

44. Melville E. Webb Jr., "Champion's Crown Harvard's Very Own," *Boston Globe*, November 23, 1914.

45. James Vautravers, "1914 College Football National Championship," *Tiptop25.com*, http://tiptop25.com/champ1914.html.

46. "Dinner to the Eleven," *Harvard Alumni Bulletin*, December 2, 1914.

47. "The Athletic Year," *Harvard Alumni Bulletin*, June 30, 1915.

48. *Harvard College Class of 1915 Album*, 65.

10. POOR ELI'S HOPES WE ARE DASHING

1. Melville E. Webb Jr., "Crimson a Better Team Than It Looked to Be Saturday," *Boston Globe*, October 25, 1915.

2. Grantland Rice, "The Sport Light," *Boston Globe*, October 30, 1915.

3. Samuel Eliot Morison, *Three Centuries of Harvard* (Cambridge, Mass.: Belknap Press, 1936), 450.

4. Frank P. Sibley, "With the Boston Bunch at Plattsburg," *Boston Globe*, August 15, 1915.

5. Melville E. Webb Jr., "Wealth of Material for Harvard Football," *Boston Globe*, September 27, 1915.

6. Melville E. Webb Jr., "Experience Will Help," *Boston Globe*, October 4, 1915.

7. Albert H. Barclay, "Yale Disturbed about Her Football Outlook," *Boston Globe*, October 10, 1915.

8. "Harvard's Football Squad Given Shakeup," *Boston Globe*, October 10, 1915.

9. "Harvard Wins, 29 to 7; Indians Fighting Hard," *Boston Globe*, October 10, 1915.

10. Melville E. Webb Jr., "Cornell's Season Pointed toward Next Saturday's Harvard Match," *Boston Globe*, October 18, 1915.

11. Webb, "Cornell's Season Pointed."

12. "It Will Take All That Harvard Has to Beat This Cornell Team," *Boston Globe*, October 22, 1915.

13. Melville E. Webb Jr., "Ithaca Wins after 25 Years of Trying," *Boston Globe*, October 24, 1915.

14. "Cornell Boys Celebrate," *Boston Globe*, October 24, 1915.

15. Webb, "Ithaca Wins after 25 Years of Trying."

16. Grantland Rice, "The Sport Light," *Boston Globe*, October 26, 1915.

17. "Edward Mahan, 83," *Boston Globe*, July 24, 1975.

18. William H. Edwards, *Football Days: Memories of the Game and the Men behind the Ball* (New York: Moffat, Yard and Company, 1916), 344–46.

19. Grantland Rice, "The Sport Light," *Boston Globe*, October 27, 1915.

20. Grantland Rice, "The Sport Light," *Boston Globe*, October 28, 1915.

21. "Coach Hinkey Deposed by Yale's Captain," *Boston Globe*, November 1, 1915.

22. Mark F. Bernstein, *Football: The Ivy League Origins of an American Obsession* (Philadelphia: University of Pennsylvania Press, 2001), 54.

23. Herbert F. Reed, "Harvard: Gridiron Deceiver," *Harper's Weekly*, November 27, 1915.

24. "Harvard Beats Princeton, 10 to 6," *Harvard Alumni Bulletin*, November 10, 1915.

25. "Live Tips and Topics," *Boston Globe*, November 16, 1915.

26. Percy D. Haughton, "Coach Proud of Harvard," *Boston Globe*, November 7, 1915.

27. Reed, "Harvard: Gridiron Deceiver."

28. "Harvard Subs Humble Brown," *Boston Globe*, November 14, 1915.

29. W. D. Sullivan, "Picks Harvard to Win in a Desperate Fight," *Boston Globe*, November 18, 1915.

30. "Live Tips and Topics," *Boston Globe*, November 15, 1915.

31. "The Harvard Club of Alsace Reconquise," *Harvard Alumni Bulletin*, March 8, 1916.

32. "Harvard Given Great Send-Off," *Boston Globe*, November 19, 1915.

33. "Lucky 49,000 Receive Tickets," *Boston Globe*, November 16, 1915.

34. "Planning for Stadium Crowd," *Boston Globe*, November 20, 1915.

35. "To Aid War Sufferers," *Boston Globe*, November 20, 1915.

36. "Yale Battles with Harvard," *Yale Daily News*, November 20, 1915.

37. Charles E. Brickley, "Brickley Picks Harvard to Win in a Decisive Way," *Boston Globe*, November 20, 1915.

38. W. D. Sullivan, "King's Scoring Run a Marvel," *Boston Globe*, November 21, 1915.

39. Sullivan, "King's Scoring Run a Marvel."

40. Sullivan, "King's Scoring Run a Marvel."

41. "Cheer Mahan and Haughton," *Boston Globe*, November 21, 1915.

42. "Cheer Mahan and Haughton."

43. "Harvard Team at the Theater," *Boston Globe*, November 21, 1915.

44. Tim Cohane, *The Yale Football Story* (New York: G. P. Putnam's Sons, 1951), 198.

45. James Vautravers, "1915 College Football Top 25," *Tiptop25.com*, http://tiptop25.com/top25_1915.html.

46. *Harvard Class of 1916, First Report* (Cambridge, Mass.: Printed for the class, 1917), 215.

I I. FROM SOLDIERS FIELD TO FLANDERS FIELD, AND BEYOND

1. Grantland Rice, "The Sport Light," *Boston Globe*, November 20, 1915.

2. "Eddie Mahan Arrives at Berkeley; to Don Suit Friday," *Oakland Tribune*, August 29, 1916.

3. John P. Marquand, *Point of No Return* (New York: Little, Brown, 1949), 363.

4. Tim Cohane, *The Yale Football Story* (New York: G. P. Putnam's Sons, 1951), 200.

5. Walter Chauncey Camp Papers, MS 125. Box 12. Manuscripts and Archives, Yale University Library.

6. *Boston Globe*, November 28, 1916.

7. "Letters to the Bulletin: Stanley Bagg Pennock, '15," *Harvard Alumni Bulletin*, December 14, 1916.

8. *Harvard Class of 1915, 25th Anniversary Report* (Cambridge, Mass.: Cosmos Press, 1940), 585–86.

9. Charles E. Brickley, "Brickley Compares Three Elevens," *Boston Globe*, October 31, 1915.

10. *Boston Transcript*, March 28, 1916.

11. Harold Kaese, *The Boston Braves* (New York: G. P. Putnam's Sons, 1948), 175–76.

12. Morris A. Bealle, *The History of Football at Harvard, 1874–1948* (Washington, D.C.: Columbia, 1948), 441.

13. *Harvard Class of 1913, Third Report* (Norwood, Mass.: Plimpton Press, 1920), 139.

14. *Harvard Class of 1914, 15th Anniversary Report* (Cambridge, Mass.: University Press, 1929), 91.

15. *Harvard Class of 1914, 50th Anniversary Report* (Cambridge, Mass.: Printed at the university, 1964), 270.

16. *Harvard Class of 1913, Third Report*, xli–xlvii.

17. *Harvard Class of 1916, 25th Anniversary Report* (Cambridge, Mass.: Printed at the university, 1941), 376–77.

18. James Carl Nelson, *Five Lieutenants: The Heartbreaking Story of Five Harvard Men Who Led America to Victory in World War I* (New York: St. Martin's, 2012), 309.

19. M. A. DeWolfe Howe, *Memoirs of the Harvard Dead in the War against Germany*, vol. 3 (Cambridge, Mass.: Harvard University Press, 1922), 527.

20. Alva Johnston, "The Ghosting Business," *New Yorker*, November 23, 1935, 23. According to Walsh, Haughton had his standards. "Haughton was induced to make nominations for an All-Eastern football team, but he would not name an All-America team, because he would not guess at the merits of players whom he had not seen."

21. "P. D. Haughton Dies, Stricken Suddenly," *New York Times*, October 28, 1924.

22. "Charles E. Brickley Found Not Guilty," *Boston Globe*, May 29, 1925.

23. "Charles E. Brickley Indicted for Theft in Illegal Stock Deals in Springfield," *New York Times*, May 16, 1923.

24. "Jury Is Chosen for Brickley Case," *Boston Globe*, May 27, 1925.

25. "Charles E. Brickley Indicted for Theft."

26. "Charles E. Brickley Found Not Guilty."

27. "Brickley Describes Investment Deals," *Boston Globe*, February 24, 1928.

28. "Brickley Questioned on Deals as Broker," *Boston Globe*, February 28, 1928.

29. "Brickley Is Given 15 Months in Jail," *Boston Globe*, March 23, 1928.

30. "Brickley Is Given 15 Months in Jail."

31. "Brickley Is Given 15 Months in Jail."

32. *Harvard Class of 1915, 25th Anniversary Report*, 77–78.

33. *Time*, January 1, 1945, 16.

34. *Harvard Class of 1915, 25th Anniversary Report*, 785.

35. Confirmed to the author by Trumbull's granddaughter, Lydia Herron-Moore.

36. Edward W. Mahan student folder, UAIII.15.88.10, 1890–1968, Box 3219, Harvard University Archives.

37. *Harvard* Class of 1916, 25th Anniversary Report, 56.

38. *Harvard Class of 1912, 25th Anniversary Report* (Cambridge, Mass.: Cosmos Press, 1937), 238.

39. *Spalding's Official Foot Ball Guide for 1914*, HUD.10914.5, Harvard University Archives.

40. *Harvard Class of 1913, 25th Anniversary Report* (Cambridge, Mass.: Cosmos Press, 1938), 866.

41. *Harvard Class of 1913, 25th Anniversary Report*, 866.

42. Rick Atkinson, *The Day of Battle: The War in Sicily and Italy, 1943–1944* (New York: Henry Holt and Company, 2007), 191.

43. Atkinson, *The Day of Battle*, 191–93, 197.

44. Paul H. Mills, "The Bold Military Adventure of Maine Governor Tudor Gardiner," *Franklin County* (Maine) *Daily Bulldog*, May 27, 2012.

45. "Wife to Divorce 'Tack' Hardwick," *Boston Globe*, June 9, 1933.

46. "'Tack' Hardwick Dies Suddenly on Cuttyhunk," *Boston Globe*, June 27, 1949.

47. "Grantland Rice on Tack Hardwick," *Boston Globe*, July 5, 1949.

48. "'Tack' Hardwick Dies Suddenly on Cuttyhunk."

49. Bill Cunningham, "Strange Life of Brickley," *Boston Herald*, December 30, 1949.

50. Confirmed to the author by relatives of teammates.

51. "Brickley, 58, Ex-Football Great, Dies," *Boston Globe*, December 29, 1949.

52. "Brickley, Fair Harvard Hero, and Son Meet Blue Coat Defeat in Reuben's Aisles," *New York Times*, December 15, 1949.

53. Red Smith, "Brickley Said Harvard Needed Grid Dictator," *Boston Globe*, December 29, 1949.

54. "Brickley, Fair Harvard Hero."

55. Smith, "Brickley Said Harvard Needed Grid Dictator."

56. "Charley Brickley Dies in Hotel Here," *New York Times*, December 29, 1949.

57. "Stars of Sports, Public Officials Mourn Brickley," *Boston Globe*, January 3, 1950.

58. "Charley Brickley Dies in New York," *Harvard Crimson*, January 5, 1950. The obit is a respectful four paragraphs long. Then again, to a 20-year-old undergrad, anything that happened 35 years beforehand is ancient history.

59. Cunningham, "Strange Life of Brickley."

60. "Harvard Enshrines 50 Sons," *Boston Globe*, October 28, 1967.

61. *Harvard Class of 1938, 40th Anniversary Report* (Cambridge, Mass.: Printed for the class, 1938), 24.

62. Eric Pace, "At 100, Hamilton Fish Has Plenty of Kick," *New York Times*, December 8, 1988.

63. Clark Shaughnessy, *Football in War and Peace* (Clinton, S.C.: Jacobs Press, 1943), 77.

64. Reprinted from the *Yale Alumni Weekly*, November 1, 1924, in the *Harvard Alumni Bulletin*, November 20, 1924, 261.

SELECTED BIBLIOGRAPHY

The following books, periodicals, and websites were integral in writing this book. A few stand out: among daily newspapers, the *Boston Globe*, *Harvard Crimson*, and *New York Times*, and among magazines, the weekly *Harvard Alumni Bulletin* (predecessor to today's *Harvard Magazine*). Beginning with 1908 and continuing through 1915, I read each issue published during the football season (roughly September 15 through Thanksgiving and sometimes beyond) and many in the offseason. Moreover, I read them in order from earliest to latest. Of course, I went in knowing the outcomes in advance, but I found much to be gained from immersing myself in the particular rhythm of each season—the early hopes, the shattering triumphs, the play of illness and injury, the need to rebound from disappointment and even (in one instance) death. I hope this method has provided a keener edge to the final product.—D. F.

BOOKS

Atkinson, Rick. *The Day of Battle: The War in Sicily and Italy, 1943–1944*. New York: Henry Holt and Company, 2007.

Bealle, Morris A. *The History of Football at Harvard, 1874–1948*. Washington, D.C.: Columbia, 1948.

Bergin, Thomas G. *The Game: The Harvard–Yale Football Rivalry, 1875–1983*. New Haven, Conn.: Yale University Press, 1984.

Bernstein, Mark F. *Football: The Ivy League Origins of an American Obsession*. Philadelphia: University of Pennsylvania Press, 2001.

———. *Princeton Football*. Charleston, S.C.; Chicago; Portsmouth, N.H.; San Francisco, Calif.: Arcadia, 2009.

Bertagna, Joe. *Crimson in Triumph: A Pictorial History of Harvard Athletics, 1852–1985*. Brattleboro, Vt.: Stephen Greene Press, 1989.

Blanchard, John A., ed. *The H Book of Harvard Athletics*. Cambridge, Mass.: Harvard Varsity Club, 1923.

Bowman, John S., gen. ed. *Ivy League Football*. New York: Crescent Books, 1988.

Brown, Reginald "Reggie." W. P. Notebooks, Rare Books and Special Collections, Series No. FBC905-1-4, Hesburgh Libraries, University of Notre Dame.

Buford, Kate. *Native American Son: The Life and Sporting Legend of Jim Thorpe*. New York: Knopf, 2010.

Bundgaard, Axel. *Muscle and Manliness: The Rise of Sport in America's Boarding Schools*. Syracuse, N.Y.: Syracuse University Press, 2005.

Camp, Walter, ed. *Spalding's Official Foot Ball Guide for 1915*. New York: American Sports Publishing, 1915.

Carroll, John M. *Fritz Pollard: Pioneer in Racial Advancement*. Champaign: University of Illinois Press, 1992.

Cohane, Tim. *The Yale Football Story*. New York: G. P. Putnam's Sons, 1951.

Corbett, Bernard, and Paul Simpson. *The Only Game That Matters: The Harvard–Yale Rivalry*. New York: Crown, 2004.

Danzig, Allison. *The History of American Football: Its Great Teams, Players, and Coaches*. New York: Prentice-Hall, 1956.

Davis, Parke H. *Football: The American Intercollegiate Game*. New York: Charles Scribner's Sons, 1911.

Edwards, William H. *Football Days: Memories of the Game and the Men behind the Ball*. New York: Moffat, Yard and Company, 1916.

Fitzgerald, F. Scott. *The Great Gatsby*. New York: Charles Scribner's Sons, 1925.

Goldstein, Richard. *Ivy League Autumns: An Illustrated History of College Football's Grand Old Rivalries*. New York: St. Martin's, 1996.

Harvard Alumni Bulletin, selected issues from 1908–1909 to 1924–1925.

Harvard Athletic Association, financial statements, 1902–1918, UAV 170.283, Box 2, UAV 170.228, Harvard University Archives.

Harvard Athletic Association, "Report of the Graduate Treasurer for the Year Ending July 31, 1915," UAV 170.275, "Receipts and Expenditures, Printed and Typewritten Statements," Box 1, 1889–1905 to July 31, 1921, Harvard University Archives.

Harvard Class 50th Anniversary Reports for classes of 1898, 1899, 1909, 1910, 1911, 1912, 1913, 1914, 1915, 1916.

Harvard Class Albums for classes of 1898, 1909, 1910, 1911, 1912, 1913, 1914, 1915, 1916.

Harvard University Register, 1898–99, Volume XXV (Boston: Press of Alfred J. Mudge and Son, 1898–1899).

Harvard University Register, 1914–15, Vol. LXI (Cambridge, Mass.: Student Council of Harvard College, 1914–1915).

Haughton, Percy Duncan. *Football and How to Watch It*. Boston: Marshall Jones Company, 1922.

Howe, M. A. DeWolfe. *Memoirs of the Harvard Dead in the War against Germany*, vol. 3. Cambridge, Mass.: Harvard University Press, 1922.

Johnson, Owen. *Stover at Yale*. New York: Frederick A. Stokes, 1911.

Johnston, Alva. "The Ghosting Business." *New Yorker*, November 23, 1935.

Kaese, Harold. *The Boston Braves*. New York: G. P. Putnam's Sons, 1948.

Marquand, John P. *Point of No Return*. New York: Little, Brown, 1949.

Metzger, Sol. "When and How to Kick." *Boy's Life*, November 1931.

Miller, John J. *The Big Scrum*. New York: HarperCollins, 2012.

Mills, Paul H. "The Bold Military Adventure of Maine Governor Tudor Gardiner." *Franklin County* (Maine) *Daily Bulldog*, May 27, 2012.

Morison, Samuel Eliot. *Three Centuries of Harvard*. Cambridge, Mass.: Belknap Press, 1936.

Needham, Henry Beach. "The College Athlete: How Commercialism Is Making Him a Professional," *McClure's*, Part I: June 1905: "Recruiting and Subsidizing"; Part II, July 1905: "'Summer Ball,' The Gate-Money Evil, and 'Unnecessary Roughness' in Football."

Nelson, David M. *The Anatomy of a Game: Football, the Rules, and the Men Who Made the Game*. Newark: University of Delaware Press, 1994.

Nelson, James Carl. *Five Lieutenants: The Heartbreaking Story of Five Harvard Men Who Led America to Victory in World War I*. New York: St. Martin's, 2012.

Oriard, Michael. *Reading Football: How the Popular Press Created an American Spectacle*. Chapel Hill and London: University of North Carolina Press, 1993.

Reed, Herbert F. *Football for Public and Player*. New York: Frederick A. Stokes, 1913.

———. "Harvard: Gridiron Deceiver." *Harper's Weekly*, November 27, 1915.

Shaughnessy, Clark. *Football in War and Peace*. Clinton, S.C.: Jacobs Press, 1943.

Smith, Ronald A. *Big-Time Football at Harvard, 1905: The Diary of Coach Bill Reid*. Champaign: University of Illinois Press, 1994.

Social Register, Boston, 1905, vol. XIX, no. 5 (New York: Social Register Association, 1904).

Student folders, UAIII 15.88.10, 1890–1968, Harvard University Archives.

Synnott, Marcia Graham. *The Half-Opened Door*. Westport, Conn., and London: Greenwood Press, 1979.

Walter Chauncey Camp Papers (MS125). Manuscripts and Archives, Yale University Library.

Watterson, John Sayle. *College Football: History, Spectacle, Controversy*. Baltimore, Md., and London: Johns Hopkins University Press, 2000.

Withington, Paul, ed. *The Book of Athletics*. Rev. by Lothrop Withington. Boston: Lothrop, Lee & Shepard, 1922.

NEWSPAPERS

Boston Globe
Boston Herald
Boston Transcript
Brooklyn Daily Eagle
Chicago Tribune
Harvard A.A. News
Harvard Crimson
Harvard Lampoon
Los Angeles Times
New York Times
Time
Yale Daily News

WEBSITES

Tip top 25 www.tiptop25.com
U.S. Census www.allcountries.org/uscensus
U.S. Embassy and Consulates in Germany https://de.usembassy.gov
YouTube www.youtube.com

INDEX

ABOUT THE AUTHOR

Dick Friedman is a contributing editor for *Harvard Magazine* and the publication's primary football writer. He writes a blog after every Crimson game, as well as articles for the print publication. In a 2015 cover story, he anointed Tim Murphy the best coach in Harvard football history—better even than Percy Haughton. That year, he was awarded the magazine's Smith-Weld Prize, which honors thought-provoking writing about Harvard. He also has written for the Ivy League website.

Friedman grew up in Newton, Massachusetts, an easy T ride from Fenway Park and Boston Garden, and eight miles from Harvard Stadium. He is a 1973 graduate of Harvard, with a degree in U.S. history. He has been an editor and writer at *People*, *TV Guide*, and, beginning in 1994, *Sports Illustrated*, where he worked until 2013. At *SI*, he directed coverage, variously, of the NBA, baseball, and college basketball, and also helped edit the golf section. Friedman did a stint editing the front-of-the-book "Scorecard" section and wrote regularly for the magazine and si.com. He also worked on special commemorative issues and several of SI's books on basketball, baseball, pro football, and, most pertinent to this project, college football.

The Coach Who Strangled the Bulldog is Friedman's first book. In some respects, he began writing it on November 1, 1958—the Saturday on which, at age seven, he attended his first game at Harvard Stadium (a 19–6 loss to Penn). Ever since, as boy and man, as undergrad and old grad, through change and through storm (as the school's alma mater, "Fair Harvard," puts it), he has followed avidly (and sometimes been driven to madness by) the fortunes of Crimson football. In 2010, he had the honor to be the guest color analyst for the radio broadcast of Harvard's game at Princeton (a 45–28 win).

Friedman is married and the proud parent of a grown daughter. After almost three decades of living just outside of Princeton, New Jersey, he recently moved to Walnut Creek, California, but plans to spend much of every football season back in Ivy League territory.